You may have made one great decision. Make another.

WORLD BUSINESS NEWSPAPER

FINANCIAL TIMES

US ★ EDITION

www.ft.com

Thursday July 12 2001

USA $1.00 Canada C$2.00 Bermuda $2.25

Russia and China
How improved political relations will produce a new co-operation treaty
Page 12

Star wars returns
Reagan's warriors are back in the new missile debate
Page 6

Budget surplus
Impact of the economic slowdown on tax cuts
Page 14

WORLD

China lifts price controls to prepare for entry to WTO

BUSINESS

Emerson earnings set to fall for first time in 43 years

CONCERN OVER ARGENTINA DEBT TRIGGERS WORST TURBULENCE SINCE 1997-98 FINANCIAL CRISIS

Sell-off hits emerging markets

Early tests planned for US missile defence

The FT proudly supports the Foreign Policy Association's mission to increase awareness of foreign policy issues. Today, more than ever, an understanding of the US in isolation is no longer enough. The FT provides you with news, analysis and perspective on the issues most paramount in worldwide business, politics and economics. Join 1.6 million readers in 140 countries.

Special Offer for New Readers: 4-weeks risk-free.

The Financial Times is offering *Great Decisions* readers a special 'get acquainted' offer. Try the FT for 4 weeks (Mon-Sat) risk free. If you value what you see, you can subscribe to a full year for **ONLY $149,** *a savings of over 50% off the cover price.* If you decide not to continue your subscription, just write "cancel" across the invoice and return it to us — you owe nothing. The first four weeks of issues are yours to keep without any further obligation.

FT FINANCIAL TIMES
World business newspaper

Call 1 800 628-8088 for subscriptions or visit us online at www.FTsubs.com

FPA.org

- When you visit www.fpa.org, you are entering the world of global thinking.
- Great Decisions online allows users to be the first to get updates and breaking news related to GD topics.
- The Educators'Corner provides those committed to teaching International Studies with a wealth of resources, while Students'Corner provides young people the chance to take part in world affairs through volunteer opportunities, grants, scholarships, and study-abroad programs.
- The FPA Great Decisions guides maintain a variety of consistently updated pages on the most relevant international issues of our times.

GREAT DECISIONS 2002

Printed by Dartmouth Printing Company
Hanover, New Hampshire

Cover design: Agnes Kostro

CONTENTS

FPA gratefully acknowledges the contribution of text paper for this book by Westvaco Corporation.

**Preparation of this topic was underwritten by a generous grant from the Freeman Foundation*

FOREWORD

Two decades ago, Ronald Reagan warned: "We must take a stand against terrorism in the world and combat it with firmness, for it is a most cowardly and savage violation of peace." On September 11, 2001, we experienced firsthand the carnage of terrorism. For those of us who call New York and Washington home, the devastation was incomprehensible; the sense of violation and vulnerability overwhelming.

While September 11 may bring about many changes, the events of that day must not change America's ideals. For as President Reagan continued: "There is something else. We must remember our heritage, who we are and what we are, and how this nation, this island of freedom, came into being....Our foreign policy should be to show by example the greatness of our system and the strength of American ideals...."

An overarching challenge in projecting these ideals is to enlarge the circle of those who benefit from them. For the majority of humanity to dwell in possibility—possibility for life, liberty and the pursuit of happiness—is an imperative of our times.

Addressing the Foreign Policy Association's World Leadership Forum on September 20, 2001, Bill Clinton remarked: "We must ask ourselves what we have to do, not only to prevent terrorism and protect ourselves, but to undermine the conditions and attitudes which make terrorist foot soldiers and sympathizers." Can we be remembered not only as the country which—in the face of terrorism—freed the world from fear, but as the country which—in the face of despair and deprivation—finally freed the world from oppression and want?

Peace is a prerequisite for progress. In our introduction to the Foreign Policy Association 2000 Annual Report, FPA Chairman Dave Williams joined me in observing:

"The central importance of foreign policy to the future of all Americans cannot be overstated. Many of our greatest triumphs, including our standard of living, would not be possible without engagement with the world. But it is in conflict prevention that American leadership is especially important. By putting out little fires, we prevent big fires. And, at the end of the day, this is where an enlightened foreign policy is most critical. For the inspiring skylines of our great cities, the priceless art works exhibited in our renowned museums, the literary treasures housed in our libraries are all at risk if we do not play our role in shaping a world at peace."

American leadership in world affairs has never been more vital than today. Such leadership can be sustained only with an engaged and informed electorate. Since September 11, Americans, in growing numbers, are eager to learn about the world and its complicated tapestry. At a terrible price, we have rediscovered the world.

Noel V. Lateef

9/11
a new day for counterterrorism?

by Richard H. Ullman

Not since the early days of the cold war has foreign policy been so important for Americans, nor have foreign policy choices been so deeply enmeshed in the moral foundations of the American polity. The terrorist attacks of September 11, 2001, and the outbreaks of anthrax that followed, may or may not have given us our first glimpse of a "new world" of vastly heightened vulnerability, but they certainly have undermined Americans' sense of security and well-being to a degree not experienced since the Cuban missile crisis of 1962, perhaps since the Soviet Union exploded its first nuclear weapon in 1949. The September events and America's reaction raise fundamental questions about the ability of the U.S. to respond to radically different threats and to meet the paramount responsibility of any government—assuring the security of all persons, citizens or not, who legally reside within its sovereign territory.

The September 11 strikes by Osama bin Laden's Al Qaeda organization were the first use of fuel-laden passenger aircraft as enormous bombs. Was the country at war? Was a formal state of war possible against an enemy not itself a sovereign state? Measures put in place by all levels of government—federal, state and local—were more pervasive and intrusive than seemed the case during the Vietnam and Korean wars, if not World War II. The American people did not need President George W. Bush's message from the White House to tell them they were at war. The endlessly replayed television pictures of the twin 110-story World

Richard H. Ullman is David K.E. Bruce Professor of International Affairs, Center of International Studies at Princeton University. He is Chairman of the Foreign Policy Association's Editorial Advisory Committee.

Trade Center towers, first as gigantic torches, then, minutes later, as piles of twisted rubble must surely rank among the most affecting images of all time. Such images made it all too easy for the Bush Administration to ask—and citizens to acquiesce in—substantial infringements on civil liberties.

Who is at war?

Comparisons with previous wars are suggestive, but they are also misleading. Previous wars had been against states. Al Qaeda was a movement. Contrast that with the cold war. For all its claims of revolutionary uniqueness, the Soviet Union was also a state—one different in many respects from the U.S. and profoundly different in ideology—but an established state in a world of states. Both had an enormous nuclear force that primarily targeted the other, in particular the other's nuclear weapons. Even a small fraction of either superpower's nuclear force would have been sufficient to destroy the other and/or the polity that lay behind it. They were indeed to be feared, but for many their fearsomeness became an abstraction. The rapidity with which people came not to notice the nuclear sword suspended over their heads was due in no small measure to a widespread belief that nuclear use by one superpower would trigger a devastating response by the other. This prospect provided deterrence against nuclear use during half a century of cold war.

The terror weapons used to attack the U.S. on September 11, 2001, like the anthrax attacks that followed, differed in almost every way from the weapons that provided cold-war deterrence. But the greatest difference was political: The leaders of the two nuclear superpowers knew each other's address. President John F. Kennedy put the matter starkly during the Cuban missile crisis. If the Soviet Union launched one of its Cuba-based missiles at the U.S., the U.S. would treat the attack as if it had been launched from the Soviet Union.

In the case of the 9/11 attacks on the U.S., there was every reason to think that they were neither instigated nor executed by another state or its agents. And while it has generally been assumed that the responsible party was the Al Qaeda organization of Osama bin Laden, no one has yet stepped forward to claim responsibility. The organization has no headquarters building, nor even a labeled post office box. Because of the difficulty of finding Al Qaeda, the U.S. Administration chose to focus its wrath on the next-best manifestation of a responsible party—the Taliban government of Afghanistan, which Washington asserted (although the Taliban never admitted) had been giving bin Laden refuge on Afghan territory and material support. Like other governments, President Bush declared, the Taliban could be either with us or against us: There could be no neutrals in the war against terrorism.

Allies in a new light

The search for allies—worldwide—was crucial, and signified a profound change of course in the foreign policy of the Bush Administration. It had come to the White House deeply distrustful of the multilateralism that had been a mainstay of the policies of the Clinton Administration that preceded it. Thus, it sought to be freed from the constraints of a number of international regimes into which one or another preceding Administration had entered. And early in the Administration its spokespersons had all but promised that American troops would not much longer participate in United Nations and North Atlantic Treaty Organization (NATO) peacekeeping missions in Bosnia-Herzegovina and Kosovo. Such tasks, they asserted, would be better left to the Europeans.

All this changed on September 11. The Bush Administration quickly realized that making good on its promise to capture bin Laden "dead or alive" and to destroy the Al Qaeda organization as an effective network for carrying out acts of terror would require sustained close international cooperation. This U.S. posture drew an immediate sympathetic response. Many of the world's governments could see themselves, too, as potential victims of a terror attack. Thus, within hours of the catastrophes at the World Trade Center and the Pentagon, the UN Security Council unanimously passed a toughly worded resolution requiring all states to cooperate against terrorism. A day later, NATO's North Atlantic Council (NAC) passed a resolution invoking for the first time Article 5 of the Washington Treaty, which declared an attack on one member to be an attack on all. The NAC called on member governments to behave accordingly. The terrorist attacks, the resolution stated, comprised such an attack.

The irony was inescapable. In 1949, NATO architects had intended Article 5 to commit the U.S. to providing for the security of NATO partners in Europe. Now, when Article 5 was employed for the first time, its purpose was to make sure that the U.S. would not fight alone the war against terrorism. Moreover, cooperation would be necessary not only with traditional allies but with a wide range of other governments. These would include states such as Pakistan, India, and the former Soviet republics such as Uzbekistan, Turkmenistan and Tajikistan that abutted Afghanistan, major Islamic states such as Saudi Arabia and Egypt, with whom the U.S. had long had a close relationship, and former U.S. adversaries such as Russia and China.

Muslim allies

Pakistan's importance to the U.S. effort was obvious. It shares a long border with Afghanistan; many Pakistanis practice the Taliban's fundamentalist version of Islam. At the time of Al Qaeda's attack on the U.S. only three countries in the world recognized the Taliban as the government of Afghanistan: Pakistan, Saudi Arabia and the United Arab Emirates. There were said to be close ties between the Taliban and Pakistan's security forces, especially the powerful shadowlike Inter Services Intelligence (ISI). From Pakistan the U.S. requested the use of air bases, staging areas for ground forces, and access to at least some of the intelligence the ISI could provide. Throughout the crisis, Pakistan's president, General Pervez Musharraf, seemed genuinely willing to give Washington significant assistance. At the same time, however, he openly worried about his country's "street," the equivalent of the Arab "street" that has exerted so much influence on moderate rulers like Egypt's president Hosni Mubarak or the Palestinian entity's Yasir Arafat. Like Muslim leaders everywhere, Musharraf worried especially about the effects on his public's opinion of many Afghan civilians killed as a result of a protracted U.S. bombing campaign.

Depending upon how one assesses the strength of Islamist opposition in Pakistan, General Musharraf's assistance to the U.S. effort to hold Al Qaeda to account was either courageous and generous or fearful and begrudging. But to properly appreciate Pakistan's position it should be noted that the response by most other Muslim states to U.S. pleas for help was much less forthcoming. The most accommodating was Uzbekistan, which placed a major air base at the disposal of U.S. forces. Nearly all other Muslim states responded to the attacks on the U.S. with strong verbal condemnation of the deeds and their perpetrators and with commensurate votes at the UN, but with no material support. Most Muslim governments were made extremely anxious by injuries to civilians as a result of U.S. bombing in Afghanistan and frequently expressed the hope that the campaign would be short. When it proved to be lengthy, governments moved to distance themselves from Washington, while their domestic critics began to equate the terror of U.S. bombs with Al Qaeda's attacks on New York and Washington.

Coalition and compromise

American efforts to enlist Pakistani support were complicated by the fact that since May 1998 Pakistan had been the target of U.S. economic sanctions imposed to punish Pakistan for carrying out a series of nuclear-weapons tests. Those tests had followed by only a few weeks a similar series by India. The U.S. response to India's tests, too, had been to impose economic sanctions. However, the Clinton Administration lifted those sanctions in March 2000, when Clinton himself visited India. But Washington's sanctions against Pakistan remained in effect to express disapproval of the coup d'état that brought Musharraf to power on October 12, 1999. Moreover, U.S. sanctions remained in effect despite a nearly universal opinion in Washington—and in Pakistan, too—that Musharraf was to be preferred over the thoroughly corrupt but formally democratic and civilian government of Nawaz Sharif that Musharraf ousted. Regardless of these complicating factors, the Bush Administration lifted Pakistan sanctions as one of its first diplomatic actions following September 11. Aside from political motivations there were humanitarian ones as well. Pakistan is desperately poor. So long as sanctions continued it could not receive economic support from international financial institutions that were anxious to supply it.

Alongside the issue of whether or not to lift the sanctions the Clinton Administration had imposed on Pakistan was a similar dilemma involving other states whose support Washington sought. Their number included two permanent members of the UN Security Council, Russia and China. Both had been the object of American censure for abuses of human rights—Russia for what much of the world saw as vicious suppression of the separatist movement in Chechnya, China for similar misconduct in Tibet. It seems clear that after September 11 the Bush Administration made the decision to soft-pedal criticism of both governments for human-rights abuses. The result was an impressive warming of bilateral relations, especially at the level of heads of state, and a strong commitment from both Moscow and Beijing to share with Washington intelligence information related to terrorism.

Handshake agreement

Then, in late November, came a breakthrough agreement on strategic nuclear weapons between President Bush and Russian President Vladimir Putin. Simultaneously came a fundamental rapprochement between Russia and NATO.These moves raise the question of what the U.S. would say and do if Russia were to launch another attack on the Chechens. Given the new U.S.-Russian partnership to oppose terrorism, could Washington remain silent? Should it?

Even further complicating American efforts to assemble a coalition against bin Laden and his movement was the ongoing war between Israel and the Palestinians. Along with images of the World Trade Center towers in flames, television broadcasts around the world showed Palestinians in the West Bank and Gaza dancing with joy in the streets. Meanwhile, the savage tit for tat of killings by both sides continued without noticeable abatement, while the peace process seemed moribund. Both President Bush and Secretary of State Colin Powell called for an end to the violence. Although their appeals purported to be evenhanded, it was clear that their calls for restraint were directed more to the Israelis than to the Palestinians. Meanwhile, columnists and editorial writers across the country came forward with a message not previously heard—that the international community should impose a settlement on the warring sides. Who pulled the trigger first in this latest and most vicious round of Israeli and Palestinian bloodletting is lost in the mists of time. But regardless of which side should bear responsibility, now that the U.S. is at war with an Islamist movement it can no longer afford to appear to be giving Israel something like a blank check to prosecute its own war of retribution on the Muslim Palestinians.

The issue was an example of the choice between principle and expediency that so often marks the conduct of foreign policy in general but which is likely to characterize counterterrorism in particular. Governments will pay premium prices for seats at the devil's table when the main course may be information regarding a potential terrorist outrage or the location of a terrorist cell. And governments may find that civil rights—in particular, freedom of speech and assembly—are a temptingly accessible currency in which to pay, including backing away from criticisms of foreign governments.

Military coalition

The coalition cobbled together by Bush and Powell was a mix of diverse states united by the horror they all felt in the face of the events of September 11 and anxious to demonstrate their solidarity with the U.S. It was an army tied together by outrage and largely unmindful of the actual military roles and missions of its troops.

The U.S. played the lead role. This led to a thorny dilemma. On the one hand, American political and military leaders were anxious that, to Americans and foreigners alike, the U.S. should not be thought to be alone in its quest for justice and revenge. On the other hand, however, American commanders did not wish to compromise U.S. military planning in order to meet demands of other members of the coalition.

While the U.S. had few partners in the conduct of military operations other than Britain, intelligence seems to have been another story. There seems to have been substantial sharing of information and also of sources. This sharing came from states in the region and also from traditional allies. Such sharing of intelligence must be at the foundation of any antiterrorism regime. Such a regime must reflect two realities. *Individuals* will find that their domain of privacy will be smaller and more circumscribed than it has previously been. State authorities will be able to track citizens' movements, habits, and associations to a far greater extent than previously. The same technologies that make possible the interception of terrorist communications has already made possible the interception of private communications of all sorts. Meanwhile, *states* will find it more difficult to maintain zones of information security against the efforts of agents of other governments—and of gifted hackers. Moreover, not only state agencies but private organizations will make use of the same resources and technologies.

Counterterrorism: international and domestic

From the outset, following the September attacks, the Administration had two political goals. One was to make the counterterrorism coalition as broad as possible so that the image it conveys does not become one of Islam versus the rest of the world. This was to be a major goal of U.S. diplomacy. A second goal was domestic: to make sure that there would be no domestic reaction that would affect the conduct of the war or relax the pressure on the terrorists.

The domestic counterterrorism program had another aspect: The President put forward by executive order a number of measures designed to expedite the identification, arrest, indictment and conviction of persons who had been or still were terrorists or facilitators of terrorism. Central to the program was a proposal to try such persons by military tribunals with virtually none of the safeguards provided in civilian courts.

A new world? No, the old world, repackaged. Americans have previously come across many of its features, both political and technological. American history also points up the fact that the country has been strongest when expression has been most unfettered. Administrations bent on curtailing civil liberties are all too familiar a phenomenon in American history, and the technologies that destroyed the World Trade Center towers were not new. What was new was the realization that 10,000 gallons of jet fuel in the belly of an airliner could become a weapon of mass destruction-in-waiting. Equally new was the realization that a young unemployed man from the streets of Cairo could be motivated to steer that airliner into a skyscraper filled with people. Similarly, to find a would-be pilot also willing to commit suicide on demand is not new: Japanese kamikaze pilots during World War II probably held that dubious honor.

The destruction of September 11 was not only the result of masterful planning. It was also the consequence of an airport/airline safety system that had become hopelessly lax. September 11 was a wake-up call that has led to changed repertoires and routines that are unlikely to decay again. Many ordinary household items can be deadly weapons. They are much less likely to be so now.

September 11, 2001, may have seemed the dawn of a new day for terrorism. That will not necessarily be the case. If the proper conclusions are drawn and adequate resources devoted to the problem, America may find itself present at the dawn of a new day for counterterrorism as well. ■

Why do they hate us? the roots of terrorism

Fear of the modern world and resentment and hostility toward the U.S. run deep in many Muslim societies, and the U.S. must address these concerns.

by Bruce Stokes

APWIDE WORLD PHOTOS

AFTERMATH OF THE SEPTEMBER 11, 2001, *terrorist attacks: devastating images of the World Trade Center in New York City and the Pentagon in Washington, D.C.*

THE SEPTEMBER 11 terrorist attacks on the Pentagon and the World Trade Center generated many emotions around the world: anger, shock, sadness, incomprehension, and in a small minority, jubilation. For those few, a blow had been struck against the U.S., the ally of their enemy Israel and the embodiment of the modern, secular world that many among them rejected.

And they were not alone. A week later, thousands of Pakistanis, adamantly opposed to U.S. military retaliation against suspected terrorist camps in Afghanistan, marched in the streets of Islamabad, Pakistan's capital, chanting "Down with America."

For average Americans watching these images on CNN or reading about such sentiments over their morning coffee, these foreign reactions, although they reflected the attitudes of a distinct minority, raised disturbing questions. "Americans are asking, why do they hate us?" President George W. Bush stated in his September 20 address to Congress.

Much of his audience—still stunned by the horrific attacks on American soil—wondered the same thing. At a time when U.S. pundits and politicians were portraying the new war on terrorism as a struggle between good and evil, many people asked: "Why were some foreigners casting the U.S. as the devil?" And they wondered: "What degree of economic deprivation and political resentment could lead someone, whatever his or her religious or political convictions, to revel in the deaths of so many innocent civilians?"

In the immediate aftermath of the September 11 terrorist attacks, the military and diplomatic efforts to capture Osama bin Laden, to destroy his terrorist network and to overthrow the Taliban regime in Afghanistan that gave bin Laden a safe haven understandably preoccupied the American public and the Bush Administration. But in the end, an army is of little value in fighting ideas. It was the anti-American sentiments found in many parts of the Islamic world, compounded by fears of globalization, modernization and secularism, that created the poisonous environment in which the September 11 terrorists came of age. To understand the hatred and resentment, the sense of deprivation and alienation that could fuel such odious behavior requires both an accurate assessment of the depth of such feelings and an acute understanding of what motivated it.

In so doing, there are important distinctions to be made. Understanding why people committed such acts in no way condones them. Explaining the sources of such frustration and malevolence in no way excuses it. There is no justification for acts of terror. But it is imperative to understand what it is that creates such a burning rage to hurt Americans. The perpetrators are criminals. But they were not born that way. They are a product of their environment. And that physical and philosophical environment is only likely to continue to produce terrorists unless and until the swamp that produced them is drained.

Anti-Americanism has multiple origins: resistance to Western values, reaction to perceptions of American cultural predominance, resentment of the U.S.

BRUCE STOKES *is an adjunct fellow at the Council on Foreign Relations and a columnist for the* National Journal, *a Washington-based public policy magazine.*

for propping up corrupt governments around the world, stationing U.S. troops in Arab countries and a sense that America has been utterly insensitive to Arab suffering both in Palestine and Iraq.

These sources of anti-Americanism can be classified into two general categories: resentment against who Americans are—modern, democratic, materialistic, culturally diverse—and anger at what people believe Americans do—ignore others' poverty, appear insensitive to foreign cultures, support Israel.

There is little the U.S. can do about the former set of concerns. Just as those who live in Islamic societies are the children of Muhammad and his culture, American values are a product of the Enlightenment and the evolution of Western tradition. Those values are too deeply rooted to be easily changed. Nor would most Americans want them to change. The best that can be hoped for is that Americans come to understand that the values they hold as universal truths are not necessarily shared by others. The problem, of course, is that even such a "live and let live" pluralistic sentiment is itself not shared by everyone, Islamic fundamentalists, for example. So some ongoing friction over core values is unavoidable.

But the U.S. can decide, if it so chooses, to change or moderate those actions that fuel anti-Americanism. Once the current phase of the war on terrorism has run its course, American-led economic and cultural globalization will remain in much of the world. The challenge that lies ahead for the U.S. is to decide what exactly it is that Americans want to do to address such resentment.

History teaches how hard it can be to reduce poverty or to foster representative government. These are challenges that make the current war on terrorism look like child's play in comparison. But unless they are addressed, all the U.S. knows about "why they hate us?" suggests it will be only treating the symptoms, not the disease.

Hardly new

Anti-Americanism is far from new. The 1958 novel *The Ugly American,* by William J. Lederer and Eugene Burdick, characterized Uncle Sam as a bumbling Babbitt in Southeast Asia, mindlessly mishandling his newfound role as leader of the cold-war world. In the 1960s, the unpopular war in Vietnam cast the U.S. on an anti-Communist crusade bent on crushing indigenous wars of liberation to impose a *Pax Americana* on the world. In the 1970s, Washington incurred the enmity of the Islamic world for its support of Israel against the Arabs and the Palestinians and for its support of the Westernized shah of Iran in his losing battle against the fundamentalist ayatollah, Khomeini. In the 1980s, the Reagan Administration's support for the contras in their fight against the left-wing Nicaraguan government revived old fears of U.S. meddling in Latin American affairs. The last decade saw resentment build toward the New World Order many thought the U.S. was attempting to impose in the wake of its decisive victory over Iraq in the Persian Gulf war. Immediately prior to September 11, there were in the eyes of many a vision of America as an arrogant global hegemon, trampling other cultures and economies in a willful pursuit of narrow U.S. economic and corporate self-interest in the name of irresistible globalization.

But such a broad-brush view of anti-American sentiments over the last half century obscures a much more subtle and complicated set of foreign attitudes toward the U.S. To best understand anti-American, antisecular, antiglobal concerns, and to be most effective in dealing with such sentiments, it is important to listen quite closely to the contradictory and internally inconsistent things that people say about the U.S. and the values Americans hold dear. The challenge in doing so is that different people are saying different things. Those sentiments vary from one country to another. And they are volatile, easily influenced by the news of the day.

For this reason, it is quite dangerous

SEPTEMBER 27, 2001, *demonstrators waving the Pakistani flag protest against possible U.S. military actions against Afghanistan.*

to make sweeping generalizations about public attitudes toward the U.S. A Frenchman's frustration with seeing one-too-many McDonald's on the Champs Élysées is not comparable to the visceral anger manifested by an Indonesian student protesting the bombing of Afghanistan outside the American embassy in Jakarta. The best that can be hoped for is to draw some general conclusions about attitudes toward the U.S. after sifting through public opinion data from overseas.

Contrary to television images of flag burning and embassy demonstrations, until recently most people around the world held relatively favorable attitudes toward the U.S. There is intense admiration for the American people and what American society has achieved for its citizens, such as providing an adequate standard of living and maintaining law and order. And they appreciate American aid in times of trouble.

More specifically, a 1999 survey of Islamic countries by the U.S. State Department found that more than half the Turks, Uzbeks, Nigerians and Indonesians questioned were favorably disposed toward America, holding the U.S. in higher esteem than France or Russia, for example. The Saudis express pro-American sentiments in return for Washington's help during the Persian Gulf war.

Other polling shows Muslim publics more divided in their attitudes toward the U.S. They tend to be pro-American in Central Asia, West Africa and India and remarkably unfriendly in countries such as Jordan and Turkey.

And polling data show that anti-Americanism tends to spike in times of crisis, during a war, when U.S. bombers accidentally bomb the Chinese embassy in Belgrade in May 1999 or when the U.S. imposes trade sanctions on a country's exports. But there is little evidence of a long-term rise in such animosity. Once a crisis is over, anger at America usually recedes.

And the everyday actions of foreigners belie the assumption that America is universally hated. McDonald's may be the symbol to many people around the world of all that is bad about American cuisine and economic domination. But there are now more McDonald's in other countries than there are in the U.S. Someone is eating all those burgers and fries and it's not American tourists. Citizens of other countries may question U.S. foreign policy or resent certain aspects of America's culture, but they value what they can learn from American society. Tens of thousands of foreign families send their children to American universities for an education (some 50,000 per year come from China alone). And, in a reflection of strong pro-American sentiment, the hundreds of thousands of immigrants, both legal and illegal, who come to the U.S. every year are in essence voting with their feet, choosing America as the place to build a better life.

AP/WIDE WORLD PHOTOS

A PAKISTANI PARAMILITARY *forces soldier guards a McDonald's restaurant in Karachi, Pakistan, September 25, 2001. Tensions of Karachi residents rose against the U.S. in anticipation of a possible attack on neighboring Afghanistan.*

Moreover, the recent emergence of antisecularism, antimodernism and antiglobalism in parts of the Islamic world in particular should not necessarily be equated with anti-Americanism. While the U.S. is a target of such sentiments, America is often only a convenient symbol of that which is feared and resented: rapid economic, cultural and technological change. It is the 21st century, with all of its challenges and its shortcomings, that is the enemy. And the U.S. is most identified with all of the attributes of the modern world, both good and bad.

Finally, of course, anti-American sentiment is often shallow and fickle. Prior to September 11, the strongest critiques of the U.S. were heard in Paris or Berlin, where both the governments and the average person in the street chastised the Bush Administration's opposition to the Kyoto treaty on global warming, the White House plan for missile defense and the new unilateralist mode of American leadership in the world. By wide margins, people in Germany, France, Britain and Italy disapproved of President Bush's handling of international policy, according to a survey by the Pew Research Center for the People and the Press in Washington. But in the wake of the terrorist attacks, American popularity has soared. ■

Who Americans are

IT IS TEMPTING TO SEIZE UPON conflicting foreign sentiments, their volatility and the apparent contradiction between the resentment many foreigners' voice and their practical embrace of many aspects of American culture in their daily lives, to simply discount current criticism of the U.S. But pollsters and regional experts say that would be a mistake. Anti-Americanism, and closely related public backlashes against globalization, modernization and secularism, are a potent cocktail that threaten to bedevil U.S. interests abroad for some time to come.

As such, it is essential to better understand public attitudes toward those phenomena of public life that many people associate with the U.S.

"People equate globalization with Americanization," said Shaun Breslin, a professor of political economy at Warwick University in Britain. "It is seen as the imposition of American values, standards and ideology, not just economics."

There have been no single worldwide surveys of public opinion about globalization although the Pew Research Center for the People and the Press plans to

AP/WIDE WORLD PHOTOS

AFGHAN REFUGEE WOMEN *wear veils in a tent camp near the village of Khwaja-Bahauddin in Takhar province, Afghanistan, October 29, 2001.*

do one in the near future. So the best information comes from smaller national and multicountry research.

In France, where the terms globalization and Americanization are often used interchangeably, a poll conducted in 2000 found that half of those questioned felt that globalization was a bad thing for France, while a third thought it was a good thing. And globalization ranked as one of the top ten "worrying modern phenomena" facing France, although near the bottom of the list, in ninth place. Opinion moderated when asked about globalization more generally. Overall, the French public thought globalization was slightly more positive than negative.

Unfortunately, even less is known about the attitudes and core values that anchor such opinions about globalization. The Dentsu Institute for Human Studies in Japan has conducted Comparative Analysis of Global Values surveys in Tokyo, New York, London and Berlin. The results show that in all the areas surveyed people think morals and ethics are worsening; in Germany and Japan it is thought the terms of employment have declined; in the U.S. and Britain it is felt they have improved and that, in terms of institutions that can deal with globalization-related problems, the private sector is generally held in greater esteem than the public sector.

The pulse of the bazaars and the universities in the Middle East also reflects antipathy toward globalization, modernization and secularism. Two thirds of Egyptians and Iranians and four fifths of Jordanians consider a "cultural invasion" by the West to be very dangerous, according to a small 1999 survey of Egypt, Jordan and Iran by sociologist Mansoor Moaddel of Eastern Michigan University. These findings track the results of State Department polls taken in the mid-1990s, which showed that in Mali, Turkey, Lebanon, Jordan and Saudi Arabia roughly three quarters of the publics agreed that Western popular culture was a bad influence on their societies.

Moreover, there are powerful religious sentiments in Islamic countries at odds with what they perceive as the secular attributes of American society.

To best understand this relationship it is essential to distinguish the role the Islamic faith plays, and doesn't play, in people's lives and their attitudes toward the U.S.

In his trailblazing article "The Clash of Civilizations?" which appeared in *Foreign Affairs* in 1993, Harvard University professor Samuel P. Huntington contended that "the fundamental source of conflict in this new world will not be primarily ideological or primarily economic. The great divisions among humankind and the dominating source of conflict will be cultural....Conflict between civilizations will be the latest phase of the evolution of conflict in the modern world," rather than the ideological tensions that were the source of the cold war.

Other observers have pointed to many of the tenets of fundamentalist Islamic belief—that women must be covered and, in places like Afghanistan, are denied an education and the chance to work, that secular law is superceded in many areas by the sharia, the often harsh Islamic legal code derived from the Quran—to argue that there is an unavoidable incompatibility between extreme forms of Islam and Western culture.

For many observers, the events of September 11 are an unfortunate, stark confirmation of the inevitability of this clash between the Christian, materialistic, modern U.S. and the Islamic Middle East. But Islamic scholars and public opinion data among Muslims paint a much more complicated picture.

History teaches that Islam is a religion of tolerance and respect for other beliefs. After the rise of Islam in the 7th century, Jews and Christians were long protected in the Middle East, because they too believed in one God and were descendants of Abraham. Unlike Osama bin Laden, most Islamic scholars do not interpret the prophet Muhammad's teaching of *jihad* as preaching "holy war," which many terrorists claim to justify their actions. Rather, moderate Muslims believe jihad to mean an inner striving to follow God's will, for justice and self-purification. This, they say, is the "greater jihad" and holy war is the "lesser" one. Islamic experts also argue further that the Quran prohibits killing civilians under any circumstances, in-

AP/WIDE WORLD PHOTOS

EXILED SAUDI DISSIDENT *Osama bin Laden speakes at a meeting at an undisclosed location in Afghanistan, 1998. In the background is a banner with a verse from the Quran.*

cluding in a defensive jihad. People in the street seem to share such beliefs. Two out of three Palestinians surveyed after the September 11 atrocities, for example, said they believed the attacks on the U.S. were not consistent with Islam.

But there is clearly a dissonance within Islam. "There is something in the religious culture of Islam which inspired, in even the humblest peasant or peddler, a dignity and a courtesy toward others never exceeded and rarely equaled in other civilizations," Bernard Lewis, the great scholar of Islam, has noted. "And yet, in moments of upheaval and disruption, when the deeper passions are stirred, this dignity and courtesy toward others can give way to an explosive mixture of rage and hatred which impels even the government of an ancient and civilized country... [to] try to find, in the life of their prophet, approval and indeed precedent for such actions."

This dissonance is evident in the views of the Islamic public.

Moaddel's polling found that religion was a more important basis of personal identity than nationality in countries like Egypt, Jordan and Iran. And parents there viewed religious faith as a more important value to impart to their children than hard work, independence or tolerance, all values that Americans rate very highly.

There seems to be a definite connection between Muslims' attitudes toward religion and opinions of the U.S. The people in relatively secular Islamic states are more pro-American; less-secular Islamic states have more critical views about America.

Only about one in ten Turks and Indonesians who say they are unfavorably disposed toward the U.S. attribute their feelings to religious factors, such as the allegedly anti-Islamic attitudes of Americans or because of what they view as the dissolute nature of American society. On the other hand, in Pakistan, nearly half of those with an overall negative view of the U.S. cite their Islamic beliefs as the reason.

There is an irony in this stereotyping of America as the embodiment of secularism. The American public is actually quite devout. Surveys consistently show that the portion of the American public who say religion is important in their lives is almost as great as the devout portion in Islamic nations, such as Egypt, Jordan and Iran.

But for most Muslims, religion is something that they think has to be kept somewhat separate from other aspects of the broader society. Muslims tell pollsters, for example, that they generally favor Islam playing a greater role in the schools, but they also believe that religion should be kept separate from government policy.

Islamic fundamentalism

Of course, the most salient concern at this moment is the influence of Islamic fundamentalism in Muslim societies. It would be a mistake to equate devotion to Islam with fundamentalism or Islamic fundamentalism with terrorist extremism. At best, the role fundamentalism plays in anti-Americanism, antisecularism, antimodernism can only be measured indirectly.

Nearly half the publics in Muslim nations such as Pakistan, Uzbekistan, Turkey, Nigeria and Indonesia support traditionalist, but not necessarily fundamentalist, tenets. For example, they tell pollsters that there can be only one interpretation of the Quran. And in Pakistan, Nigeria, Indonesia and the Palestine-administered territories, at least three out of five people believe that the *sharia* is the best basis for governance.

But contrary to American misconceptions, such Islamic fundamentalism is not a product of ignorance or backwardness. In fact, throughout the Islamic world, the better-educated people are, the more observant they become—measured by praying or the keeping of Ramadan. In Pakistan, for example, people with a university degree are twice as likely as those who are illiterate to support the use of the Islamic legal code. In Egypt, the fundamentalist religio-political Muslim Brotherhood has made great inroads among professionals, with many of its members in legal and engineering societies. So it should come as no surprise that many of the World Trade Center and Pentagon terrorists were well educated.

Economic globalization has accelerated the pace of economic and social change in many Islamic countries. Not knowing what will happen next creates a sense of insecurity. Fundamentalists "are knowledgeable enough to know something is wrong," said Moaddel, who has interviewed many Muslim Brotherhood members, "but [lacking exposure to the humanities or social sciences, never having read Jean-Jacques Rousseau, John Locke, John Stuart Mill or Thomas Jefferson] they are not knowledgeable enough to be able to devise solutions for their societies."

Lost in a disorienting world, without the tools to reshape their societies to adapt to the rapid pace of a global economy, fundamentalism offers some in the Islamic world structured solutions that provide a sense of meaning and direction. Throughout history, millenarian movements, such as Islamic fundamentalism, have arisen in such times of extreme insecurity. ■

What Americans do

THE SECOND WELLSPRING of anti-Americanism—reaction to how the U.S. acts in the world—is a bit easier to define and assess and thus may well afford more opportunities to actually do something about "why they hate us."

The prominent role the U.S. plays in the Middle East—as Israel's principal ally, as a major regional military force with bases in Saudi Arabia and naval vessels in the Persian Gulf, and as an ally of various governments in the region—is clearly a source of ongoing friction.

"The call to wage war against America," said Osama bin Laden in 1998, "was made because America has spearheaded the crusade against the Islamic nation, sending tens of thousands of its troops to the land of the two holy mosques, over and above its meddling in its affairs and its politics and its support of the oppressive, corrupt and tyrannical regime that is in control."

And those sentiments are shared by at least some of the people in the streets of the Middle East. Not surprisingly, three quarters of those living in the Palestine-administered territories label the U.S. as "hostile to Muslim countries."

APWIDE WORLD PHOTOS

PILGRIMS VISIT THE PROPHET'S MOSQUE *in Medina, Saudi Arabia, December 1, 1999. Each year thousands of pilgrims stop at the prophet's grave before traveling on to Mecca.*

A quarter of Indonesians and Pakistanis and a third of Turks feel the same way. These polls were all taken before the war against Afghanistan, so it is safe to assume this anger against the U.S. has only grown since then.

This resentment has been compounded by a profound sense of Islamic humiliation inflicted by Israel's repeated defeats of Arab armies. The popular assumption in much of the region is that Israeli success was only possible because of U.S. military support. As a result, for many Arabs, the U.S. has replaced Europe as the embodiment of evil in their eyes. The U.S. is the source of the ills and misfortunes that befall their world in the second part of the past century.

"Most people in the region define this as the single most important issue to the region," said Shibley Telhami, professor of peace and development at the University of Maryland. "It's an identity issue. It defines how Arabs see themselves and their identity."

America-bashing became an even more popular sport in much of the Middle East in the wake of the recent collapse of the Palestinian-Israeli peace process. When the process had some future, Islamic activists in Egypt and Jordan told pollsters that they thought they could have some kind of dialogue with America. But when the new *intifada* (or major uprising) broke out in late 2000, those sentiments quickly dissolved.

"...Anti-Americanism in the Middle East is clearly tied to U.S. support for Israel and people's resentment of the status quo between Israel and the Palestinians," said Richard N. Haass, then the director of Foreign Policy Studies at The Brookings Institution, now the head of the policy planning staff in the Bush State Department, in an interview with *Al-Ahram* newspaper in late October 2000. "I am quite concerned about anti-Americanism," he warned, "because if the peace process doesn't move forward, anti-Americanism will grow, fairly or not, maybe not, but it will grow all the same."

Of course, it would be a mistake to directly link the breakdown of the peace process to the September 11 terrorist incidents. The investigation of the perpetrators of those attacks shows that they had been planning their actions, training to fly airplanes and so forth, for years, even at the time when peace in the region seemed a definite possibility.

There is also mounting resentment throughout the region toward America's seeming indifference to the suffering of average Iraqis. A decade after the Persian Gulf war, it is the plight of women and children in Baghdad, Iraq's capital, not the fate of Kuwait, that stirs public emotions in the region. And it is the ongoing, American-supported economic embargo that is blamed for the Iraqi people's plight, not President Saddam Hussein's failure to use his available oil money to buy food and pharmaceuticals for his people. Half of all Pakistanis, Turks and Indonesians believe the sanctions should be stopped, even though some acknowledge that Iraq remains a threat to its neighbors.

And in foreign relations, as in much of life, it is unfortunately true that no good deed goes unpunished. Many Americans cannot understand why the contributions the U.S. has made to the world—the rebuilding of Europe and Japan after World War II, standing up to and eventually defeating the Soviet Union during the cold war, humanitarian efforts in Central America and Africa—have not elicited more lasting, good feelings toward America. There is no explanation, but it is indisputable that America's good works are often ignored or soon forgotten. Gratitude can be a short-lived public sentiment in foreign relations.

For example, in 1999 the U.S. led a multinational military campaign to save from genocide the overwhelmingly Muslim population of Kosovo in the Balkans. But subsequent surveys showed that three out of five Indonesian Muslims said that they had heard "not that much" or "nothing at all" about U.S. efforts. A similar portion of Pakistanis voiced no opinion about the U.S. stand on the side of Muslims. Most disturbingly, among Pakistanis who had an opinion about what Washington did in Kosovo, a quarter of those questioned thought less of the U.S. as a result.

But anti-American resentment extends beyond the perception that Washington has taken sides in the Middle East. The world, said Huntington, "is a dangerous place, in which large numbers of people resent our wealth, power and culture."

In most societies, the biggest guy on the block is generally not well liked. And throughout history, no one has had much love for the nation that is that era's economic and cultural hegemon. Jewish zealots chafed under Roman rule. American patriots in the 18th century and Indian nationalists in the 20th century resented British power. The U.S. is now the dominant global force, militarily, economically and culturally. Americans do not like to see themselves as the new Roman or British empire. They protest that the U.S. rejects such imperial ambitions. But Americans may not be the best judge of their own power and influence. And some degree of public antipathy toward the U.S.—at times justified, at times not—is simply another burden of being a superpower.

In the post-cold-war era, after the breakup of the Soviet Union and before the possible rise of China, the U.S. stands unchallenged. As such, it is seen by others to live beyond the normal constraints on other nations. To many foreign eyes it was simply arrogant of the U.S. to refuse for years to pay its UN dues (a default recently corrected), to fail to sign the chemical weapons and the antilandmine treaties or to renounce the Kyoto agreement on global warming. Such behavior is hard for much of the rest of the world to swallow.

Resentment has been further fueled by U.S. economic success in recent years, by the relative lack of economic success in parts of the Islamic world and, to some of those who have not been so successful, by America's failure to share more of the benefits of America's economic good fortune.

Economic deprivation

Poverty in itself does not immediately and directly lead to terrorism. Rather than responding to deprivation by lashing out at others, the vast majority of the world's poor devote their energy to the daily struggle to secure income, food and opportunities for their children. But extremism does take root where economies collapse, as in Afghanistan, or when states, such as many of those in the Middle East, fail to provide basic services like heath care, education, and law and order. Economic deprivation creates an environment that nurtures radicalism.

The dramatic rise in oil prices in the 1970s brought enormous riches to the Middle East. Subsequent images of Arab shaikhs driving Cadillacs in the desert shaped the popular American misperception of the Islamic world. It is true that many of the world's wealthiest families derive their fortunes from the oil pumped in Saudi Arabia, Kuwait, Qatar and Bahrain. But such riches belie the failings of their economic systems and are too dependent on volatile oil prices, still tightly held in the hands of a small minority of countries and people, and have not been used to create jobs and an educated workforce prepared for the global economy of the 21st century.

For the most part, the Middle East is not marked by the kind of income inequality found between countries and within the societies of Latin America and Africa. But the oil wealth of the Persian Gulf states, where per capita income exceeds that of Greece and Portugal, contrasts sharply with the poverty found in Yemen. Even within relatively wealthy countries, there can be disparities between regions. Many of the hijackers involved in the attacks on the World Trade Center and the Pentagon came from one of the poorer regions in southwest Saudi Arabia, for example.

Conditions are worse in many of the non-oil-producing Islamic states. In Pakistan, a third of the population still lives on less than a dollar a day. In Yemen, less than half the population has access to essential drugs or to adequate sanitation.

And economic prospects are worsening. Since the early 1970s, the populations of Egypt and Iraq have doubled, and those of Jordan and Saudi Arabia have nearly tripled. As a result, per capita income in Arab states has grown at an anemic annual rate of 0.3%. With the labor force growing faster than that of any other region in the world, far outstripping available jobs, there is a deepening pool of restless, unemployed young men, a ripe breeding ground for terrorism.

Individual countries' relative success may be even more psychologically galling than absolute economic distress because public perceptions can often be more important than reality. The fundamental question that troubles many people in the Islamic world today: "Are we better or worse off than we should be?"

In the 1950s, per capita income in Egypt was similar to that in South Korea. Today it is less than one fifth that of the Asian economic tiger. A half century ago, Saudi Arabia's per capita income was higher than Taiwan's. Today, Saudi income is only half that of the Asian island nation, compounding Islamic humiliation. The Arab world as a whole has made great strides in extending life expectancy and lowering infant mortality. But it still trails Latin America and the Caribbean, which are generally perceived to be poorer.

Finally, the outmoded, state-controlled economies found in most Islamic countries are incompatible with the emerging global economy. Overly rigid markets lack the diversification to produce modern goods and services, constraining growth. Average tariffs in Egypt, Morocco and Tunisia, for example, are up to four times higher than those in their regional neighbor Israel. Governments in Arab nations, on average, employ more than one out of every six people, double the world norm. Nontariff-related trading costs—such as government paperwork and corruption—are estimated to account for up to 10% of the price of most goods, making them uncompetitive internationally and

BY DEERING FOR THE ARKANSAS DEMOCRAT-GAZETTE

out of the reach of many domestic consumers. State-owned banks still control a large share of total banking assets. Financial regulatory supervision is poor. Capital markets are underdeveloped.

"In such circumstances," said Jessica Stern, a lecturer on terrorism at Harvard University's Kennedy School of Government, "terrorists are drawn to extremist movements out of a feeling of severe deprivation."

Unfortunately, the governments of most Islamic states lack the democratic institutions necessary to help them deal with the sense of hopelessness and abandonment their people feel in the emerging global economy. Compared with almost every other region, the Arab world has failed to undergo a democratic transformation that would have created the institutions necessary to mediate these social and economic tensions.

Generals and kings and other hereditary rulers still run many Islamic societies. Elected leaders tend to hold their jobs for life. Parliaments have little power. It's little wonder that Freedom House, the New York–based think tank that specializes in tracking democracy around the world, ranks most Islamic nations as "not free."

Average people feel frustrated and cut off from power. A majority of Turks, two fifths of Egyptians and a third of Iranians distrust their governments. Tellingly, the more education people have, the less faith they have in their elected leaders.

Nevertheless, there is a broad Islamic public consensus that democracy is the best form of government. More than four out of five people in the region express such sentiments. Of course, definitions of democracy vary markedly from country to country. In Turkey, for example, only one in twenty people place great store in being free to criticize the government or in having a multiparty political system. So it would not be safe to assume that an Islamic democracy would necessarily bear any resemblance to its American cousin.

And the U.S. has done very little to help foster democratic institutions in many of these societies. In Egypt, Saudi Arabia, Kuwait and elsewhere in the Middle East, the U.S. has preserved close ties with autocratic regimes that serve short-term U.S. interests: access to oil, acquiescence in the Arab-Israeli peace process and resistance to Islamic fundamentalist groups.

In 1995, for example, Washington was mute when Egyptian President Hosni Mubarak steamrolled his way through yet another parliamentary election with little sign of a democratic opposition or later when he imprisoned human-rights advocates (1995–97). Nor did the U.S. effectively protest when Jordan postponed parliamentary elections because of the recent intifada.

Such U.S. support for authoritarian regimes has arguably arrested the evolution of democratic institutions in the region, incurring the wrath of the disadvantaged and those interested in democratic reforms.

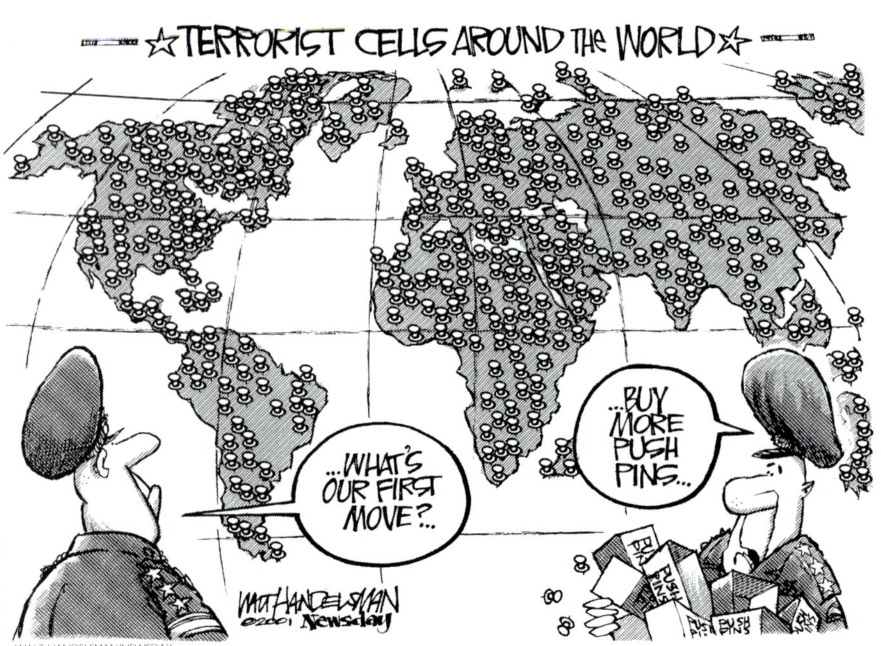

WALT HANDELSMAN/NEWSDAY

What can be done

There is little the U.S. can do about anti-Americanism rooted in who Americans are: modern, democratic, materialistic, culturally diverse. Those attributes can not and will not be changed. America can do something about the anti-Americanism evoked by how the U.S. acts or fails to act in the world. But Washington's track record in dealing with these issues leaves much to be desired.

Countering anti-Americanism requires both better U.S. public diplomacy—to be sure that people around the world understand who Americans are and what they stand for—and substantive economic and democracy-promoting initiatives to relieve economic and political frustration that nurtures anti-American hatred.

First must come better understanding. "The British, the French, even the Romans had a more subtle grasp of the nature of the countries in the Middle East than does the U.S.," said Valpy FitzGerald, a professor who specializes in globalization at Oxford University in Britain. "It's not the case that the U.S. is incompetent. You displayed a deep understanding of local politics in France and Germany after the war." Washington simply has not tried hard enough.

The paucity of Arab speakers and Islamic experts in the U.S. government, in American think tanks and in the media has been obvious for a generation. There are few American officials who can talk to Arab audiences through the media in Arabic. There is a need to speak directly to the Arab masses to make the case that the U.S. is not responsible for the high price of vegetable oil in the markets of Egypt or Yemen and that the U.S. cannot transform that situation overnight. In the wake of September 11, that effort has begun. But there is a long road ahead.

At the same time, the U.S. needs to encourage mainstream Islamic scholars from the Middle East to explain to their own people that Osama bin Laden's concept of a holy war against the American infidels is a grotesque misrepresentation of Muslim doctrine.

Tackling the region's underlying economic woes will be a tougher nut to crack.

The Bush Administration has crafted

a major economic aid package for nations on the front lines of the war on terrorism, such as Pakistan, and countries with large, potentially volatile Muslim populations, such as Indonesia. Assistance includes more foreign aid, new loans from the International Monetary Fund, a quick rollover of existing foreign debts and greater access to U.S. and European markets for the textiles and apparel these nations produce. In addition, the U.S. has already entered into a free-trade agreement with Jordan that could serve as a model for closer commercial ties with the region.

Focus on education

One important target for U.S. and other foreign aid could be education. Ignorance, not just poverty, is a fertile ground for extremism. Throughout the Middle East and other Islamic nations, secondary-school enrollment is relatively low and adult illiteracy is disproportionately high. Fundamentalist Islamic sects have frequently stepped into the void.

In Pakistan, for example, education is not mandatory. In many rural areas of that nation, for example, free government schools are not available. As a result, the World Bank estimates that only 40% of Pakistanis are literate. Islamic religious schools—*madrasas*—on the other hand, are located all over the country. Pakistani officials estimate there may be 50,000 such academies. They provide not only free education, but also free food, housing and clothing. In the poor areas of southern Punjab, madrasas reportedly even pay parents for sending them their children. In so doing, fundamentalist religious schools win converts to their brand of Islam. Most of these academies offer only religious instruction, ignoring math, science and other secular subjects important for functioning in a modern society. Pakistani officials estimate that at least one in ten of these schools also promote extremism, including holy war.

In Egypt and Jordan, where the state controls religious schools, jihad cannot be taught. The U.S. could lean on the Pakistani government to get control over its educational system and to equip women, as well as men, with modern skills. Washington could also provide Islamabad with the resources to succeed. One obstacle may be that surveys show majorities in a number of Muslim countries strongly believe that religion should have greater influence over education, not less.

In the end, however, economic aid is only a Band-Aid. To get these economies growing faster, profound economic reform—including trade liberalization and an overhaul of their domestic economies, revamping everything from the banking to the transport systems—is long overdue. And it is a reform that only these nations themselves can accomplish.

Finally, to change its image in the Islamic world, the U.S. may have to finally bite the bullet and press democratic reform in the region.

In recent history, the U.S. has done very little to promote democracy in Islamic societies. Instead, it has aligned itself with authoritarian regimes. Such support has arguably arrested evolution of democratic institutions in the region, incurring the wrath of those interested in democratic reform.

Obviously, over the next few months, the Bush Administration has little choice but to move cautiously on the democratization front. It must handle Pakistan, in particular, with kid gloves, to avoid toppling an already unstable regime. The last thing Washington needs in Islamabad is a new, fundamentalist Pakistani government with its hands on some two dozen of its own nuclear bombs. Similarly, the U.S. needs a stable Saudi government to sustain world oil production. Moreover, in the short run, if there were fair and free elections in many of these countries, it is not at all clear what kind of governments many of these electorates would choose. Some would undoubtedly be antithetical to U.S. interests.

But there are pro-democracy initiatives that can be launched. Over the last eight years, the U.S. has invested only $300 million in democracy promotion in the region, primarily in Egypt and the West Bank, focusing on free and fair elections, judicial and legislative reform and bureaucratic decentralization. More money could be used.

But some activities require political capital, not taxpayer dollars. The U.S. government could have great success in fostering democracy in Islamic societies simply by forcefully encouraging its Arab allies to engage in more dialogue with their citizens for the sake of alleviating pressure from below. At the very least, it could respond boldly whenever there is an unexpected weakening of a dictator or the threatened breakdown of what democracy exists in the region.

Conclusion

In the weeks and months since September 11, an overwhelming majority of the American public has supported the U.S. bombing campaign against Afghanistan and the overthrow of the Taliban government there. Such support has remained strong even in light of the possibility of terrorist retaliation against the U.S., American battle casualties, the killing of innocent civilians and prospects for a long war. What the American public has not demonstrated is support for dealing with the underlying issues that engender frustration and resentment toward the U.S. and foster terrorism. In fact, a recent Pew Research Center survey found that while the American public's support for a multilateral foreign policy has increased in the wake of the terrorist attacks, its support for humanitarian efforts—combating AIDS in Africa, or fighting world poverty—has actually gone down.

If September 11 was this generation's Pearl Harbor, there may also be a need for a modern Marshall Plan for economic recovery to root out the causes of terrorism. The failure to boost economic development and democratization in Western Europe after World War I led to World War II. And America's success in dealing with such problems in the wake of World War II avoided World War III.

So, coping with anti-Americanism, antiglobalism and antisecularism in the Islamic world has to be a fundamental component of the new U.S. "war on terrorism." Telling America's story, spurring economic development and promoting democracy will not be as compelling as an air war or as satisfying to America's current need for justice. But fear of the modern world and resentment and hostility toward the U.S. run deep in many Muslim societies. U.S. military actions in Afghanistan and possibly elsewhere are only likely to intensify such feelings. Unless Washington addresses those concerns, the economic and psychological conditions that gave birth to terrorism will remain and possibly worsen. ■

OPINION BALLOTS are on pages 19–20

DISCUSSION QUESTIONS

1. Is recent anti-Americanism primarily sparked by what the U.S. does in the world—supports Israel, promotes economic globalization, conducts superpower foreign policy—or is it driven by opposition to fundamental U.S. values—pluralism, democracy and secularism?

2. Should the U.S. change its behavior abroad—moderate its support of Israel, increase its foreign aid and so forth—to address the concerns reflected in anti-Americanism?

3. What can the U.S. do about anti-Americanism that is rooted in who Americans are?

4. To what degree do you think resentment of the U.S. reflects anti-Americanism and to what degree does it reflect broader frustration with globalization and modernization?

5. Are the antisecular sentiments expressed by Islamic fundamentalists a reflection of a deeper cultural clash between the Islamic and Christian civilizations?

6. Should the U.S. promote democracy in autocratic countries that happen to be U.S. allies, even at the risk of destabilizing the current governments of those nations?

READINGS AND RESOURCES

Ajami, Fouad, "The Sentry's Solitude." **Foreign Affairs,** Nov./Dec. 2001, pp. 2–16. Against the backdrop of rampant anti-Americanism in the Middle East, which governments can the U.S. count on and at what price?

Armstrong, Karen, **Islam: A Short History.** New York, Random House, 2000. 272 pp. $19.95. This brief overview lays to rest Western prejudices that Islam is a backward, intolerant, violent religion. Armstrong traces Muhammad's rise, subsequent splits in Islamic religious practice between Sunnis and Shiites, and the rise of Islamic fundamentalism.

Barber, Benjamin R., and Schultz, Andrea, **Jihad vs. McWorld: How Globalism and Tribalism Are Reshaping the World.** New York, Ballantine Books, 1996. 400 pp. $15.00 (paper). An analysis of the conflict between consumer capitalism and religious fundamentalism. The authors highlight the paradoxical interdependence of these two forces and show how their tensions contribute to anti-Americanism.

Harrison, Lawrence E., and Huntington, Samuel P., eds., **Culture Matters: How Values Shape Human Progress.** New York, Basic Books, 2001. 384 pp. $18.00 (paper). The point of the various essays is not to denigrate any particular culture but to offer insights into why some countries and ethnic and religious groups have done better than others.

Huntington, Samuel P., **The Clash of Civilizations and the Remaking of World Order.** New York, Simon and Schuster, 1997. 367 pp. $15.00 (paper). Based on the author's seminal article in **Foreign Affairs** (Summer 1993), this book is a provocative polemic, arguing that Islamic, Sinic (East Asian) and other "civilizations" have replaced nations and ideologies as the driving force in global politics in the post-cold-war era.

Lewis, Bernard, **The Multiple Identities of the Middle East.** New York, Schocken Books, 2001. 176 pp. $12.00 (paper). Lewis, the foremost Western historian of the Middle East, discusses the evolving identity of people in the Middle East caught between imported Western concepts of individual political freedoms and loyalty to community traditions.

Miller, Judith, **God Has Ninety-Nine Names: Reporting from a Militant Middle East.** New York, Simon and Schuster, 1997. 476 pp. $15.00 (paper). This survey of militant Islam, by the former bureau chief for **The New York Times** in Cairo covers eight Arab countries, plus Iran and Israel. She argues, presciently, that Islamic fundamentalists are threatening Middle Eastern stability. She paints a picture of floundering, incompetent governments, corruption and repression that shows why Arab states are vulnerable to a fundamentalist movement promising social justice and moral righteousness.

BROOKINGS INSTITUTION, 1775 Massachusetts Ave., NW, Washington, DC 20036; (202) 797-6000; Fax (202) 797-6004. **www.brookings.org** ■ This private nonprofit think tank has dedicated a site to analysis of the recent terrorist activity, with links to Weekly Terrorism Briefings.

CENTER FOR STRATEGIC AND INTERNATIONAL STUDIES, 1800 K St., NW, Suite 400, Washington, DC 20006; (202) 887-0200; Fax (202) 775-3199. **www.csis.org** ■ This public-policy research institute provides a description and analysis of known terrorist groups and activities.

CHEMICAL AND BIOLOGICAL ARMS CONTROL INSTITUTE, 1747 Pennsylvania Ave., NW, 7th fl., Washington, DC 20006; (202) 296-3550; Fax (202) 296-3574. **www.cbaci.org** ■ This organization is dedicated to research, analysis, publication and education on issues related to arms control, nonproliferation, counterterrorism and new national security challenges.

THE NATIONAL ENDOWMENT FOR DEMOCRACY, 1101 Fifteenth St., NW, Suite 700, Washington, DC 20005; (202) 293-9072; Fax (202) 223-6042. **www.ned.org.** ■ The endowment is a private, nonprofit organization funded by the U.S. government to strengthen democratic institutions around the world.

U.S. STATE DEPARTMENT, Coordinator for Counterterrorism, Office of Public Affairs, Room 2507, Department of State, 2201 C St., NW, Washington, DC 20520. **www.state.gov/s/ct** ■ This website contains information on U.S. policy toward terrorist activity and links to State Department reports on global terrorism.

½ OPINION BALLOTS

Please submit only one ballot per person, per topic. *Ballots must be received by June 30, 2002.*
Vote online at ***www.greatdecisions.org*** *(code: gd2002fpa) or mail ballots to:*

FOREIGN POLICY ASSOCIATION, 470 PARK AVENUE SOUTH, NEW YORK, NY 10016-6819

TOPIC 1 Roots of terrorism

ISSUE A. What do you think was the most significant factor sparking the acts of terrorism on September 11? (choose one)

___ **1.** Opposition to U.S. policies

___ **2.** Opposition to American values

___ **3.** Neither

Comment: ______________________________

ISSUE B. How much blame for the acts of terrorism on September 11 would you assign to Islamic fundamentalism? (choose one)

___ **1.** A great deal

___ **2.** Some

___ **3.** None

Comment: ______________________________

Your zip code: ___ ___ ___ ___ ___

Date: / /2002 *Ballot continues on reverse side…*

TOPIC 1 Roots of terrorism

ISSUE A. What do you think was the most significant factor sparking the acts of terrorism on September 11? (choose one)

___ **1.** Opposition to U.S. policies

___ **2.** Opposition to American values

___ **3.** Neither

Comment: ______________________________

ISSUE B. How much blame for the acts of terrorism on September 11 would you assign to Islamic fundamentalism? (choose one)

___ **1.** A great deal

___ **2.** Some

___ **3.** None

Comment: ______________________________

Your zip code: ___ ___ ___ ___ ___

Date: / /2002 *Ballot continues on reverse side…*

TOPIC 2 Korean security issues

ISSUE A. In dealing with North Korea, the U.S. should:

	YES	NO
1. Renounce the Agreed Framework of October 1994.	❑	❑
2. Insist that North Korea first reduce its conventional forces before negotiating with it.	❑	❑
3. Offer political and economic inducements to North Korea to expedite nuclear inspections and halt its export, testing, production and deployment of missiles.	❑	❑
4. Withhold any assistance until North Korea reforms its economy.	❑	❑

ISSUE B. As for relations between North and South Korea, the U.S. should (choose one):

___ **1.** Promote reconciliation between the two Koreas.

___ **2.** Impede reconciliation unless both Koreas allow U.S. troops to stay.

___ **3.** Oppose reconciliation between the two Koreas.

Your zip code: ___ ___ ___ ___ ___

Date: / /2002 *Ballot continues on reverse side…*

TOPIC 2 Korean security issues

ISSUE A. In dealing with North Korea, the U.S. should:

	YES	NO
1. Renounce the Agreed Framework of October 1994.	❑	❑
2. Insist that North Korea first reduce its conventional forces before negotiating with it.	❑	❑
3. Offer political and economic inducements to North Korea to expedite nuclear inspections and halt its export, testing, production and deployment of missiles.	❑	❑
4. Withhold any assistance until North Korea reforms its economy.	❑	❑

ISSUE B. As for relations between North and South Korea, the U.S. should (choose one):

___ **1.** Promote reconciliation between the two Koreas.

___ **2.** Impede reconciliation unless both Koreas allow U.S. troops to stay.

___ **3.** Oppose reconciliation between the two Koreas.

Your zip code: ___ ___ ___ ___ ___

Date: / /2002 *Ballot continues on reverse side…*

ISSUE C. Do you agree or disagree with the following statements?

	AGREE	DISAGREE
1. The U.S. war in Afghanistan is an example of the "clash of civilizations."	❑	❑
2. The U.S. should change its policies abroad to alleviate anti-American sentiments.	❑	❑
3. The U.S. should promote democracy in the Middle East even if that may destabilize some of those regimes.	❑	❑

Comment: ______________________________

A. *How many years have you participated in the* Great Decisions *program (that is, attended one or more discussion sessions)?*
- ❑ **1.** This is the first year I have participated.
- ❑ **2.** I participated in one previous year.
- ❑ **3.** I participated in more than one previous year.

B. *What is your age?* ❑ **1.** 17 or under ❑ **2.** 18 to 30 ❑ **3.** 31 to 45 ❑ **4.** 46 to 60 ❑ **5.** 61 or over

C. *Your sex?* ❑ **1.** Female ❑ **2.** Male

D. *Have you been abroad during the last two years?* ❑ **1.** Yes ❑ **2.** No

E. *Do you know, or are you learning, a foreign language?* ❑ **1.** Yes ❑ **2.** No

F. *What is the highest level of formal education you have completed?*
❑ **1.** Some high school ❑ **2.** High-school degree ❑ **3.** Some college ❑ **4.** College graduate ❑ **5.** Advanced degree

G. *How often are you asked for your opinion on foreign policy matters?*
❑ **1.** Often ❑ **2.** Sometimes ❑ **3.** Hardly ever

H. *How many **hours**, on average, do you spend reading one* Great Decisions *chapter?*
❑ **1.** Less than 1 hr. ❑ **2.** 1–2 hrs. ❑ **3.** 3–4 hrs. ❑ **4.** More than 4 hrs.

I. *Do you have access to the Internet (check all that apply)?*
❑ **1.** Yes, at home. ❑ **2.** Yes, at work. ❑ **3.** Yes, at school. ❑ **4.** Yes, at the library or Internet café. ❑ **5.** No.

J. *Would you say you have or have not changed your opinion in a fairly significant way as a result of taking part in the* Great Decisions *program?*
❑ **1.** Have ❑ **2.** Have not ❑ **3.** Uncertain

ISSUE C. Do you agree or disagree with the following statements?

	AGREE	DISAGREE
1. The U.S. war in Afghanistan is an example of the "clash of civilizations."	❑	❑
2. The U.S. should change its policies abroad to alleviate anti-American sentiments.	❑	❑
3. The U.S. should promote democracy in the Middle East even if that may destabilize some of those regimes.	❑	❑

Comment: ______________________________

A. *How many years have you participated in the* Great Decisions *program (that is, attended one or more discussion sessions)?*
- ❑ **1.** This is the first year I have participated.
- ❑ **2.** I participated in one previous year.
- ❑ **3.** I participated in more than one previous year.

B. *What is your age?* ❑ **1.** 17 or under ❑ **2.** 18 to 30 ❑ **3.** 31 to 45 ❑ **4.** 46 to 60 ❑ **5.** 61 or over

C. *Your sex?* ❑ **1.** Female ❑ **2.** Male

D. *Have you been abroad during the last two years?* ❑ **1.** Yes ❑ **2.** No

E. *Do you know, or are you learning, a foreign language?* ❑ **1.** Yes ❑ **2.** No

F. *What is the highest level of formal education you have completed?*
❑ **1.** Some high school ❑ **2.** High-school degree ❑ **3.** Some college ❑ **4.** College graduate ❑ **5.** Advanced degree

G. *How often are you asked for your opinion on foreign policy matters?*
❑ **1.** Often ❑ **2.** Sometimes ❑ **3.** Hardly ever

H. *How many **hours**, on average, do you spend reading one* Great Decisions *chapter?*
❑ **1.** Less than 1 hr. ❑ **2.** 1–2 hrs. ❑ **3.** 3–4 hrs. ❑ **4.** More than 4 hrs.

I. *Do you have access to the Internet (check all that apply)?*
❑ **1.** Yes, at home. ❑ **2.** Yes, at work. ❑ **3.** Yes, at school. ❑ **4.** Yes, at the library or Internet café. ❑ **5.** No.

J. *Would you say you have or have not changed your opinion in a fairly significant way as a result of taking part in the* Great Decisions *program?*
❑ **1.** Have ❑ **2.** Have not ❑ **3.** Uncertain

VIEW POINTS

Korean security issues

APWIDE WORLD PHOTOS

AT SUNAN INTERNATIONAL AIRPORT, PYONGYANG, *North Korean leader Kim Jong Il, left, and South Korean President Kim Dae Jung shake hands prior to their historic three-day summit meeting in June 2000.*

PLEASE NOTE: In response to interest from our participants, we are experimenting with a new format for this topic. Instead of the treatment of an issue by one author, we present two differing perspectives. Leon V. Sigal argues that the problem with engaging North Korea stems partly from U.S. misinterpretation of Pyongyang's negotiating strategy, which Washington should test through diplomatic give-and-take, and John E. McLaughlin discusses the difficulties of engaging North Korea because of its own instability and negative behavior.

Cooperative security in Korea

by Leon V. Sigal

LEON V. SIGAL *is director of the Northeast Asia Cooperative Security Project at the Social Science Research Council and author of* Disarming Strangers: Nuclear Diplomacy with North Korea, *published by Princeton University Press. His work is supported by the Carnegie Corporation, the W. Alton Jones Foundation and the Plowshares Foundation.*

When Americans think of North Korea, what comes to mind are goose-stepping troops parading past a reviewing stand, a regime motivated by paranoid hostility to menace the world with nuclear weapons and missiles, a command economy that makes little for the world to buy except missiles, a terrorist state that committed horrifying acts, like the 1983 bombing in Rangoon, Myanmar, that barely missed South Korea's president and killed 17 members of his entourage and 4 bystanders. Yes, in many respects, North Korea fits the image of a rogue state.

Rogue state is another name for enemy, and the way to treat enemies is to isolate and coerce them, not engage and cooperate with them. The problem with that approach is that since the late 1980s, North Korea has been trying to end its lifelong enmity with the U.S. In exchange, it has demonstrated willingness to halt its nuclear-arms and missile programs and it may even be prepared to end its artillery threat to Seoul, South Korea—but only if Washington cooperates.

What U.S. interests are at stake with North Korea at this time? First, the U.S. wants to guarantee that, whatever happens internally in North Korea, the artillery Pyongyang has emplaced within range of Seoul is never fired in anger. Second, it wants to stop Pyongyang from acquiring nuclear arms. Third, it wants to prevent North Korea from developing, testing, deploying and selling any more ballistic missiles. Fourth, it seeks reconciliation between the two Koreas and peaceful reunification of the peninsula.

The only way to achieve these aims—and reduce uncertainty about North Korea's intentions—is to engage in diplomatic give-and-take, testing whether North Korea is willing to cooperate with the U.S. Coercion will not work; it will only ensure that North Korea deploys more artillery near the demilitarized zone (DMZ), seeks more aggressively to acquire nuclear arms and tests, deploys and sells more missiles.

Encouraging the collapse of North Korea, which some people think is in the American interest, is far too risky a course, especially if the first three aims have not been achieved. Others want to condition U.S. aid on reform in North Korea. Does the U.S. care how North Korea runs its economy so long as it does not threaten its neighbors? Besides, conditioning aid is counterproductive. Change will come as more outsiders begin working in North Korea. That, too, will be possible only if Pyongyang cooperates. A careful look at its last decade of interaction with Washington suggests Pyongyang has been willing to do just that.

Blackmail or tit for tat?

Militarily, ever since the mid-1980s, North Korea has been no match for South Korea alone, even without U.S. help. Pyongyang fears Japan's growing military might, a fear that recent actions by Japan have done little to dispel. Meanwhile, North Korea has lost its friends: Russia is no longer a strong and reliable ally and China will help only in the event of an attack. Economically, with the collapse of communism in the Soviet Union and Eastern Europe and with China on a capitalist road, North Korea has had to turn elsewhere for aid, investment and trade. What better way to provide for its own security than to befriend the U.S., South Korea and Japan?

Faced with ever-worsening prospects, then North Korean leader Kim Il Sung decided in the late 1980s to reach out to all three rivals—only to have the first Bush Administration impede closer South Korean and Japanese ties to the North and insist that Pyongyang would have to stop developing nuclear arms before its isolation could end. Concluding that Washington held the key to open doors to Japan and South Korea, Pyongyang decided to trade in its nuclear-arms program in return for better relations. At the same time, it kept its nuclear option open as leverage on Washington to live up to its end of the bargain.

Critics concluded that Pyongyang was engaging in blackmail in an attempt to obtain economic aid and had no intention of giving up anything in return. It was not. It was playing tit for tat, cooperating whenever the U.S. cooperated, retaliating when the U.S. reneged, in an effort to get the U.S. to put an end to enmity.

If North Korea had been determined to acquire nuclear arms early in the 1990s, as most people in Washington believed at the time, it could have shut down its nuclear reactor at Yongbyon anytime between 1991 and 1994, removed the spent nuclear fuel and quickly reprocessed it to extract plutonium, the explosive ingredient in bombs. Yet international inspectors have verified that North Korea did no reprocessing there from 1991 on. Nor did it shut down the reactor until May 1994, long after it was expected to. These actions indicate that Pyongyang was exercising some self-restraint in hopes of concluding a nuclear deal with the U.S. In May 1992 it offered to trade in its reactor at Yongbyon.

Uncertain about North Korean nuclear intentions and slow to recognize its change of course, Washington ignored the offer and threatened sanctions or worse if North Korea did not fulfill its obligations under the Nuclear Non-Proliferation Treaty of 1968. Pyongyang, in turn, warned it would renounce the treaty. The International Atomic Energy Agency demanded special inspections and warned of sanctions. The North, in turn, restricted but did not foreclose the inspectors' access to Yongbyon.

That drove both sides to the brink. Only a bold mission to Pyongyang in June 1994 by former President Jimmy Carter averted war by undermining the U.S. sanction strategy and convincing Kim Il Sung to attend a summit meeting with South Korea and to suspend nuclear arming. In the Agreed Framework of October 1994, the North agreed to freeze and eventually dismantle its nuclear-arms program in return for two

(continued on page 27)

North Korea: engagement or confrontation

by John E. McLaughlin

JOHN E. McLAUGHLIN *is Deputy Director of Central Intelligence. In his previous position as Deputy Director for Intelligence he was responsible for the analysis of political, economic and military events worldwide. The following is excerpted from a speech at the Texas A&M Conference on "North Korea: Engagement or Confrontation."*

The full text of this speech is available online at
www.cia.gov/cia/public_affairs/speeches/ddci_speech_04172001.html

Confrontation has been a virtual constant in U.S. relations with North Korea for more than half a century. The far newer phenomenon is engagement—cautious, tentative, guarded, halting—apply the adjective of your choice.

Engagement or confrontation? Ultimately, they describe policy options. It is, of course, not the mission of U.S. Intelligence to prescribe policy.... But, on our best days, we do hope to inform policy.

That said, let me say explicitly that no one should comb through these remarks for clues about the future direction of U.S. policy on Korea. These are personal reflections on one of the most complex and significant issues of our time.

When it comes to North Korea, conditions there clearly hold the potential for both engagement and confrontation. For a state like the North—often reflexively hostile to the outside world, yet in need of it as never before—engagement and the potential for confrontation can coexist—and are likely to coexist—even in the best of scenarios.

The nature of the challenge

What are the elements of the problem? For the U.S., North Korea is—first and foremost—a challenge. It was throughout the cold war, and it is so now. In fact, it could be said that North Korea was a metaphor for some of the most extreme aspects of the cold war and is today a metaphor for the most challenging aspects of the new world that has come in its wake.

Let's look back for a moment and then talk about how the picture has changed. As you all know, the armistice of July 1953 created on the Korean peninsula a long pattern of tense standoff, punctuated by occasional crisis. For U.S. Intelligence, North Korea became—as much as anything—an order-of-battle problem. Count the troops. Count the tanks. Count the guns. Add up the capabilities. Estimate their intentions. I know I'm making this sound easier and simpler than it was, but my point is that we were dealing with a much less fluid picture back then.

Like everyone else, we knew the regime was brutal within its borders and a menace beyond. Its commando raids into South Korea and its assassination attempts against successive South Korean presidents—including the 1983 bombing in Rangoon that killed 21 people—were clear windows into the minds and morals of North Korean leaders.

And yet, North Korea's status as a client of the Soviet Union and China—a prickly client, to be sure—did impose constraints on its behavior. With the end of the cold war and the scaling back of the subsidies that went with it, those constraints began to erode. Today, it may be a fragile regime, but it is one that operates with fewer constraints on its behavior and often outside international norms. And, as I implied earlier, it operates in a world where the reference points—technological, geopolitical, economic, military—are themselves in flux.

In short order, the challenge that North Korea poses to us and our allies has grown in complexity and peril. Its traditional feature—the conventional threat—remains in place. And—as we saw in September 1996 and June 1999—the North has found it hard to abandon tactics like commando incursions and naval confrontations—even when they fail miserably.

But added into this mix is an increased threat from weapons of mass destruction and the humanitarian challenge we could face, given the increased stress that poverty and economic decline must be creating in the North.

The conventional threat...

Let's talk for a minute about the conventional military picture. I reveal no secret when I say that on the battlefield North Korea cannot defeat the South and the U.S. But it could inflict tremendous damage in a losing cause.

The North Korean military, like all but the most elite of North Korean society, has suffered the effects of the country's economic implosion. It does not exercise often or well. Its equipment is aging. Its military production is scant. But it is large, and most of it is forward deployed.

Its artillery could rain havoc down on Seoul, a mere 30 miles from the DMZ. It has the biggest pool of special forces in the world—not the best, as we have seen, but with enough punch to sow panic and destruction.

These are capabilities. The intention to use them is a very different matter, and this has been debated thoroughly for years. The case can be made that it would be foolish for the North to use these capabilities. And the case can be made that it would be foolish to make that assumption. But, the bottom line is that like any military commander, we in the intelligence profession can ill-afford to ignore capabilities.

In fact, I can tell you that we tend to make our mistakes not when we convince ourselves that a foreign group or leader might do something, but when we convince ourselves that they will not.

Here is a short passage from one of our intelligence assessments: "...an invasion of South Korea is unlikely unless North Korean forces can develop a clear-cut superiority over the increasingly efficient South Korean army." That judgment came out on the 13th of January—1950. It had a fairly short shelf life.

No matter what we think the North Korean leadership might do with its military, it is a linchpin of their state. They take it very seriously. And so must we—as the ally of South Korea and its democracy, and as a nation with 37,000 of its own troops serving, working, and living among 45 million friends in what could one day be harm's way.

That holds true whether we believe the North sees its armed forces as a mark of prestige, a constituency to be satisfied, a tool that might bring respect, or even one that might bring conquest. The military has priority on whatever resources the North has. This is stated policy, the so-called "military first" policy. But it is hardly the whole story.

...and unconventional ones

Were Kim Jong Il and his lieutenants simply sitting atop a large collection of conventional forces, they would still be a grave concern. But it would be one whose destructive power and geographic reach the U.S. and South Korea have together understood and managed for decades.

As real as the conventional threat may be, North Korea's challenge to regional and global security is magnified by two other factors I've already mentioned.

First, the North's pursuit of weapons of mass destruction and long-range missiles, and its readiness—even eagerness—to become missile salesman to the world. And second, the economic and humanitarian disaster that has afflicted the people of the North—a catastrophe whose effects will endure for generations, no matter how the Korean situation finally plays out.

Weapons of terror

Looking first at those advanced weapons: as we all know, it was not a brigade of tanks or division of infantry that riveted our attention and concern on the Korean peninsula early in the last decade. It was the nuclear plant at Yongbyon.

The Agreed Framework has frozen activity there. But we still cannot account for all of North Korea's plutonium. And—with an opaque regime in which the practice of denial and deception is embedded in national strategy—we still cannot say for sure that nuclear-weapons-related work is not going on somewhere else.

Indeed, the North probably has one or two nuclear bombs—and it may also have biological weapons alongside its chemical ones.

Regarding missiles, the outlines of the North's program are far less mysterious, for the leadership sees the No Dong and Taepo Dong as tools of public diplomacy as well as national defense.

It has so far held to its missile launch moratorium and it has signaled its interest in negotiating a missile deal with us. At the same time, the North's proliferation activities remain robust—for a profit and for a purpose: To keep our attention, to underline their greatest source of leverage, and to remind us of what it is they are willing to haggle over.

North Korea continues to aggressively market its ballistic missiles, equipment and technology. We find the No Dong and its variants in places like Iran and Pakistan, where they have the potential to alter geopolitical and military calculations in important ways throughout the Middle East and South Asia.

In short, the North has accelerated the pace at which other countries acquire and refine potential delivery systems for weapons of mass destruction.

The flight of a Taepo Dong over Japan more than two years ago added a new and worrisome dimension to the North's own definitions of deterrence and power projection. And it is busy at work on new models that could reach the U.S. itself with nuclear-sized payloads.

The humanitarian challenge

Turning to the second factor I mentioned: even as the North challenges the world in one small but lethal field of modern technology, it presents another challenge as old as life itself: malnutrition and starvation.

A combination of natural calamity and human mismanagement may have claimed up to a million lives in the 1990s. Even today, the North's sputtering economy remains unable to provide remotely sufficient food or work for its people.

Even with the charity of other nations, malnutrition is widespread. Without this charity, famine would be epidemic. Many North Koreans must simply fend for themselves, seemingly forgotten by a system that nonetheless demands their obedience. Some just flee.

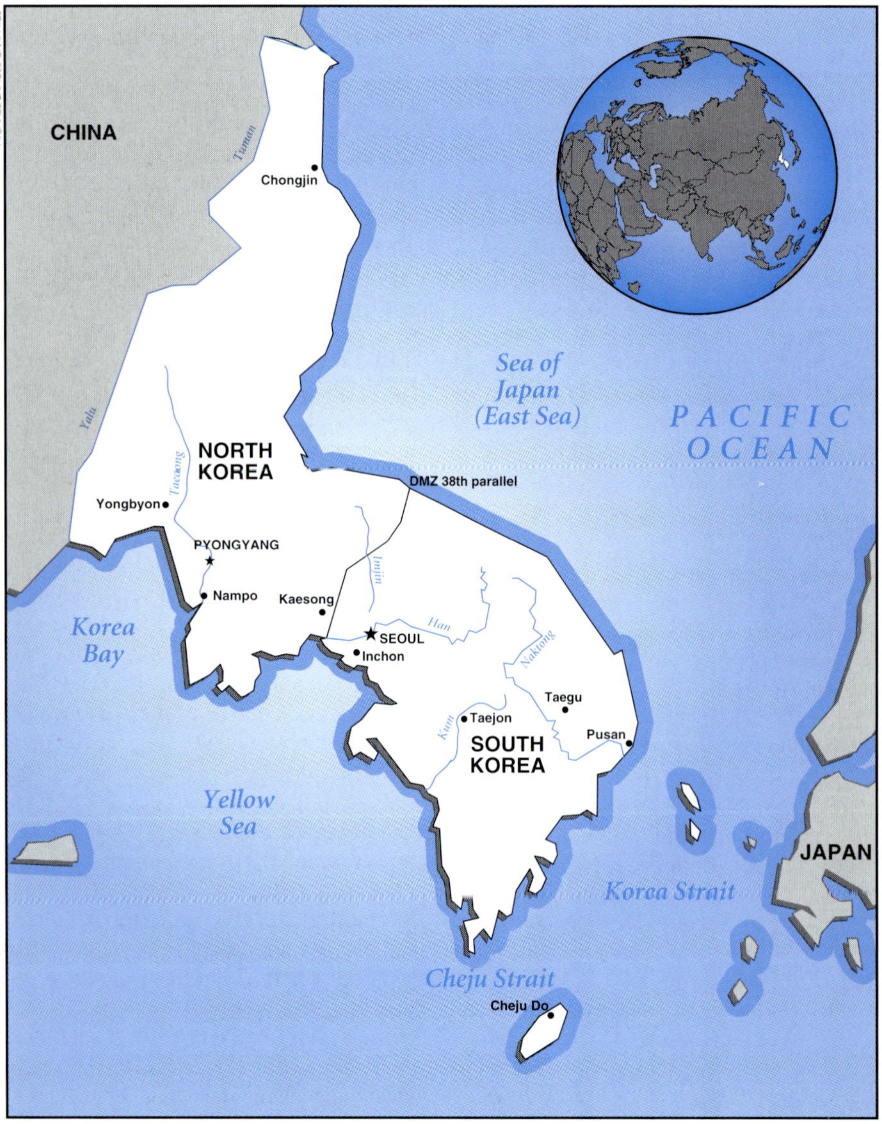

MICHAEL SAMUEL GRAPHICS

As for the others, their dire poverty is captured in a single picture—one that I am sure many of you ... have seen. It is a satellite photo of the Korean peninsula at night. North China and South Korea are a blaze of lights. North Korea is totally dark outside the single dot that is Pyongyang. The fishing fleets in the Sea of Japan give off far more light than does all of North Korea.

No one who looks at that photograph should forget that there are some 23 million human beings struggling in that darkness.

North Korea's leadership: tactical flexibility...

And what of the small group in that dot of light, the small group that commands North Korea? . . . No matter what you make of Kim Jong Il's diplomatic opening, it does at least reflect a tactical flexibility. His words and actions are well worth weighing and watching. We have all seen the signposts.

His behavior at the North-South summit. His dispatch of Vice Marshal Cho to Washington and his reception of American diplomats in Pyongyang. His acceptance of foreign aid and foreign aid workers. His efforts to attract foreign money to his investment enclaves. His small adjustments to the domestic economy.

But the key is whether any of these steps signal the start of a process. For in and of themselves, they have yet to bring real improvement to the North. Yet they do suggest the leadership there knows it must do something to better conditions in the country—for its own survival, if nothing else.

Kim's trips to China in January of this year and May of last year are also significant. But so is the fact that China's economic reform was made possible in large part by the passing of Mao and the deemphasis of major portions of his legacy. In North Korea, we have yet to see any comparable movement away from the legacy of Kim Il Sung and all that it represents. Real change will not come until that happens.

...Risky strategy

So far in Pyongyang, the son has held fast to the father's legacy, including the goal of Northern preeminence in a reunified Korea.

It is easy to caricature Kim Jong Il—either as a simple tyrant blind to his dilemma or as a technocratic champion of sweeping change. But the extreme views of him tend to be the product of bias, ignorance or wishful thinking. The reality is more complex.

AP/WIDE WORLD PHOTOS

NORTH KOREA LAUNCHED THE SATELLITE *Kwangmyunsung One over a Japanese island in August 1998.*

At home, he has shown his hard side—through his purges of the elite, his light regard for the suffering of ordinary Koreans and the swift destruction of any expression of popular discontent. Abroad, he has shown his pragmatic side—through his willingness to engage old enemies and his skilled brinkmanship as he does so.

Like his father, he has been shrewd enough to make bad behavior the keystone of his foreign policy. He knows that proliferation is something we want to stop. Thus, Kim Jong Il has tried to drum up outside assistance by trading off international concerns about his missile programs and sales. He has—more subtly, of course—done much the same thing with foreign fears of renewed famine and the chaos that could accompany any unraveling of his regime.

These are the wild cards he adds to strengthen what would otherwise be a deuce-high hand. This is his leverage with the world. Along the way, he will seek to exploit any daylight he can find between the U.S., South Korea, Japan, the European Union, or anyone else who might be inclined to offer him economic help. And from his perspective, it makes good sense.

Decisive to the success of this strategy is the projection of a credible threat. And here—as we know—the North has its bases covered. But, like any policy founded on threats, it comes with the built-in possibility of accident or miscalculation—by those who conduct it, or by those who react to it.

The nature of the regime

Before I can say anything about the future of the North Korean regime—and its challenge—a few words are in order about what makes it tick today.

It is a peculiar creation. The leaden, bureaucratic Marxism we saw falter in the late 20th century—with its gray Central Committees and half-forgotten Central European ideology—is an imperfect guide to North Korea and offers few reliable analogies for how the North Korean regime might some day experience transformation.

The transformation of the Central European countries at the beginning of the last decade was eased by at least three things not present in the North Korean equation: extensive exposure to and penetration by the outside world (East Germany is the best example); economies already on the road to privatization (Hungary was the extreme case); and the presence of dissident movements powerful enough in a country like Poland to represent an effective parallel society.

Instead of these cushioning factors, in North Korea, the command economy, central planning, and other familiar features introduced there long ago by the Soviets exist alongside something else. A single story makes the point. A foreign visitor asked a North Korean what he thought of Kim Il Sung. "He is God,"

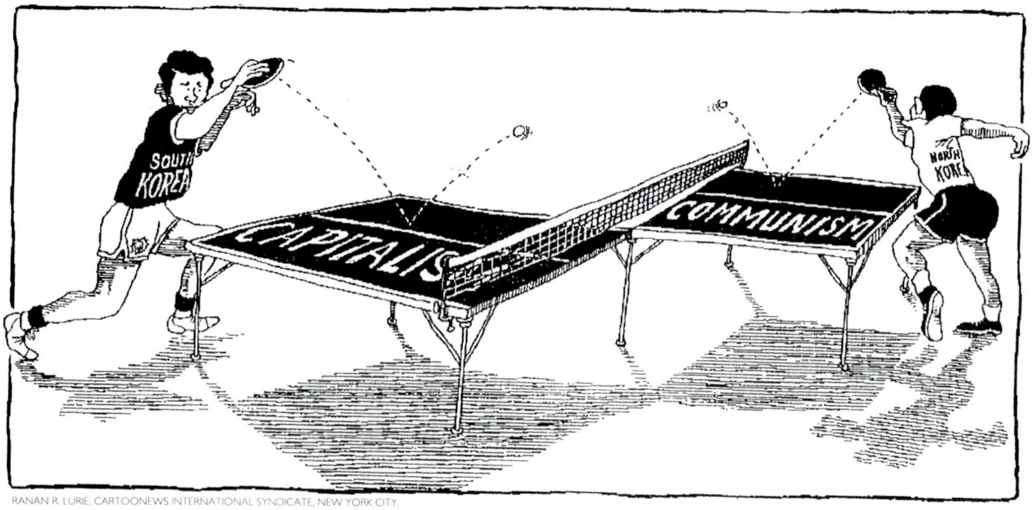

RANAN R. LURIE, CARTOONEWS INTERNATIONAL SYNDICATE, NEW YORK CITY.

came the answer. Then a tougher one. "What do you think of Kim Jong Il?" The Korean thought a moment, looked around, and replied: "He is 70% God."

Those answers might be very different were the North Korean outside the country. But they do say something about the tone and tenor of the regime on the inside.

Now I'm sure there are subtleties and complexities about the regime that we can neither discern nor appreciate. But that aside, the key is that power continues to reside with Kim Jong Il and the cluster of relatives and allies who run the military, the security forces, and the rest of the state and party apparatus.

No matter how you view them, it is evident they rule a state that is simultaneously impoverished and addicted to living beyond its means. They preach the values of self-reliance, but they rely on foreign aid. The priorities they set and enforce have delivered a huge army, a broken economy, widespread hunger, and a challenge for all of us.

...and its future

Because totalitarian elites tend to mask their own policy deliberations and drive opposition underground, the health and stability of their regimes are notoriously difficult for outsiders to gauge. North Korea is no exception. Predictions of its collapse have come and gone, and I will not venture one here now.

But I will say the North faces tough choices. Kim Jong Il probably recognizes the obvious truth that the economic competition with the South is lost. And he has seen for himself the economic gains brought by reform in China.

Yet he also knows the security risks involved and he knows the fates of other leaders who fell victim to change they could not control. He may have seen images of Gorbachev in retirement. Of Honecker in exile. Of a startled Ceausescu on his palace balcony the day the crowd stopped cheering.

At this point, Kim Jong Il may have a toe in the river of change. And he is moving just as we would expect him to: Slowly, carefully, with plenty of room to bargain, maneuver, or pull back.

After a decade of deprivation, the real story may be the durability of the North—a grim testament to the power of a people's ability to endure hardship.

Clearly, the North is under serious stress and it is likely to remain so. But frankly, no one can be confident about when, how, or even whether that stress might achieve critical mass and lead to fracture.

That formulation may not be intellectually satisfying. But I hope you will agree that it is intellectually honest.

The regional context

As the situation in the North unfolds, there is a final element of change we must consider: The regional context, which . . . was reshaped by the close of the cold war.

Russia and China are each redefining their power, their influence, and their reach, and their relationship with each other. Japan is focused on ending its long economic recession and has heightened security concerns in the aftermath of Pyongyang's missile tests. And South Korea has emerged as a vibrant society with a strong democracy and the world's 12th-largest economy—a stark contrast to the stagnation in North Korea, whose economy barely registers on the charts.

And East Asia as a whole is looking anew at the U.S., now the only global superpower. In that capacity, we are still often called on to be partner, protector or honest broker. But we are also seen as a nation whose interests and priorities do not always coincide with the other major actors in the region.

It is in this fluid environment that the U.S. must work the problem of North Korea. We find in the immediate neighborhood friends and allies like South Korea and Japan, and others, like Russia and China, whose interests may converge less frequently with ours but who nonetheless share with us a common, significant stake in the ultimate destiny of North Korea. No one will benefit from prolonged instability. . . . The cost of reconstruction—whenever the time comes to tally it up—will demand the resources of more than one country.

If we ever face a crisis in the North, its solution will fall to the nations of East Asia and the U.S. We will together have the chance to resolve it in concert, not conflict. It is a chance none of us can afford to miss.

Conclusion

Intelligence officers like to say that change typically brings uncertainty, and that uncertainty raises the odds of surprise. With so much change in and around the Korean peninsula, that old truth certainly applies. But none of us should be surprised by the prominence of North Korea as a challenge for policymakers and intelligence analysts.

In a very real sense, it is one of the inevitable issues of American foreign policy. Inevitable because—no matter what level of engagement we may want—the North seems sure to engage us. It could be across a table. It could be with the consequences of its negative behavior or its own instability. Or it could be some combination of them all.

What is clear . . . is the complexity, gravity and importance of the North Korean issue and its very certain role as a signpost for the future of East Asia. ■

(continued from page 22)
new light-water reactors for generating nuclear power, an interim supply of heavy fuel oil, some relaxation of U.S. economic sanctions, and modest movement toward diplomatic ties.

When Republicans took control of Congress in elections just weeks later, they denounced the deal as appeasement. Unwilling to challenge Congress, the Clinton Administration backpedaled on implementation. Pyongyang was deeply disappointed. After all, it reasoned, if Washington was willing to supply nuclear reactors, it would surely put an end to enmity. When the U.S. was slow to live up to the terms of the accord, North Korea threatened to break it. Pyongyang also resolved to try again to end enmity, this time using its missiles as inducement.

Had Pyongyang wanted missiles worth deploying or selling, it should have been testing and perfecting the No Dong, Taepo Dong-I and Taepo Dong-II. Yet it conducted just two longer-range missile tests of its own over the past decade—both of them failures. Both tests were examples of tit for tat. Washington opened missile negotiations of its own with Pyongyang in 1996, but in the ensuing two years it held just two rounds of talks. Again, the North resorted to tit for tat. On June 16, 1998, it made public an offer to negotiate an end not only to its missile exports, but also to testing and production.

The statement carried by the Korean Central News Agency in English said: "The discontinuation of our missile development is a matter which can be discussed after a peace agreement is signed between the Democratic People's Republic of Korea [DPRK, North Korea] and the U.S. and the U.S. military threat [is] completely removed. If the U.S. 'concern' about our missiles is truly related to the peace and security of Northeast Asia, the U.S. should immediately accept the DPRK-proposed peace agreement for the establishment of a durable peace mechanism on the Korean peninsula."

By "peace agreement" the North did not mean a peace treaty but a declared end to enmity and a pledge to respect each other's sovereignty. Nor was "the U.S. military threat" synonymous with the U.S. troop presence in South Korea. Only a basic change in political relations with Washington would remove the threat as Pyongyang perceives it; the withdrawal of U.S. forces from South Korea would not since the North would remain at risk from U.S. forces based offshore. The "peace mechanism" is a military-to-military channel that Pyongyang has sought to replace the Military Armistice Commission set up to monitor the cease-fire at the end of the Korean War in 1953. The new channel, which would involve the U.S., South Korea and North Korea, would do more than resolve disputes—like the 1994 shootdown of an American reconnaissance helicopter that strayed across the DMZ, repeated incursions by Northern spy submarines, or the 1999 firefight sparked when fishing boats from the North ventured south and were rammed by the South Korean navy. It would also serve as a venue to negotiate detailed force cuts and other measures to reduce the risk of war on the Korean peninsula.

The North Korean peace offer came with a threat to resume tests, a threat the North carried out on August 31, 1998, when it launched a three-stage Taepo Dong-I in a failed attempt to put a satellite into orbit.

Perry tries cooperation

This time, tit for tat worked, thanks to the new South Korean president, Kim Dae Jung. The South's aim had long been reunification, a synonym for collapse of the North. From his inauguration in February 1998, Kim proclaimed that his "immediate objective" was "to put an end to the cold-war confrontation and settle peace rather than attempting to accomplish reunification." Food aid and engagement, he believed, would reassure the North that the South did not seek its collapse and would lead to an end to adversarial relations. President Kim resolutely maintained his cooperative course in the face of relentless partisan attack.

During his 1999 policy review, former secretary of defense William Perry became persuaded of the wisdom of Kim's course. Instead of the collapse or reform of North Korea, Perry concluded that "the urgent focus of U.S. policy toward the DPRK must be to end its nuclear weapons and long-range missile-related activities." Instead of coercing Pyongyang, Perry chose to cooperate with it. "In a step-by-step and reciprocal fashion," he said, Washington will "move to reduce pressures on the DPRK that it perceives as threatening," starting with the economic embargo. Around Washington, Perry's ends won wider acceptance than his means. Seoul was enthusiastic, Tokyo less so, but for the first time in a decade, all three allies began working in tandem to reassure North Korea.

Perry went to Pyongyang in May 1999 and proposed high-level talks to convene in Washington, affirming that the U.S. was at last ready to negotiate in earnest and make good on its promises. The Perry policy paid off in September 1999 when the DPRK agreed to suspend its missile tests while negotiations proceeded. In return, the U.S. promised to end sanctions under the Trading with the Enemy Act, a pledge it was slow to carry out.

Meanwhile, Kim Dae Jung was initiating quiet contacts of his own that culminated in June 2000 in the first ever North-South summit meeting. The South and North pledged to reconcile, an irreversible step toward ending a half century of internecine conflict. That was an important milestone, and not just for the Koreas. By reaching an accommodation, the longtime foes were realigning relations in all of Northeast Asia.

Cooperation on terrorism?

As soon as the summit was over, the Clinton Administration carried out its promise to relax sanctions. Pyongyang also wanted Washington to end sanctions under U.S. antiterrorism law. "We cannot visit the U.S. [wearing] the cap of a terrorist," the North Korean ambassador to China put it, underscoring Pyongyang's view that the two sides had to be treated as sovereign equals for talks to succeed.

There is no conclusive evidence of Pyongyang's involvement in any terrorist act since 1987. In recognition of that, the Bush Administration in October 1990 dropped "abandoning terrorism" from its list of preconditions for holding high-level talks with the North. North Korea remains on the list of state sponsors of terrorism mainly because Pyongyang still harbors a handful of aging Red Army members whom Tokyo holds responsible for the 1970 hijacking of a Japanese airliner. Pyongyang is ready to repatriate them, but Japan did not address the issue in its normalization talks with the North. The Clinton Administration considered issuing a presi-

APWIDE WORLD PHOTOS

SOUTH KOREAN *soldiers on 12-day maneuvers in a joint annual exercise with U.S. troops.*

dential waiver to take North Korea off the list, but to avoid allied loss of face, it instead asked the DPRK to condemn terrorism in talks in mid-March 2000. The talks led to a joint statement issued on October 6 in which the North renounced terrorism and the two sides "underscored their commitment to support the international legal regime combating international terrorism and to cooperate with each other in taking effective measures to fight terrorism," in particular, "to exchange information regarding international terrorism." Pyongyang is now moving to act on that pledge.

An end to enmity

These steps prompted Kim Jong Il, who replaced his father as North Korea's leader, to send his second in command, Vice Marshal Cho Myong Rok, to Washington on October 10. After three days of talks, the two sides pledged that they no longer harbored any "hostile intent" toward one another. The declared end to enmity opened the way to a missile deal and to negotiations on conventional force—once a missile deal was concluded and implemented.

A joint communiqué read: "The two sides agreed that resolution of the missile issue would make an essential contribution to a fundamentally improved relationship between them." The DPRK, it continued, understood that "resolution of the missile issue" meant no exports, no tests, no production and no deployment of medium- and longer-range missiles. "A fundamentally improved relationship" meant to the DPRK that, as part of the missile deal, the U.S. would commit itself to establish full diplomatic relations in due course.

The North hinted at its readiness to put its conventional forces on the negotiating table as well, by agreeing that "there are a variety of available means, including four-party (North and South Korea, the U.S. and China) talks, to reduce tension on the Korean peninsula and formally end the Korean War by replacing the 1953 Armistice Agreement with permanent peace arrangements," which alludes to the North's proposed "peace mechanism" for defusing the armed standoff along the DMZ.

The missile deal

Secretary of State Madeleine Albright became the first U.S. official to meet with Kim Jong Il when she went to Pyongyang on October 23, 2000. In the course of talks, Kim agreed to end exports of all missile technology, including existing contracts, and to freeze testing, production and deployment of all missiles with a range of 500 kilometers. That would cover the No Dong, Taepo Dong I and II and, arguably, the SCUD-C. In return, the U.S. agreed to arrange for the launch of two or three North Korean satellites a year. To replace the revenue forgone by halting missile exports, the North agreed to accept compensation in kind, not cash.

Pyongyang's missile offer was clear evidence that diplomatic give-and-take can safely dispose of its missile threat long before missile defenses are ready for deployment. It was also a testament to Kim Dae Jung's faith that cooperation would work—that, as Secretary Albright put it on November 2, "The North should find it easier to address concerns about the size of its military and the status of its weapons programs if tensions with the South relax and fears about its own security diminish." As if to underscore the point, Foreign Minister Paek Nam-Sun told a visiting Chinese delegation that week that the North was ready to resume four-party talks.

To turn the freeze into an outright ban, significant issues remained to be resolved in the missile talks: "elimination" of North Korea's missiles, on-site monitoring to verify a freeze on production and deployment—what negotiators were calling "transparency" and "confidence-building measures on missiles"—and extending the freeze to cover all missiles with a range of over 300 kilometers, the standard used in the Missile Technology Control Regime. That would ban shorter-range SCUD-B missiles, which Pyongyang regards as part of its conventional deterrent. Those would have to be dealt with in the course of conventional force negotiations with Seoul and Washington.

The U.S. can monitor a freeze on testing and deployment by surveillance satellite, but unless the North is willing to freeze production of all SCUDs, effective verification will require monitoring at production sites. Although it has yet to say so in negotiations, Pyongyang might be induced to accept on-site monitoring similar to that conducted at a suspect nuclear site at Kumchang-ni. North Korea let U.S. inspectors visit there twice to ascertain that nothing was amiss and expressed interest in setting up a joint venture that would allow permanent monitoring at the site. Extending similar arrangements to missile plants and other sites will take time to work out. The freeze can be turned into a verifiable ban, but not if Washington asks for more access to North Korea than it needs.

North Korea will likely withhold its commitment to dismantle No Dong missiles until Japan accelerates normalization talks and declares an end to enmity.

During the negotiations, the U.S. held back two commitments of its own, to arrange to provide up to $300 million a year in investment and aid for Pyongyang—a far cry from the $1 billion North Korea sought as compensation for ending its missile exports and a pittance by comparison to missile defenses. The compensation in kind, not cash, could take the form of investment in agriculture and energy or forgiveness of North Korea's debt. The aid would be phased in and could be stopped if

Pyongyang proved not to be forthcoming on elimination and transparency.

Above all, North Korea wanted President Bill Clinton to come to Pyongyang to seal the deal. A presidential visit would have consummated North Korea's 10-year campaign to end enmity with the U.S. American willingness to end enmity is Pyongyang's sine qua non for relaxing the armed confrontation in Korea. Why would North Korea give up its artillery threat to Seoul if the U.S. remained its foe?

'Let George do it'

With the 2000 election outcome uncertain, the White House got cold feet. Without Clinton's commitment to visit, negotiations stalled.

Instead of picking up the ball where Clinton dropped it, new President George W. Bush moved the goalposts. First and foremost, more than a year later, no Administration official has reaffirmed the October 12, 2000, joint communiqué and its pledge of no "hostile intent." It also discouraged Seoul from discussing a peace agreement with Pyongyang. In talks with Japanese Prime Minister Junichiro Koizumi, President Bush impugned Kim Jong Il's trustworthiness, an undiplomatic way to respond to his offer to give up missiles for an end to enmity. Second, the Administration seeks "improved implementation" of the Agreed Framework of October 1994. That accord stipulates when a "sufficient portion" of the light-water reactor project is complete, but before key nuclear components can be delivered, North Korea must come into full compliance with its safeguards agreement with the International Atomic Energy Agency. The Administration, in effect, wants to rewrite the accord to expedite North Korean compliance without offering anything in return. Third, the Administration seeks "a less threatening conventional military posture" from the North. Given its military inferiority, Pyongyang cannot do that unilaterally. Instead, that would require Seoul and Washington to take more far-reaching measures than what they have proposed so far. The Administration has yet to study the reciprocal arrangements that would be needed. Finally, the Administration has decided that, as a matter of policy, progress toward a missile deal will depend on progress on the other issues of concern. The White House announced its "comprehensive approach" to North Korea on June 6, 2001.

In response to the White House announcement, Pyongyang's Foreign Ministry issued a statement on June 18, calling on Washington to implement the provisions of the Agreed Framework and the October 12 joint communiqué. It followed that up with a June 28 statement that linked the U.S. demand for inspections with its own demand for electricity to compensate for the delay in completing the first promised replacement reactor. That suggested a quid pro quo: electricity for expedited compliance. Pyongyang accompanied its offer with a threat: "If no measure is taken for the compensation for the loss of electricity, the DPRK can no longer keep its nuclear activities in a state of freeze and implement the Agreed Framework." It was yet another instance of tit for tat.

Is cooperative threat reduction worth pursuing?

This history suggests that cooperative threat reduction is the way to enhance security in Asia. Yet the Bush Administration's stance is the latest sign that that idea has been slow to catch on in Washington. Is cooperation always an appropriate strategy for achieving American aims abroad? Of course not. Sometimes conciliation has to be combined with coercion, or at least a threat of coercion. Yet cooperation can work where coercion would fail. It is cheap by comparison. It is particularly appropriate for the strong in dealing with the weak.

Cooperation is also the way to induce countries to forswear arming themselves with nuclear weapons and missiles. Such countries are insecure. Trying to isolate them or force them to forgo arming could well backfire. They usually respond better to inducements than to threats. Indeed, American reassurances and inducements have a long record of accomplishment in stopping the spread of nuclear arms, having helped convince South Korea, Taiwan, Brazil, Argentina, South Africa, the Ukraine, Belarus and Kazakhstan to abandon nuclear arming. Only in Iraq and Pakistan did they fail.

Notwithstanding the successes, cooperative threat reduction will not gain easy acceptance in Washington. Aversion to cooperation has been an article of faith among unilateralists in the right wing of the Republican party, who believe the U.S. should go it alone in the world, unfettered by allies and unbound by treaties. It is also prevalent among realists who run foreign policy for President Bush and who are skeptical, if not hostile, to making deals with North Korea. Some in the Administration still see North Korea as a useful pretext for missile defense, despite its expressed readiness for a freeze and eventual ban on missiles.

North Korea seems unlikely to negotiate in earnest until it is convinced that the President is willing to cooperate in ending enmity. That means restarting missile talks, reaching an agreement, and faithfully implementing it.

Concluding that the Administration is not serious about diplomatic give-and-take, Pyongyang has instead resumed high-level dialogue with Seoul in hopes that the way to Washington lies through Seoul. If so, a return visit to Seoul by Kim Jong Il seems a possibility. That would mark an important shift for Pyongyang, which for the past decade has engaged seriously with Seoul only when it was sure Washington was cooperating as well.

The risk is that realists in the Bush Administration may get in the way of North-South reconciliation. They wrongly assume that if the North and South begin to ease hostility, U.S. troops will have to leave. Far from insisting on their withdrawal, Kim Jong Il told Kim Dae Jung in June 2000 what Pyongyang has in effect been saying to Washington since 1992—that so long as the U.S. remains its enemy, U.S. troops are a threat and must leave Korea, but once the relationship is no longer hostile, U.S. troops are no longer a threat and could remain. Conversely, for Washington to be seen as impeding North-South reconciliation will erode support in South Korea for that presence and jeopardize the American position in Northeast Asia.

Given uncertainty, President Bush may distrust North Korea, but he would be wrong to pick a fight with America's ally in South Korea rather than reach accommodation with North Korea. Over a decade ago, doctrinaire realists in Paris and London tried to keep the two Germanys from getting back together. A prudent George Bush knew better than to stand in their way. Should George W. Bush follow his lead in Korea? ■

OPINION BALLOTS are on pages 19–20

DISCUSSION QUESTIONS

1. Should the primary goal of U.S. policy toward North Korea be to compel its collapse, to reform its economy, or to seek an end to its nuclear and missile programs and a relaxation of the conventional military confrontation in Korea?

2. Should the U.S. continue to contribute food aid to prevent famine in North Korea or should it insist on quid pro quos?

3. Should the U.S. continue to implement the Agreed Framework of October 1994? Should it seek to accelerate North Korea's compliance with the Nuclear Non-Proliferation Treaty, and if so, should it be willing, in return, to compensate North Korea with some electricity?

4. Should the U.S. rush to deploy missile defenses, using North Korean missiles as justification, or should it seek to expedite missile talks with North Korea, allowing more time to test missile defenses?

5. Should the U.S. be prepared to offer political and economic inducements to North Korea in return for a halt to its missile exports? For a freeze on its medium- and longer-range missile programs? For a verifiable ban on all its missile activities?

6. Should North Korea be taken off the list of state supporters of terrorism?

7. As part of a missile deal, should the President of the U.S. hold a summit meeting with North Korea's Kim Jong Il as a sign of American willingness to end hostile relations?

8. Should the U.S. promote reconciliation between North and South Korea? Should it insist on a continued American military presence in South Korea?

9. Is a change in relations with North Korea an opportunity to improve the security of the U.S. and its Asian allies?

10. Should the U.S. be willing to pursue a strategy of cooperative threat reduction, using reassurances and inducements in an attempt to dissuade other states from seeking nuclear, chemical or biological arms and missiles? For instance, Iran?

READINGS AND RESOURCES

Axelrod, Robert M., **The Evolution of Cooperation.** New York, Basic Books, 1985. 256 pp. $20.00. The classic study of tit for tat.

Carter, Ashton B., and Perry, William J., **Preventive Defense: A New Security Strategy for America.** Washington, D.C., Brookings Institution Press, 1999. 243 pp. $24.95. Two leading practitioners discuss cooperative threat reduction.

Cumings, Bruce, "Divided Korea: United Future?" **Headline Series** No. 306. New York, Foreign Policy Association, 1995. 88 pp. $5.95. Contrasts the politics of the two Koreas and places them in historical context.

———, **Korea's Place in the Sun: A Modern History.** New York, Norton, 1997. 527 pp. $25.00. A history of modern Korea by a leading scholar.

Eberstadt, Nick, "Hastening Korean Reunification." **Foreign Affairs,** March/April 1997, pp. 77–92. The case for compelling North Korea's collapse.

Lim Dong Won, **Kim Dae Jung's "Three-Stage" Approach to Reunification,** trans. by Rhee Tong-Chin. Los Angeles, University of Southern California Center for Multiethnic and Transnational Studies, 1997. 424 pp. $19.95 (paper). The so-called "sunshine policy" followed by South Korea, set out by its architect and implementer.

Oberdorfer, Don, **The Two Koreas,** rev. ed. Cambridge, Mass., Perseus, 2002. 528 pp. $18.00. A contemporary history of North-South relations by a longtime Korea observer.

Sigal, Leon V., **Disarming Strangers: Nuclear Diplomacy with North Korea.** Princeton, N.J., Princeton University Press, 1999. 321 pp. $17.95 (paper). A detailed account of negotiations leading to the October 1994 Agreed Framework between the U.S. and the DPRK.

ASIA FOUNDATION, 465 California St., 14th fl., San Francisco, CA 94104; (415) 982-4640; Fax (415) 392-8863. **www.asiafoundation.com** ■ The foundation strives to promote the mutual interests of Asia and the U.S. and focuses on governance and law, women's political participation and regional relations. The site contains links to organizations focusing on specific issues.

ASIA SOCIETY, 725 Park Ave., New York, NY 10021; (212) 288-6400; Fax (212) 517-8315. **www.asiasociety.org** ■ This site provides information about current issues in Asia and focuses on developing a greater understanding between Asians and Americans. The society publishes the **Asian Update Series** as well as country briefings. It also maintains the information website **www.asiasource.org.**

KOREA SOCIETY, 950 Third Ave., 8th fl., New York, NY 10022; (212) 759-7525; Fax (212) 759-7530. **www.koreasociety.org** ■ This nonprofit organization promotes understanding and information about Korea and its relations with the U.S. It publishes the **Korea Society Quarterly.**

NATIONAL BUREAU OF ASIAN RESEARCH (NBR), 4518 University Way, NE, Suite 300, Seattle, WA 98105; (206) 632-7370; Fax (206) 632-7487. **www.nbr.org** ■ This site contains information and analysis of current Asian issues, and also has links to hundreds of websites dealing with Asia, including several on South Korea.

THE NAUTILUS INSTITUTE, 125 University Avenue, Berkeley, CA 94710; (510) 295-6100; Fax (510) 295-6130. **www.nautilus.org** ■ Its website Northeast Asia Peace and Security Net (NAPSNet) contains a daily compendium of newsstories from the region.

LEARN MORE ABOUT THIS TOPIC AT www.greatdecisions.org

Access links to online resources • Order the recommended readings • Take the GD Quiz • Find maps in the online atlas • Submit your opinion ballots • Read the latest National Opinion Ballot Report • and more ...

U.S. and the Middle East: elusive quest for peace

To maintain alliances necessary to facilitate the war against terrorism, the differences that divide Israel and the Palestinians must be resolved. Reviving the peace process will require a major diplomatic commitment.

by Augustus Richard Norton

AP/WIDE WORLD PHOTOS

ISRAELI SETTLERS *protest in Jerusalem next to an armored bus ambushed by Palestinians in the Gaza Strip, October 2000.*

"We will bring Al Qaeda to justice, peace or no peace in the Middle East," President George W. Bush promised at a November 2001 joint news conference with British Prime Minister Tony Blair. Despite Blair's encouragement that the U.S. shoulder a more active role in Middle East peaceseeking, Bush's comments revealed his hesitance to pursue a potentially thankless task. In one form or another, the Arab-Israeli conflict has persisted for more than half a century, and while peace has sometimes seemed tantalizingly within reach, in the first months of Bush's four-year term, the prospects for peace seemed doubtful. Rather than moving closer to peace, there was growing polarization and mistrust between Israelis and Palestinians, punctuated by horrible acts of terrorism by Palestinian militants and widespread killing by Israeli forces (as well as by Jewish settler vigilantes).

When Bush was inaugurated in January 2001, the al-Aqsa *intifada* (uprising) was already in its fourth month. Protests had erupted the previous September, following General Ariel Sharon's provocative visit to the Haram al Sharif (the noble sanctuary, which is the site of the al-Aqsa mosque and the revered Dome of the Rock mosque, the third-most sacred site in Islam), and developed into a familiar violence-revenge-retaliation cycle. By September 2001, the quest for peace in the Middle East had become intertwined with the security of the U.S. in a way that even the most prescient presidential advisers could not have imagined.

America's defeat of the Taliban in Afghanistan is a bittersweet triumph, only a partial redress for the horrible losses inflicted on New York City and the Pentagon. President Bush has emphasized that the victory in Afghanistan is only the first campaign in a war against terrorism that will continue for years to come. Meanwhile, much diplomatic work remains to be done in the Middle East. If America's resolve, "peace or no peace," should not be doubted, momentum toward peace in the Middle East is more important than ever. The continuing conflict between Palestinians and Israelis has undermined the credibility of U.S. foreign policy in the eyes of tens of millions of Muslims around the world.

This is not a question of rewarding the hate-fueled men who incinerated thousands of innocent souls; these permanent enemies of America would not have been dissuaded from their errands of destruction by peacemaking. The larger real challenge is how to dissipate the anger that is so widely expressed in

AUGUSTUS RICHARD NORTON *is a professor in the departments of anthropology and international relations at Boston University. He holds a Ph.D. from the University of Chicago and taught political science at West Point.*

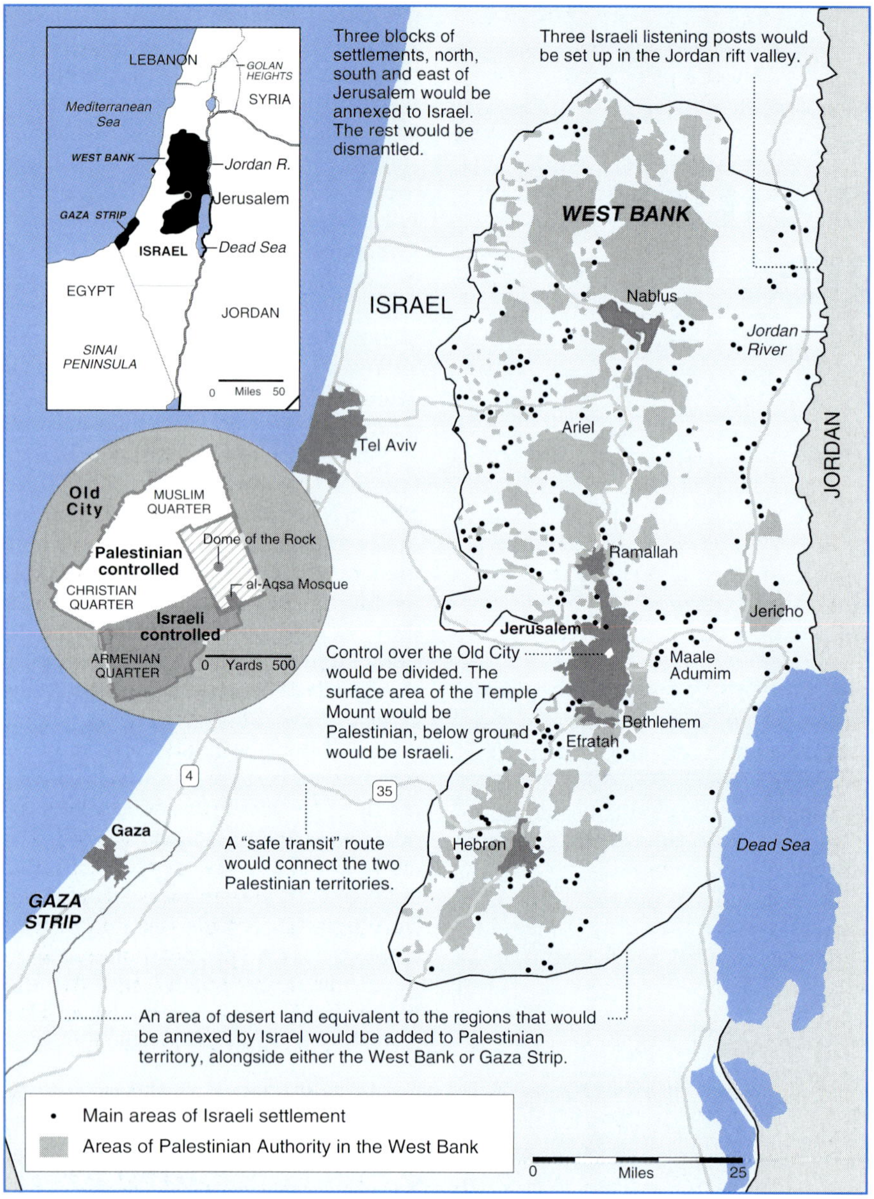

NYT GRAPHICS

the Muslim world, and especially in the Middle East. In some cases, the intrusion of Western cultural values spawns resentment. However, there is often a tendency to exaggerate this factor; many Muslims are fascinated with the Western media, music and film, not to mention technology.

More important, anger is certainly a by-product of the frustration that grips many Muslim societies, where one's life chances are stymied by rigid political systems and stale economies. There is no debating the fact that the U.S. is often resented for propping up unpopular and corrupt regimes. Notwithstanding much Washington rhetoric about promoting democracy in the world, for the Middle East, Washington policymakers have preferred assured stability to the promotion of freedom and reform. Given the popularity of oppositional Islamist movements that are not only vocal in their criticism of the U.S. but are often hostile to the survival of Israel, the promotion of free elections and widespread political participation is often viewed by policymakers as tantamount to courting disaster.

The risk of self-fulfilling prophecy is obvious: excluded opposition groups, whether Islamist or secular, are prone to conclude that peaceful change is not possible. In the absence of a more nuanced and inclusive policy, the U.S. is left in the embrace of entrenched, self-interested authoritarian regimes that rule through oppression. When U.S. support for dictatorships is combined with the widely unpopular sanctions against Iraq and the regression in the peace process between Israel and the Palestinians, U.S. policy in the region is often viewed as hostile to Muslims and insensitive to their suffering.

Skepticism of U.S. policy is not a new development. It was brewing throughout the 1990s and came to a head after the September maelstrom. Americans were justifiably appalled, even embittered, to view images of young Palestinian refugees greeting news of the disaster with delight and celebration. Was the source of their delight a deep-rooted religious or ideological hatred of America? If so, the future of America's relationship with the Muslim world—which is inhabited by over one billion souls—may be dark and violent. There is no doubt that hatred has been inculcated in some Muslim quarters, particularly in fundamentalist schools and seminaries where young Muslims are often exposed to a puritanical, xenophobic and uncompromising version of Islam. These places have proliferated in recent decades, not least in Pakistan. The preponderance of Muslims, including most Palestinians, is no more comfortable with these intolerant variants of their faith than non-Muslims. One merely needs to recall the rejoicing of Afghans over the recovery of simple freedoms long forbidden by the Taliban to catch a glimpse of mainstream Muslims. That is the good news.

The bad news is that over the course of the 1990s, U.S. policy in the Middle East lost momentum. In the Arab-Israeli conflict, the credibility of the U.S. as an honest broker has been badly tarnished. In the Persian Gulf, the U.S.-steered sanctions against Iraq have not decisively weakened the grip of Iraqi President Saddam Hussein but have occasioned great suffering by innocent Iraqis. Osama bin Laden tapped into this anger in his professionally choreographed video riposte to the launching of U.S. air attacks on Afghanistan, October 7, 2001. No doubt, his comments were self-serving, but his references to a million children dying in Iraq or Israeli tanks invading the towns of Palestine reverberated in Arab audiences, where there is much sympathy for the people of Iraq as well as the Palestinians.

Well before September 11, some

U.S. policymakers were becoming more attentive to these criticisms of America's foreign policy. This is why Secretary of State Colin Powell attempted to sharpen the Iraq sanctions by focusing more narrowly on matériel of potential military use rather than continuing the broader sanctions that often hurt Iraqi civilians rather than the government. Powell's efforts to shift to "smart sanctions" were thwarted in June by Russia. Russia enjoys a privileged trading relationship with Iraq thanks to the current trade restrictions, and if the range of products covered by sanctions shrinks, so would Russian trade.

On the Arab-Israeli front, the new Bush Administration did make several skittish forays into peacemaking in the spring of 2001, but reticence triumphed over will. Unlike his predecessor, President Bush is unaffected by idealistic images of the Middle East. He had kept his Administration at arm's length from the burdens of peacemaking, but September 11 "changed" everything. Criticism of America for neglecting the suffering of Palestinian Arabs in the West Bank and Gaza now matters greatly. In the Arab world, there has always been sympathy for the plight of the Palestinian refugees, even if views run hot and cold on the Palestine Liberation Organization (PLO) or leading PLO personalities, such as Yasir Arafat. Credible polling data collected in mid-2001 emphasize that the Palestinian cause enjoys broad popular support in Egypt, Kuwait, Lebanon, Saudi Arabia and the United Arab Emirates, ranging from 79% of Egyptians, who describe the Palestinian cause as the most important issue, to 58% in Kuwait, who shared the same view. Among those who did not describe the Palestinian issue as the most important, most said it was one of the top three.

What is different now is that the burden of blame is widely ascribed to America. Pat Lang, the Pentagon's veteran Defense Intelligence Officer for the Middle East (now retired), notes: "Even though in a lot of places like Egypt, ordinary folks may not care about the Palestinian people personally at all, the idea of the collective wrong inflicted on Islam and the Arab world by the action of the Israelis, and us as their sponsors, in their view, is something that is resented deeply."

The Arab public now enjoys alternatives to the state-controlled media and access to enormous amounts of information about events around the Muslim world and the region. The profile of the electronic and print media in the Arab world has been transformed. Arab intellectual elites have a serious newspaper, *Al Hayat* (Life), which is widely available in the region as well as in Europe and North America. Other regional papers, such as *Al Sharq al-Awsat* (The Middle East), join *Al Hayat* in offering informative newsstories and critical commentary on events. The contrast with lifeless state-controlled papers in countries such as Jordan, Syria and Egypt is dramatic.

More important, ubiquitous and inexpensive satellite dishes now bring a variety of programming to millions of Arab households. Soap operas and "B" movies are standard fare, but viewers also have access to in-depth news programming and commentary. State television persists in broadcasting boring reports about which foreign leader sent the king or the president a birthday greeting. The station that attracts many viewers and widely influences opinion is the CNN-style Al Jazeera, which is based in the Persian Gulf state of Qatar. Other stations, including the Lebanese LBC and the Saudi-owned MBC, have followed Al Jazeera's lead with provocative talk shows and interviews. Al Jazeera is iconoclastic and eclectic and it attracts many avid viewers. Real-time images from the intifada (or from the war in Afghanistan) are standard fare. There is little question that the eruption of widespread Arab protests in the autumn of 2000 was provoked by televised images of Israelis using deadly force against Palestinian civilians. Governments did not prompt the demonstrations. They were a grassroots response.

It is very troubling that the U.S. response to the Al Qaeda terrorism has prompted more attention in the Muslim world to the charge of America's "double standards." Is America insensitive to the Muslim victims of violence? Many Muslims think so, although, in fact, the evidence is mixed. In spite of the fact that the origins of Islam are in the Middle East, the overwhelming majority of Muslims live outside the region, in South Asia and Southeast Asia (Indonesia, Bangladesh, Pakistan and India account for fully half of all the world's more than one billion Muslims). Bin Laden and his ilk urge that the world's Muslims see the conflict between Israelis and Palestinians as a campaign in a religious war. A conflict between rival nationalisms, Zionist versus Palestinian, offers some promise of resolution through compromise. Religious wars reject compromise by definition. Eradication or conversion is the aim of religious war, prompting some

APWIDE WORLD PHOTOS

PALESTINIANS HURL STONES *at Israeli soldiers in a demonstration after Ariel Sharon visited the Temple Mount compound (inset), site of the revered al-Aqsa mosque, September 2000.*

thoughtful Arab intellectuals to warn of the dangers should the Arab-Israeli conflict fester much longer.

The key is to shrink the base of sympathy upon which America's enemies may draw. Thus, the war against terrorism is not only a matter of draining the swamp in terms of denying finances, bases and shelter to terrorists, but it must also be a battle for the minds of Muslims, as the Bush Administration has come to realize. The phenomenon of public opinion is not limited to countries covered by Gallup pollsters. Even authoritarian rulers have constituencies and must pay attention to shifting public moods and rising public anger. Arab delegations played to those home audiences at the United Nations racism conference in Durban, South Africa, in September 2001, when they urged stridently anti-Israel resolutions. The U.S. condemned the Arab position and withdrew its delegation rather than legitimate the meeting by being present. Nonetheless, the incident underlined how the Arab-Israeli conflict corrodes constructive international dialogue, not to mention cooperation with the U.S.

Dennis Ross, President Bill Clinton's point man in the quest for peace, notes: "Our Arab allies would feel less defensive about their ties to us if anger and frustration over the Palestinian situation were not so pronounced in the Arab world." If the U.S. is to sustain a pattern of Middle East alliances that will facilitate the war against terrorism, there will need to be substantial progress in attaining a solution that bridges the differences dividing Israel and the Palestinians. The absence of such progress only lends legitimacy to America's opponents. The record of the last decade includes successes to build upon and pitfalls to avert. ■

The Spirit of Madrid (and Moscow)

ONLY A DECADE AGO, with the Soviet Union in collapse and a victory by the U.S.-led coalition against Iraqi aggression in Kuwait, hopes ran high that there could be a "new Middle East," marked by peace and prosperity rather than war and woe. President George Bush, the elder, and his Secretary of State James A. Baker III showed real imagination in creating an impressive structure for seeking peace. Rather than adopting the incremental, step-by-step approach that marked U.S. diplomacy in the 1970s, in the era of President Richard M. Nixon and Secretary of State Henry A. Kissinger, Bush and Baker adopted a more ambitious two-track structure. Bilateral negotiations between Israel, on the one hand, and Jordan, Lebanon, Syria and the Palestinians, on the other, were launched in Madrid, Spain, in the fall of 1991. Then, in January 1992, in Moscow, Russia, a series of innovative multilateral forums were launched to deal with broad regional issues: security, economic development, refugees, water and the environment. The complex structure evoked real excitement in the region, where the idea of peace then seemed truly feasible.

The multilateral talks were an encouraging if limited success. Many extraregional states became involved in the multilaterals, including Canada, Italy, Japan and Russia, and regional participation was impressive. While Syria and Lebanon boycotted the multilaterals, arguing that they were a form of implicit recognition of Israel that should succeed not precede bilateral treaties, and Iraq was not invited, most Arab states enthusiastically participated. By late 1992, heretofore novel meetings—at the level of technicians, scientists and experts, not high-profile diplomats—between Israelis, Saudis, Moroccans, Omanis, Kuwaitis and others became common. Granted, the multilaterals were never intended to address the hard land-for-peace issues that could only be settled bilaterally, but they represented an opportunity for the states of the region to begin dialogues with former enemies. By the time Prime Minister Benjamin ("Bibi") Netanyahu took office in 1996, Israel not only enjoyed full diplomatic relations with the two Arab states that had signed peace treaties (Egypt in 1979 and Jordan in 1994), but also quasi-diplomatic ties with five other Arab countries. For a few years, at least, the idea of peace between Arabs and Israelis, and even a new Middle East, no longer seemed farfetched.

Meeting under U.S. auspices, usually in Washington, the bilateral tracks made some substantial progress, but only Israel and Jordan succeeded in reaching a peace agreement. Lebanon, under Syria's sway since the end of the 15-year civil war in 1990, would make no progress until "sister" Syria did. Syria and Israel held a series of significant negotiations to find a fitting solution to Israel's security priorities and Syria's unconditional demand for the return of the Golan Heights, which Israel has occupied since 1967. Rabin's assassination in 1995 sidetracked these talks.

The heart of the Arab-Israeli conflict is the Palestinian question, as the respected U.S. diplomat Harold Saunders explained in turning-point testimony before Congress in 1975. If Israelis, Americans and Arabs could agree on this premise, they could not agree on who represented the Palestinian people diplomatically into the 1990s. Although the Arab League anointed the PLO in 1974 as the "sole legitimate representative of the Palestinian people," neither Washington nor Israel were willing to deal with the PLO, given its record of terrorism and anti-Israeli violence. It was only in 1988 that the PLO—emphatically coached by then Secretary of State George P. Shultz—formally renounced terrorism and acknowledged Israel's right to exist. The year before, the first intifada had shaken Israel's complacency about maintaining control of the occupied territories, and the Reagan Administration seized the moment in order to remove an impediment to negotiations under the aegis of the next U.S. Administration. Nonetheless, the pro-Saddam Hussein stance that PLO Chairman Arafat adopted in the 1990–91 Persian Gulf war ruined any chance for the PLO to participate in the Madrid conference of 1991. Whether Arafat was trying to stay on the right side of Palestinian public opinion is immaterial. He blundered magnificently and he lost support in many Arab capitals following the Persian Gulf war.

Israelis were long captivated by the idea that they could find alternative Palestinian interlocutors, men and women with no links to the PLO, who would prove less adamant about creating a Palestinian state and therefore more pliant to Israel's interests. The assumption, shared by the U.S. and by Israel, was that a solution to the fate of the West Bank and Gaza would be found in a confederal arrangement with Jordan. At Madrid, Israel adamantly refused to accept a separate Palestinian delegation and insisted that Palestinian personalities with no overt ties to the PLO should represent their people as part of the Jordanian delegation. The PLO therefore seemed to be effectively shut out of the two negotiating tracks.

While King Hussein of Jordan agreed to the arrangement, his diplomats declined to negotiate on behalf of Palestine. Accommodating State Department officials moved chairs, couches and coffee into the corridors so that "informal" talks between Israelis and Palestinian members of the Jordanian delegation could begin without implying that Israel recognized a separate delegation from Palestine. For their part, the Palestinian members, distinguished men and women including the late Faisal al-Husseini, Haidar Abdel-Shafi and Hanan Ashrawi, were wary of Israeli divide-and-rule tactics and any appearance that they were "selling out" Palestinian aspirations for statehood. Throughout the negotiations they stayed in regular contact with Arafat and the PLO headquarters in Tunis. Israel was effectively conducting indirect negotiations with the PLO, although it persisted in refusing to openly negotiate with it. ■

The Oslo process

By 1993, the Israeli-Palestinian track had reached its limit. Meantime, in Gaza and the West Bank, militant Islamist organizations, especially Hamas (Islamic Resistance Movement), gained popular support. Hamas rejects negotiations with Israel, which it vows to destroy. Although Israel had previously turned a blind eye to the Islamist organizations that it calculated would undermine the PLO's support in the occupied territories, by 1993 it viewed Hamas as an existential threat. Under these circumstances, Prime Minster Rabin agreed, with skepticism, to secret arm's length talks in Norway under the wing of the late Johan Joergen Holst, the brilliant Norwegian foreign minister. For Arafat, considering the declining fortunes of the PLO after the Persian Gulf war, this was a chance to reestablish the bona fides of the PLO. The U.S. was duly informed of the discussions, but U.S. Secretary of State Warren G. Christopher and his advisers were dubious. The last thing they expected was a diplomatic breakthrough in distant Scandinavia.

Of course, the Oslo talks did succeed beyond Israeli and American expectations. In September 1993, President Clinton hosted the signing of the first of a series of agreements collectively referred to as the Oslo accords. The White House lawn image of Rabin reluctantly shaking hands with Arafat, his longtime nemesis, remains an indelible image of the peace process.

The forward momentum of the peace process was impressive with Rabin at the helm, but the prime minister's assassination in 1995 (by a Jewish fanatic intent on sabotaging peace) put the Oslo accords in jeopardy. Rabin's death propelled Shimon Peres into the position of prime minister, but a series of terrorist attacks in early 1996 lent credibility to his right-wing opponent, Netanyahu. Netanyahu, an avowed opponent of the Oslo process, ran his campaign for prime minister on the pledge of "making a secure peace." He beat Peres in a razor-close election, and for the next three years progress slowed markedly. Netanyahu's Likud party rejected the idea of a Palestinian state, and the new prime minister recommitted himself to

AP/WIDE WORLD PHOTOS

AN ULTRA-ORTHODOX JEWISH MAN *passes posters showing Palestinian leader Yasir Arafat and Israeli Foreign Minister Shimon Peres shaking hands. The text on the poster reads, "Put the Oslo criminals on trial."*

THE OSLO ACCORDS

Declaration of Principles on Interim Self-Government (September 1993): This is the formative agreement that was negotiated in Oslo, Norway. It provides for the establishment of an interim Palestinian Authority (PA), and it establishes a five-year period for the negotiation of the so-called "final status" issues (Jerusalem, refugees, settlements, security arrangements and borders). Israel agrees to withdraw from Gaza and the West Bank town of Jericho.

Cairo Accord (May 1994): This agreement deals with implementation. It permits Arafat's return to Gaza and establishes the terms of reference for the transfer of limited power to the PLO as Israeli forces withdraw from Jericho and most of Gaza. With this accord, the five-year clock starts ticking. The final-status issues are to be concluded by May 1999.

"Oslo II" (September 1995): Signed in Washington, this agreement permits the election of a Palestinian Legislative Council (which occurs in January 1996), and divides the West Bank into areas A, B and C. The first is under the civil and security control of the PA, the second is under Palestinian civil government while the Israelis retain security control, and the third refers to areas that remain under full Israeli occupation. Seventy-two percent of the West Bank comprised area C, although most Palestinians were found in areas A and B. Israel commits itself to three further redeployments at six-month intervals. Oslo II also set May 1996 for the beginning of final-status talks (but this was subsequently postponed by Prime Minister Netanyahu).

Hebron Protocol (January 1997): Hebron is the last Palestinian city, other than East Jerusalem, to remain under Israeli occupation. This protocol divides the city center—where 400 Israeli settlers from the right-wing Gush Emunim live—between the PA and the Israeli military authority, and restores most of the city to the PA. (In a separate letter, Secretary of State Christopher emphasized that Israel solely would define the extent and location of subsequent withdrawals.)

Wye River Memorandum (October 1998): This document emphasizes the commitment of the PA to step up its security measures and it requires that those sections of the PLO charter that challenged Israel's right to exist be again repudiated by the PLO (Netanyahu asserted that this had not happened, although the Israel Oslo team disagreed). In return, Israel committed itself to a further withdrawal from 13% of the West Bank. President Clinton visited Gaza to witness the revision of the charter.

Sharm el-Sheik Memorandum (September 1999): Lays out a timetable for the delayed withdrawals beginning in September 1999 and concluding January 2000. Two safe passages between Gaza and the West Bank are agreed upon, and the Israelis agree to the further release of Palestinian prisoners. September 2000 was set as the deadline for final-status talks. ■

expanding settlement construction, not least in the contested environs of Jerusalem.

Netanyahu's election was a nasty surprise for the Clinton team, and relations between the prime minister and the President were often strained. Clinton, however, was intent on avoiding even the suggestion that the U.S. was dictating or imposing the terms of reference for progress. Instead, he attempted to work with Netanyahu, but it was transparent that the Israeli leader had little interest in seeing the Oslo accords succeed except on terms that were wholly unacceptable to the Palestinians. Thoughtful observers of the peace process frequently suggest that a firmer, more assertive American role might have undercut Netanyahu's obduracy. Clinton was determined to continue to play the role of facilitator, coordinator and messenger. Only in the last days of his presidency did he offer publicly his own ideas about the framework for a settlement.

General Ehud Barak was swept into office in 1999. The former army commander was known for his military daring and his tough-minded commitment to security, but he also promised the electorate progress on several fronts: in Lebanon, where Israel was facing stiff resistance from Hizbullah (the "Party of God"), and in the peace process, which had made little progress during his predecessor's term in office. By 1999, the Israeli public had wearied of Israel's involvement in southern Lebanon, which had cost the lives of hundreds of Israeli soldiers. From Israel's perspective, its "security zone" protected its northern border, but from the standpoint of the Lebanese, Israel had been occupying parts of their country since 1978. Barak promised the voters that he would have Israel out of Lebanon within a year of his election, even if Israel had to withdraw unilaterally and without the agreement of Syria. He kept his word, and by May 2000, the Israeli Defense Force withdrew from Lebanon and the proxy militia that Israel had trained and equipped crumbled in a matter of hours. To the surprise of many analysts in Israel and the U.S., Israel's northern border has been peaceful, with the exception of a contested area (claimed by Lebanon) in the occupied Golan Heights.

Before the withdrawal from Lebanon, Barak attempted to reach an agreement with Syria, picking up the threads that had been woven by Israeli and Syrian negotiations during Rabin's tenure. Barak acknowledged Rabin's 1995 promise to return the Golan Heights to Syria in return for peace. By the end of 1999, a draft Israeli-Syrian treaty was leaked in the Israeli press, revealing that tremendous progress had been made. President Clinton and Syrian President Hafez al-Assad met in Geneva, Switzerland, in March 2000 in a much anticipated summit meeting, which was preceded by a flurry of diplomatic contacts, including a dozen phone calls between the two presidents. Even so, the summit failed. To the surprise of Assad, as well as Clinton, Barak was unwilling to return a sliver of Syrian land on Lake Tiberius. Clinton valiantly explained to the Syrian leader that Barak concluded that he could not gain public support for a deal that gave Syria access to Israel's largest watershed. Assad was unwilling to countenance anything less. There has been no progress since.

Israel had unfinished business with the PA, and Barak turned his attention to the Oslo accords. Barak was never a fan of the incremental withdrawals envisaged in the Oslo accords. He preferred to jump to the final-status issues once and for all rather than fight a series of domestic political battles over every phase of withdrawal. In fact, even when authorized by the Knesset (parliament) to withdraw from three Palestinian villages around Jerusalem, he declined to implement the withdrawals. Equally important, Barak did not trust Arafat, and he preferred a comprehensive agreement that would require the Palestinians to accept the full parameters of peace, instead of proceeding from one interim step to another and postponing the tough compromises that both sides would eventually have to swallow.

The chemistry between Barak and Arafat was not good at all. While Rabin maintained a viable working relationship with his Palestinian counterpart based on a ration of mutual respect, Barak seemed to find dealing with Arafat distasteful. In contrast, Clinton developed a solid dialogue with Arafat, who sensed considerable empathy on the part of the President. Initially, Barak wanted to keep the U.S. in the background, but by summer 2000 he needed Clinton's help. Barak was losing political support in Israel and he calculated that a deal with Arafat would not only be in Israel's interest, but would reverse his fortunes. He prevailed on Clinton to host a summit meeting at Camp David, Maryland, the presidential retreat where Jimmy Carter had overseen trailblazing negotiations between Israel and Egypt in September 1978.

The meeting was convened in July 2000, despite Arafat's expressed anxiety that the groundwork had not been prepared. If the mood was not particularly auspicious to begin negotiations, it bears recalling that Israeli Prime Minister Menachem Begin and Egyptian President Anwar Sadat felt positive disdain for one another and hardly ever spoke during the earlier Camp David negotiations. Barak and Clinton were intent to move forward, and Clinton assured the Palestinians that no one would be held to blame if the talks failed. Even so, Arafat and the Palestinian delegation brought considerable distrust and suspicion with them to Camp David. The interim agreements had only been partially implemented by Israel, and, among other things, the Palestinians worried that they would be forced to renegotiate arrangements that had been already settled. Barak's cavalier approach to fulfilling the Oslo accords did not inspire confidence. Nor, from Israel's perspective, had the PA fulfilled its security responsibilities under the accords. Arafat failed to move strenuously against violent militants and terrorists. He also often failed to grasp that indiscriminate attacks on Israeli civilians poisoned the negotiating environment.

The Palestinian scholar Salim Tamari notes that security was the "jewel in the crown" of Oslo for Israel. Without security, Israel's commitment to the accords is in question. In fact, both sides have suffered terrible losses, as the box below shows.

THE HORRIBLE PRICE IN LIVES

From the September day in 1993 that Arafat and Rabin signed the Declaration of Principles until October 31, 2001, 440 Israelis have died in the hostilities. Of these victims, 116 Israeli civilians were killed by Palestinians in the West Bank or Gaza, 184 Israeli civilians were killed within Israel; 84 security-force personnel were killed in the occupied territories and 56 members of the security forces were killed in Israel.

During the same eight-year period, 1,032 Palestinians lost their lives in the conflict. Of these victims, 866 were Palestinian civilians killed by Israeli security forces or civilians in the occupied territories; 137 were members of the Palestinian security forces who died at the hands of the Israeli security forces; and, 29 were Palestinian civilians killed in Israel.

The first 10 months of 2001 were bloodier than any previous year for Israel and for the Palestinians: 137 Israelis have died at Palestinian hands, either in the occupied territories or in Israel, and 364 Palestinians have been killed by Israelis.

It is difficult to say precisely what was offered by Barak at Camp David. Offers were never put on paper, nor has Barak himself addressed the topic in any specificity. Nonetheless, by sifting through participants' accounts, it is possible to assemble the outlines of the package that was on offer. To begin, it should be underlined that a number of taboos were broken. This Camp David meeting was the first occasion when the question of Jerusalem was put on the table. The long-standing Israeli argument is that the city is the eternal and undivided capital of Israel. In international law, the question of eastern Jerusalem (the predominantly Arab part of the city that includes the spiritually important old city) is unsettled. The Palestinians claim the city as the rightful capital of their envisaged state. Barak was willing to concede significant chunks of the city to the PA, including control but not sovereignty over the Haram al Sharif, and sovereignty for the Arab neighborhoods of the city. Whatever the dimension of the areas involved, this was a pathbreaking offer by an Israeli prime minister precisely because it demonstrated that the fate of the revered city was negotiable.

There are more than 3.7 million Palestinians living outside of historic Palestine. The question of "return" is therefore a burning issue for Palestinians and a matter of grave concern to Israel. Arafat's insistence that the right of return extend not just to the West Bank and Gaza but to Israel as well was disquieting, to say the least. The very nature, not to say the survival, of Israel would be jeopardized by the return of millions of Palestinians. Most serious Palestinians understand this is a redline issue for Israel, and few expect that more than limited numbers will ever be able to return to their former homes in Israel. What the Palestinians were demanding however, was a right, in principle, that Barak was not willing to provide.

In the West Bank, Barak offered to withdraw from over 90% of the territory (with the caveat that the precise dimensions of the offer were never spelled out at Camp David). The territory retained by Israel would include most of the extensive settlements. In compensation, Israel offered a small land swap accounting for about 1% of the West Bank. Since the Oslo accords also specify safe-passage routes between Gaza and the West Bank, one needs to presume that those routes would require from 1% to 3% of Israel's territory. Thus, the Palestinians were being offered the equivalent of more than 90% of the occupied territory.

As for Gaza, it has always been presumed that the settlements—occupying 20% of the land area of the strip—would be evacuated. The settlements are only tenable with a large security force protecting them. Plus, they are a constant irritant in cheek-to-jowl Gaza, which has a Palestinian Arab population of 1.2 million people, compared to nearly 7,000 Jewish settlers.

The Palestinian negotiators began with the assumption that they had already conceded 78% of historic Palestine to Israel in 1988 when they renounced terrorism and accepted Israel's legitimacy. The signing of the 1993 declaration of principles made this acceptance explicit. They felt that they should not be required to sacrifice any more territory. One also has to presume that the

UNOCCUPIED TERRITORY

backs of the Palestinians were stiffened by the developments two months prior in Lebanon, when Israel unilaterally withdrew from the country. During the summer of 2000 there was speculation in the Israeli press that Barak, should he fail to reach agreement with the PA, would impose a settlement on the Palestinians. In this scenario, Israel would retain its large settlement blocks around Jerusalem and concede segments of the West Bank to the PA. This is a variant of ideas about unilateral separation that has been debated in Israel, but given the patterns of settlement, and the economic and resource interdependence of the two peoples, feasibility is problematic.

The combination of Barak's negotiating style, which included extending, rescinding, replacing, revising offers through Clinton rather than face-to-face with Arafat, and Arafat's failure to produce any counterproposals, lends a somewhat surreal aspect to the Camp David negotiations. Barak insisted that the Palestinians accept his offer in good faith. Nothing would be on offer after Camp David unless Arafat agreed on the spot. But good faith was in short supply. After an extraordinary 14 days, Arafat would not accept the package proffered by Barak.

The failure of Camp David did not turn on one issue, such as the right of return, as many of the press reports have indicated. In point of fact, this valiant attempt to jump to the big issues was not well prepared diplomatically or psychologically. Equally important, Clinton allowed himself to become a mailman for Barak rather than actively attempting to give shape and direction to the negotiations. U.S. credibility suffered tremendously in the process. Clinton's angry words at the conclusion of the summit, when he made plain his frustration that Arafat did not contribute more to the negotiations, worked to undercut his credibility as an honest broker. The President said that he might decide to move the U.S. embassy to Jerusalem (a step that would signify acceptance of Israeli claims on Jerusalem), but he backed away from this threat over the ensuing weeks.

As for Arafat, just as he failed to articulate a position at Camp David, he has also failed to enunciate a path toward peace to his own public, either before or after the summit. Arafat has abdicated responsibility for preparing his people for compromise and peace. The result of this dereliction of responsibility is a diminishment of moderate voices and an elevation of radical ones, which, in turn, undermine Arafat's moral authority as a peacemaker.

Once the dust settled, and particularly after the al-Aqsa intifada erupted on September 28, 2000, the negotiations resumed. While the world's attention focused on Camp David as a singular event, the negotiations there were part of a process. Despite Barak's adamant take-it-or-leave-it position at Camp David, he recommitted himself to negotiations, as did the PA. During the next five months, Israeli and Palestinian negotiators met, often under U.S. auspices, and they moved much closer to common ground on the tough issues of Jerusalem, territory and refugees.

After nearly eight years of avoiding staking out a U.S. proposal, Clinton offered his own views on the outlines of a settlement on December 23, 2000. Clinton's bridging proposals were accepted by Barak provided that the Palestinians also accepted them as offered. In January, Arafat indicated his acceptance, with reservations. Both sides continued negotiating in Taba, the Egyptian resort town. All participant accounts point to impressive progress. While technical issues remained to be solved, the shape of an agreement closely following Clinton's December proposals emerged.

Israel agreed to return 94% of the West Bank, as well as a swap representing 3% of the territory to compensate for annexed settlements. In addition, the Gaza-West Bank corridor was calculated as equal to 3% of the territory. Jerusalem would be the capital of two states, Israel and Palestine. Complex arrangements would be made to protect Palestinian control of Haram al Sharif and Israeli control of the underlying land of the Temple Mount, including the Western or Wailing Wall. Israel would agree to limited numbers of Palestinians returning to Israel, and there would be an unlimited right of return to the West Bank and Gaza (although it was anticipated that many Palestinians would stay where they were, or emigrate to the West). Unfortunately, the Taba breakthroughs came too late in the day. Barak was about to be defeated in the February elections by Sharon. Barak's credibility had shrunken to the point that he suffered the most lopsided electoral defeat in Israel's history.

As for Clinton, his uncritical acceptance of Barak's positions prompted the Palestinian negotiators to publish an extraordinary critique of the U.S. President's approach to the peace process. Historians will weigh whether a more assertive, more balanced U.S. role might have moved the belligerents much closer to peace. From the standpoint of the Palestinians, Clinton and his team of advisers were so committed to sustaining momentum in the peace process that they lost sight of the miserable conditions in which many Palestinians were forced to live as well as Israel's selective application of the Oslo accords. ■

The new President Bush

AFTER FINALLY gaining the White House in one of America's most bizarre elections, George W. Bush might be excused for wishing to avoid yet another contentious arena—the Middle East. The presidential battle between Vice President Al Gore and Bush did not turn on foreign policy, but both candidates made every effort during the campaign to affirm their credentials as friends of Israel. During the 2000 presidential debates, Bush expressed appreciation for the Clinton Administration's peacemaking efforts, but he also signaled less enthusiasm for pushing the negotiation process: "This current Administration's worked hard to keep the parties at the table. I will try to do the same thing. But it won't be on my timetable." Candidate Bush was eager to leave the timetable to the belligerents, and as President he has stuck to that approach. He made no secret of his desire to stay at a comfortable distance from the Arab-Israeli conflict.

Bush's reticence to get involved in Middle East negotiations contrasts sharply with President Clinton's enmeshment in Middle East peacemaking. Clinton's down-to-the-wire failure was a warning bell for Bush and his advisers who insisted that the expenditure of valuable diplomatic capital, not to mention the President's time, required that a dispute must be "ripe" for resolution. Deputy Secretary of State Richard Armitage expressed the dominant sentiment in the Administration: "You can't want peace more than two parties want peace....What does Mr. Clinton think about having spent the waning days of his presidency locked at Camp David to no effect?"

The new President's initial aversion to set the diplomatic pace in Middle East peacemaking was not in doubt. Of course, if the combatants decide on their own to faithfully negotiate, or if others, especially European powers, defuse the dangers, the U.S. could successfully evade deeper engagement and the associated domestic political tolls. These conditions are unlikely to be met.

The two parties to the conflict have shown little ability to end the conflict on their own. No other actor, whether a state, the European Union, or the UN secretary-general, has the leverage and the influence that the U.S. does. America is the indispensable matchmaker in the Middle East. David Kimche, the renowned Israeli diplomat, put it succinctly: "It should, by now, be clear to all and sundry that there is no possibility of ending the nightmare that we share with the Palestinians unless the U.S. takes on a more active role." Even French diplomats—hardly routine proponents of U.S. dominance in the region—readily argue that America's leadership is essential.

Diverging perspectives

Yet, at a time when the support of fellow democracies in Europe is vitally important to the U.S., European and American perspectives on the Arab-Israeli conflict often diverge. The Israeli settlements are a case in point. For most European capitals, the settlements are a violation of the Fourth Geneva Convention, which prohibits annexation of occupied land, while the U.S. is more inclined to revert to euphemistic language about the settlements being "unhelpful" or "counterproductive." Of course, it is precisely America's ability to be more sensitive to Israeli concerns that elevate it to a privileged position as peacemaker.

Quelling the violence requires heavy diplomatic lifting, and pressure will have to be applied to both sides, not just the unpopular Palestinian leadership. Reengagement of an active U.S. mediation role is an obvious prescription, but the political price is not trivial when there is broad disagreement among U.S. policy elites concerning the possibility of peace, or even stemming the violence. Bush finds himself outflanked by congressional Democrats and Republicans in the theater of Arab-Israeli issues. His dilemma is that he has only a narrow Republican majority in the House while the Democrats hold a majority in the Senate. Pressure on Israel is unacceptable to Congress, so contentious excursions toward a balanced foreign policy in the Middle East will jeopardize his domestic political agenda. It is a measure of just how far official Washington leans in supporting Israel, that the suggestion of a balanced Middle East policy is itself a poison formula.

The path of least resistance is to do as little as possible while calling on the belligerents to end the "cycle of violence," which is precisely what the Bush Administration did when it assumed power. Given the relative strength of Israel and the Palestinians, this leaves the Israelis in the driver's seat, which suits Prime Minister Sharon. Friendly Arab governments are exasperated by this laissez-faire diplomacy, which "encourages Israeli intransigence" in the view of Egyptian President Hosni Mubarak among other Arab leaders. Bush is intent to postpone if not avoid any contretemps with Israel and its domestic supporters. The President and his domestic advisers easily anticipate the backlash from pro-Israeli quarters, not least the Congress, should the U.S. lean on Israel. They prefer not to "go there." No world region is connected to as many domestic political minefields as the Middle East.

Partisans of Israel may claim one of the most formidable lobbying organizations in Washington, Aipac (the American Israel Public Affairs Committee), which is not shy about publicizing its influence or flexing its muscles. While Arab-American and American Muslim groups have organized lobbying efforts as well, they often are poorly coordinated and sometimes working at cross-purposes. In the national capital, the leading forum for the discussion of Arab-Israeli issues is the Washington Institute on Near East Policy (Winep), which grew out of Aipac in 1985 and regularly hosts high-profile appearances by leading Israeli and American policymakers. The first director of Winep, Martin S. Indyk, filled major positions during the Clinton Administration in the National Security Council and the State Department, and he twice served as ambassador to Israel. Winep has earned a privileged place at the high table and, as its self-designated "Presidential Study Group" implies, there is no shyness about presuming a formative role in U.S. Middle East policy. As in most of its work, the report of the Presidential Study Group presumes a neat overlap between U.S. and Israeli interests.

AN ISRAELI TANK SHELL SCORES *a direct hit on a building in the Palestinian-controlled town of Beit Jala, May 14, 2001.*

In fact, the overlap is not always so neat, as the Bush Administration may testify, especially after September 11. The challenge for the Bush Administration is to juggle U.S. interests that are not necessarily complementary: maintaining a special relationship with Israel; sustaining the unimpeded flow of Persian Gulf oil and a strategic presence in the gulf, and containing and undermining Saddam Hussein's regime in Iraq. So long as serious momentum toward peace in the Arab-Israeli zone continued in the 1990s, it was possible to keep U.S. interests in equilibrium. As the prospects for peace deteriorated (beginning in the late 1990s), the contradictions in U.S. policy became harder to camouflage and the double standards more obvious.

The U.S. and Israel certainly share a deep cultural affinity and they are joined by a skein of strategic and intelligence dialogues and extensive diplomatic coordination. They also share a deep commitment to defeating terrorism. Yet, the other U.S. interests in the region dictate that America pay attention to the bigger picture, including the views of other friends in the Middle East. Saudi Foreign Minister Prince Saud al-Faisal underlined that the U.S. cannot escape coming to terms with the conflict between Israel and the Palestinians. "Undoubtedly, the sore that festers in the Middle East, that taints every aspect of life in the Middle East is the continuing conflict between Israel and the Palestinians."

One legacy from the Clinton Administration is a fact-finding committee that grew out of the October 2000 Sharm el-Sheikh summit. The summit was convened by the U.S. to try to bring an end to the al-Aqsa intifada. It was agreed that the U.S. would appoint an international committee to investigate the causes of the violence and recommend steps to end it. Chaired by former Democratic Senator George J. Mitchell (who played a key role in the successful negotiations in Northern Ireland), the committee included a former president of Turkey, a foreign minister of Norway, another former senator (Warren Rudman) and a representative from the European Union. The Mitchell Committee Report is a major contribution to understanding the Israeli-Palestinian conflict, and the Bush Administration has embraced the findings of the April 2001 report as a blueprint for moving toward a solution.

A key condition

Among the important recommendations is the resumption of security cooperation between Israel and the PA. To this end, Bush dispatched Central Intelligence Agency Director George J. Tenet to the region to oversee the restoration of cooperation. Tenet, who had made nine trips to the region, produced a "work plan" in June that was accepted by both sides, but it has yet to be implemented. A key condition is not just an end to the violence, but a cooling-off period during which both sides may prepare to resume negotiations. Prime Minister Sharon insists the implementation of the committee's recommendations must be preceded by seven days of absolutely no violence by the Palestinians. Many people, including a number of U.S. and Israeli officials, believe this is an impossible condition, but Secretary Powell accepted it while visiting Israel in June. Sharon, though under quiet pressure from the U.S. to loosen the requirement, has not relented.

As the process continues, assuming it does, the report calls on the Palestinians to condemn and discourage incitement and make an all-out effort to stop violence. For its part, Israel is to freeze all settlement building, which is a hard pill for some Israelis to swallow, especially for Prime Minister Sharon, who has dedicated much of his public life to promoting settlements in order to maintain control of Judea and Samaria, the biblical terms he and other right-wing Israelis use to refer to the West Bank. Israel is also called upon to lift the persistent closures that made Palestinian movement between cities and often between and within villages impossible. Since last year, Israel has withheld the payment of taxes paid by Palestinians working in Israel. Those taxes should now be transferred to the PA, as required by the Oslo accords. The Mitchell committee has provided a road map for restoring the essential elements of security and mutual respect that are preconditions for meaningful negotiations.

Throughout the summer of 2001, the Bush Administration maintained a low profile in the Middle East. Official spokespeople often ducked behind soothing exhortations. Both sides should avoid provocative acts that propel the cycle of violence. Ari Fleischer, White House spokesman, offered the following sample of boilerplate: "Violence is violence and the President has deplored the violence in the region...." President Bush sometimes mounted the "bully pulpit" to express his support for Israel and exhort the PA to make a bigger effort to end the violence. Like many in his Administration, Bush blames the PA for inflaming the violence and for failing to do enough to stop anti-Israeli terrorism. From the western White House in Crawford, Texas, where Bush vacationed in August, he offered some free advice: "And if Mr. Arafat is interested in having a dialogue that could conceivably lead to the Mitchell process, then I strongly urge him to urge the terrorists, the Palestinian terrorists, to stop the suicide bombings, to stop the incursions, to stop the threats." In Israel, the President's advice to Arafat was widely interpreted as a strong rebuke to the Palestinian leader, and as an endorsement of Sharon's efforts to provide security for Israel.

While nearly three quarters of American voters support the establishment of an independent Palestinian state, only 39% have a favorable view of Palestinians (compared to 60% who view Israelis favorably) and only 18% have a favorable view of Arafat (29% view Sharon positively). Judged by their rhetoric, Washington-based elected officials not only share the voters' bleak assessment of Arafat but also tend to have a less-balanced view of the contestants than the electorate. Whereas 78% of voters polled believe that both sides are responsible for the breakdown of the peace process, members of Congress are far more inclined than the broader population to publicly ascribe blame to Arafat and the PA for the violence that has persisted since September 2000.

For his part, Bush has refused to meet with Arafat at all, even going so far as to pass up a chance to simply say hello during the November session of the UN. Unlike Clinton, who hosted Arafat in the White House frequently, Bush is withholding any meeting with Arafat until the PA moves more strenuously than it has against violence. Withholding the implied approval that a meeting with the President represents is a powerful symbolic tactic, and it has the political benefit of keeping the President's public image unbesmirched by contact with an unpopular personality. There are risks, or course, since Arafat has already been weakened considerably by the failure of the Oslo process and the vitality of contending Palestinian voices. No single Palestinian has the political base and the credentials to replace Arafat, so he remains an indispensable participant in the negotiations. There is no question that a meeting with Bush would bolster his political standing among his own people.

Secretary of State Powell has been immersed in the crisis virtually since the inauguration. By his own admission, he spends more time on the Middle East than any other region of the world. After Israel briefly reoccupied the Palestinian suburb of Beit Jala in late August, Powell made six phone calls to Israeli and Palestinian leaders in one day in order to establish the terms of reference for an Israeli withdrawal from the Jerusalem suburb. Israel's actions, including assassinations, occupation of Palestinian territory, and disproportionate responses to Palestinian attacks sometimes earn Powell's frank disapproval:

"When you start knocking down buildings with bulldozers, don't expect people not to respond to this kind of activity. When you start announcing more settlement activity, this does not create conditions that would cause the other side to be less responsive or less violent. So this is a time for both sides to avoid all provocations that would keep us from getting into a period of quiet, that would allow us to move forward...."

More often than not, such rebukes are quickly diluted by less critical comments from the White House or Administration heavyweights. Infighting within the Bush Administration bubbled over into the press in stories meant to cast doubt on Powell's credibility as an architect of U.S. policy. One veteran of Washington trench warfare, complains: "You can't take the leadership role without the President of the U.S. And he can't cut Colin Powell off at the knees every time Colin speaks on the issue."

Discounting rebukes

Understandably, Israeli officials tend to discount U.S. rebukes from Powell or the State Department, especially when they are tempered by softer, less-critical comments from 1600 Pennsylvania Avenue. A dictionary-stretching example of Israeli discounting of Washington's demands was provided by Peres in October, when he explained, in Hebrew, to journalists that the word "'immediately,' in English, doesn't mean at once." He was responding to strong statements from the State Department calling on Israel to "immediately withdraw" from Palestinian villages and towns that it had reoccupied.

Tensions between the U.S. and Israel have become more apparent as the Bush Administration has begun to insert itself more strenuously into rejuvenating the peace process. Bush was offended when Sharon seemed to be comparing him to Neville Chamberlain, the architect of pre-World War II appeasement, and the Administration has applied strong pressure on Israel to evacuate the PA areas that it has reoccupied. Speaking to the UN General Assembly in November, President Bush envisaged two states living side by side, Israel and Palestine, which balanced his strong words about Palestinian violence having to stop.

Understandably, the Israeli government is nervous about the newly energized Bush Middle East policy. However, the U.S.-Israel relationship remains a very strong one, and at every turn the Administration has underlined its deep commitment to Israeli security. Also, there is full awareness that Netanyahu waits in the wings. Sharon, Administration optimists argue, has the merit of being more instinctively pragmatic than the former prime minister. Time will tell whether he is willing to follow the powerful example of Rabin.

Secretary Powell's fair-minded speech at the University of Louisville in November 2001 signaled a new vigor in the American role in the peace process. Powell reiterated the President's reference to two states living side by side. He included a sharp message to the Palestinians that violence has to stop and an equally sharp message to Israel that the building of settlements in the occupied lands has to stop. "We will do all we can to help the process along. We will push. We will prod." Two very capable and highly respected men are tasked with moving the prodding and the pushing: Ambassador William Burns, the State Department's top Middle East official, and retired Marine General Anthony Zinni. Zinni will spend a lot of time on the ground, filling the role of George Tenet.

Making peace between Israel and the Palestinians requires uncommon tenacity, thick political skin and the cooperation of the belligerents. That is a tall order, but on the global stage, peace in the Middle East matters more than it ever has before. The rights of the Israelis and the Palestinians to security, dignity and independence are compelling. For America, this is not only an appropriate challenge to pursue for good moral reasons, but this is an indispensable goal for sustaining the base of broad, international support that will be required in the difficult years that lie ahead. ■

OPINION BALLOTS are on pages 43–44

DISCUSSION QUESTIONS

1. Should peacemaking in the Middle East be the responsibility of the people of the Middle East? Is a U.S. role really necessary to move the peace process along?

2. The U.S. has played a leading role in the search for peace for decades. Should the U.S. adopt a more inclusive diplomatic approach and promote a larger role for Europe or the UN?

3. Annually, five billion dollars in U.S. aid flows directly to Israel and Egypt, the two largest recipients of aid by far. Is aid an effective tool of foreign policy and might it be used or withheld to gain compliance with U.S. policy?

4. The Oslo accords were all based on the assumption that Israelis and Palestinians would gain confidence in the process and move closer to peace. Has the process failed, and should it be put aside, or is it possible to rejuvenate the Oslo accords?

5. America has been widely criticized by Muslims for adopting "double standards" and turning a blind eye to outrageous behavior by its friends. The case of Israeli treatment of Palestinians is a favorite example. Is this a fair charge and what should the U.S. do about it?

6. The U.S. has declared that the Palestinian groups Hamas and Islamic Jihad are terrorists. What should PLO Chairman Arafat be expected to do to control these groups?

7. President Bush has expressed his support for a Palestinian state, a longtime goal of the Palestinians and an outcome that has been at least implicit in the Oslo process. What should be done to ensure the viability of that state and should the U.S. insist that it is a democracy?

READINGS AND RESOURCES

Agha, Hussein, and Malley, Robert, "Camp David: The Tragedy of Errors." **The New York Review of Books,** August 9, 2001. This is a revisionist account of the Camp David summit of 2000 and it is must reading.

Benvenisti, Meron, and Friedman, Thomas L., **Intimate Enemies: Jews and Arabs in a Shared Land.** Berkeley, Calif., University of California Press, 1995. 260 pp. $45.00. Former deputy mayor of Jerusalem addresses the Israeli occupation of the West Bank and Gaza and evaluates the 1993 Israeli-Palestinian accords.

Eisenberg, Laura Zittrain, and Caplan, Neil, **Negotiating Arab-Israeli Peace: Patterns, Problems, Possibilities.** Bloomington, Indiana University Press, 1998. 288 pp. $16.95 (paper). Two very capable scholars examine the background, assumptions and importance of most of the agreements in the 1980s and 1990s.

Haberman, Clyde, "Dennis Ross's Exit Interview." **New York Times Magazine,** March 25, 2001, pp. 36–39. Ross spent a decade as "point man" in the U.S. quest for a peaceful resolution of the Arab-Israeli conflict.

"The Middle East." **Current History,** January 2002. Entire issue. Leading scholars and experts offer timely essays in this respected and widely read annual review.

"Mitchell Committee" Report. 2001. Available at **www.cfr.org/public/pubs/MitchellComm_Report.pdf.** This is a penetrating and lucid report by the blue-ribbon international committee chaired by Senator George Mitchell.

Quandt, William B., and Armacost, Michael H., **Peace Process: American Diplomacy and the Arab-Israeli Conflict Since 1967,** rev.ed. Berkeley, Calif., University of California Press, 2001, 325 pp. $19.95. This is an indispensable history of America's attempt to bring peace to Arabs and Israelis.

Savir, Uri, **The Process: 1,100 Days that Changed the Middle East.** New York, Vintage Books, 1999. 352 pp. $15.00 (paper). A reliable, engaging account of the Oslo process by one of the Israeli participants.

Sayigh, Yezid, "Arafat and the Anatomy of a Revolt." **Survival,** Autumn 2001, pp. 47–60. This is a critical assessment of Arafat and the PA by a prominent Palestinian scholar.

Slater, Jerome, "What Went Wrong? The Collapse of the Israeli-Palestinian Peace Process." **Political Science Quarterly,** Summer 2001, pp. 171–99. A detailed analysis of the Camp David negotiations, preceeded by an overview of the prevailing Israeli and Palestinian "narratives" of the conflict.

Tessler, Mark A., **A History of the Israeli-Palestinian Conflict.** Bloomington, Indiana University Press, 1994. 906 pp. $29.95 (paper). One of America's leading scholars has written a comprehensive and balanced reference. This is the single best history available.

FOUNDATION FOR MIDDLE EAST PEACE, 1761 N St., NW, Washington, DC 20036; (202) 835-3650; Fax (202) 835-3651. **www.fmep.org** ■ This foundation is dedicated to aiding Americans understand the Israeli-Palestinian conflict and to finding a peaceful solution that appeals to both sides.

MIDDLE EAST INSTITUTE, 1761 N St., NW, Washington, DC 20036; (202) 785-1141; Fax (202) 331-8861. **www.mideasti.org** ■ Provides impartial information on current events in the Middle East. Publishes the **Middle East Journal.** Site contains links to other quality sites on the region.

MIDDLE EAST STUDIES ASSOCIATION OF NORTH AMERICA (MESA), University of Arizona, 1643 E. Helen St., Tucson, AZ 85721; (520) 621-5850; Fax (520) 626-9095. **www.mesa.arizona.edu** ■ MESA is a nonprofit, nonpartisan membership organization comprising academics and others interested in the Middle East and North Africa. Publishes quarterly **International Journal of Middle East Studies.**

U.S. STATE DEPARTMENT. www.state.gov/p/nea/rt/index.cfm?id=2829 ■ Bureau of Near Eastern Affairs website on the "Middle East Peace Process."

LEARN MORE ABOUT THIS TOPIC AT www.greatdecisions.org

Access links to online resources • Order the recommended readings • Take the GD Quiz • Find maps in the online atlas • Submit your opinion ballots • Read the latest National Opinion Ballot Report • and more ...

OPINION BALLOTS

Please submit only one ballot per person, per topic. *Ballots must be received by June 30, 2002.*
Vote online at ***www.greatdecisions.org*** *(code: gd2002fpa) or mail ballots to:*

FOREIGN POLICY ASSOCIATION, 470 PARK AVENUE SOUTH, NEW YORK, NY 10016-6819

TOPIC 3 Middle East peace process

ISSUE A. Do you agree or disagree with the following statements?

	AGREE	DISAGREE
1. The U.S. is guilty of a "double standard" in its Middle East policy.	❑	❑
2. Israel is justified in targeting Palestinian terrorists alleged to have committed political assassinations.	❑	❑
3. PLO Chairman Yasir Arafat is doing all he can to control extremist groups such as Hamas and Islamic Jihad.	❑	❑
4. The U.S. should use its aid to Israel and Egypt more effectively to gain compliance with American policies.	❑	❑
5. The European countries should play a larger role in the Middle East peace process.	❑	❑

Comment: ______________________________

____

Your zip code: ____ ____ ____ ____ ____

Date: / /2002 *Ballot continues on reverse side...*

TOPIC 3 Middle East peace process

ISSUE A. Do you agree or disagree with the following statements?

	AGREE	DISAGREE
1. The U.S. is guilty of a "double standard" in its Middle East policy.	❑	❑
2. Israel is justified in targeting Palestinian terrorists alleged to have committed political assassinations.	❑	❑
3. PLO Chairman Yasir Arafat is doing all he can to control extremist groups such as Hamas and Islamic Jihad.	❑	❑
4. The U.S. should use its aid to Israel and Egypt more effectively to gain compliance with American policies.	❑	❑
5. The European countries should play a larger role in the Middle East peace process.	❑	❑

Comment: ______________________________

____

Your zip code: ____ ____ ____ ____ ____

Date: / /2002 *Ballot continues on reverse side...*

TOPIC 4 Colombia and drug trafficking

ISSUE A. What is the most important step the U.S. should take in assisting Colombia in its battle with drug traffickers? (choose one):

___ **1.** Combat the armed rebel and paramilitary groups.

___ **2.** Train Colombian counternarcotics units and eradicate coca and poppy fields.

___ **3.** Correct human-rights abuses and provide economic incentives for crop substitution.

Comment: ______________________________

____

ISSUE B. Illicit drug use in the U.S. is a more important problem facing the country than:

	YES	NO
1. Environmental decline	❑	❑
2. Energy availability	❑	❑
3. International terrorism	❑	❑
4. Economic problems	❑	❑
5. Racial and ethnic conflict	❑	❑

Comment: ______________________________

____

Your zip code: ____ ____ ____ ____ ____

Date: / /2002 *Ballot continues on reverse side...*

TOPIC 4 Colombia and drug trafficking

ISSUE A. What is the most important step the U.S. should take in assisting Colombia in its battle with drug traffickers? (choose one):

___ **1.** Combat the armed rebel and paramilitary groups.

___ **2.** Train Colombian counternarcotics units and eradicate coca and poppy fields.

___ **3.** Correct human-rights abuses and provide economic incentives for crop substitution.

Comment: ______________________________

____

ISSUE B. Illicit drug use in the U.S. is a more important problem facing the country than:

	YES	NO
1. Environmental decline	❑	❑
2. Energy availability	❑	❑
3. International terrorism	❑	❑
4. Economic problems	❑	❑
5. Racial and ethnic conflict	❑	❑

Comment: ______________________________

____

Your zip code: ____ ____ ____ ____ ____

Date: / /2002 *Ballot continues on reverse side...*

ISSUE B. Should the peacemaking approach in the Oslo Accords be abandoned as a failure, or is it possible to revive that approach? (choose one)

___ **1.** Abandon the Oslo approach

___ **2.** Possible to revive the Oslo approach

Comment: ______________________________

ISSUE B. Should the peacemaking approach in the Oslo Accords be abandoned as a failure, or is it possible to revive that approach? (choose one)

___ **1.** Abandon the Oslo approach

___ **2.** Possible to revive the Oslo approach

Comment: ______________________________

ISSUE C. How likely is it that without an active U.S. involvement, Israel and its adversaries in the Middle East will ever reach a peaceful settlement? (choose one)

___ **1.** Very likely

___ **2.** Somewhat likely

___ **3.** Somewhat unlikely

___ **4.** Very unlikely

Comment: ______________________________

ISSUE C. How likely is it that without an active U.S. involvement, Israel and its adversaries in the Middle East will ever reach a peaceful settlement? (choose one)

___ **1.** Very likely

___ **2.** Somewhat likely

___ **3.** Somewhat unlikely

___ **4.** Very unlikely

Comment: ______________________________

ISSUE C. Do you support or oppose the following measures to deal with the drug problem in the U.S.?

	STRONGLY SUPPORT	SUPPORT	OPPOSE	STRONGLY OPPOSE
1. Strict law enforcement in the U.S. to curtail illicit drug use.	❑	❑	❑	❑
2. Involvement in producer nations to curtail the production of illicit drugs.	❑	❑	❑	❑
3. Interdiction campaigns to curb drug smuggling into the U.S.	❑	❑	❑	❑
4. Educational efforts to dissuade Americans from using illicit drugs.	❑	❑	❑	❑
5. Increased treatment opportunities to wean American users off drugs.	❑	❑	❑	❑
6. Decriminalization of illicit drugs.	❑	❑	❑	❑

Comment: ______________________________

ISSUE C. Do you support or oppose the following measures to deal with the drug problem in the U.S.?

	STRONGLY SUPPORT	SUPPORT	OPPOSE	STRONGLY OPPOSE
1. Strict law enforcement in the U.S. to curtail illicit drug use.	❑	❑	❑	❑
2. Involvement in producer nations to curtail the production of illicit drugs.	❑	❑	❑	❑
3. Interdiction campaigns to curb drug smuggling into the U.S.	❑	❑	❑	❑
4. Educational efforts to dissuade Americans from using illicit drugs.	❑	❑	❑	❑
5. Increased treatment opportunities to wean American users off drugs.	❑	❑	❑	❑
6. Decriminalization of illicit drugs.	❑	❑	❑	❑

Comment: ______________________________

Colombia and drug trafficking

The implementation of Plan Colombia, the U.S. initiative to help eradicate the thriving drug trafficking in that country, presents many strategic and ethical problems for Americans and Colombians.

by David C. Morrison

APWIDE WORLD PHOTOS

A PLANE FUMIGATES *poppy fields outside of Popayan in southwest Colombia, July 2001. Fumigation is part of the three-pronged Plan Colombia, which comprises military force, crop eradication and social development.*

FEBRUARY 1990: President George H.W. Bush touched down briefly in Cartagena, Colombia, to meet with the presidents of the three chief cocaine-producing South American nations—Bolivia, Peru and Colombia. Then the heyday of the Medellín cocaine cartel, with a massive war of terror being waged by Pablo Escobar and other drug lords against the central government in Bogotá, security was intense. But, backed by $2.2 billion in American aid, Bush triumphantly proclaimed the formation of an "antidrug cartel" that would exchange intelligence and bolster regional economic ties in hopes of curtailing the flow of illicit drugs to America's streets.

Today, Escobar is dead, the Medellín cartel (and the Cali cartel that succeeded it) are defunct, and coca production has shrunk dramatically in both Bolivia and Peru. However, dramatically illustrating the one-step-forward, one-step-back nature of antinarcotics campaigns, coca production in and cocaine exports from Colombia itself have sharply increased, and Colombia has since become a major player in the U.S. heroin market. Meanwhile, the large cartels of the 1980s have been replaced by hundreds of smaller trafficking operations that are in many respects more difficult to combat.

And so, a decade later, in August 2000, then President Bill Clinton followed his predecessor in making his own brief touchdown in Cartagena to inaugurate yet another U.S. antidrug campaign in Colombia. This time, the vehicle was the far more controversial "Plan Colombia," a $7.5 billion strategy designed by President Andrés Pastrana to curtail drug production there by 50% in five years through a mixed program of military force, crop eradication and social development.

Plan Colombia is about much more than just drugs, however. Most of Colombia's cocaine is cultivated and processed in two southern provinces, Putumayo and Caquetá, which are also dominated by the most powerful of the leftist revolutionary armies still waging that country's four-decade-old guerrilla war. To complicate matters, right-wing

DAVID C. MORRISON, *a reporter with* National Journal *for 10 years, is a freelance writer in Washington, who specializes in covering, among other topics, drug-policy issues.*

MICHAEL SAMUEL GRAPHICS

paramilitary groups and death squads secretly allied with elements of Colombia's official military also feed off the illicit drug business.

No question, Colombia, wracked by decades of seemingly intractable violence and lawlessness, needs some kind of a plan. But Pastrana's program is sparking region- and hemispherewide concern, largely thanks to the first and primary thrust of this three-pronged effort: the military drive that is fueled by $1.3 billion in U.S. aid, to be paid out over two years. Almost half a billion dollars of that package will pay for counterdrug operations in southern Colombia, including the importation of at least 100 U.S. advisers over the next few years to train and equip three new special antidrug battalions for the Colombian army. A similar sum will buy18 Black Hawk military helicopters, 42 Huey transport helicopters, radars, bases and other items designed to bolster American and Colombian efforts to interdict drug shipments. The balance will support efforts by the Colombian National Police to eradicate coca and poppy fields.

In a separate initiative, the 15 European Union (EU) nations are expected to channel some $90 million into Pastrana's effort to stabilize Colombia. But little of that money will actually flow through Plan Colombia, which other donor nations view as overly dominated by American military aid. The EU, together with Canada, Japan and Switzerland, has thus far contributed only $280 million, which must be channeled through private nongovernmental organizations (NGOs).

"It's the only aid package I know of where the military component was put smack in the middle of a development package," a Scandinavian diplomat has complained. "It contaminated everything in the eyes of Colombian civil society and the European Community."

Plan Colombia has generated in Washington the usual debate over any U.S. foreign intervention. And human-rights advocates are concerned that U.S. forces will inevitably become associated with abuses inflicted by Colombia's notoriously heavy-handed and corrupt armed forces and paramilitary troops. Indeed, despite guarantees by Pastrana that such would not be the case, Clinton in August 2000 had to sign a waiver bypassing certain human-rights conditions imposed by the U.S. Congress which Colombia had not yet met in order to expedite release of the large portion of the $1.3 billion aid package included in the fiscal year 2001 bill. (One of his last acts in office was essentially to repeat that process.)

Meanwhile, Republican presidential candidate George W. Bush was signaling his strong support for U.S. action in Colombia that could even surpass the Clinton effort in scope. "We cannot continue to make a false distinction between counterinsurgency and counternarcotics efforts," Robert Zoellick, now U.S. trade representative, told the Council on Foreign Relations shortly before the election. If the Colombian government officials want "to take their country back from killers and drug lords,...then the U.S. should offer serious, sustained and timely financial, material and intelligence support."

Pastrana visits Washington

One of the first foreign leaders to visit the newly installed President Bush in February 2001 was Pastrana, seeking additional funds to bolster the social development programs such as crop substitution and judicial reform that account for only 25% of the U.S. spending thus far on Plan Colombia.

"We are a poor country," Pastrana said prior to his departure to Washington. "But we are spending $1 billion a year of our money to keep drugs off the streets of Washington and New York. We need more help." Besides requesting an easing of trade tariffs (particularly on textiles, partially granted later in the year), Pastrana also sought as much as $500 million in new aid. The U.S. later responded with the $625 million Andean Counterdrug Initiative, to be shared by Colombia and six other South American nations.

Bush later engaged in a mid-2001 dispute with Congress over seeking to lift the limit on the number of U.S. contract employees allowed to work in Colombia as trainers and drug-crop eradicators. An eventual compromise capped the overall number of private contract and U.S. military personnel in Colombia at the previous level of 800, but allowed contract personnel to exceed the previous limit of 300.

Since then, of course, the U.S. seems to have lowered Plan Colombia, and many other initiatives, on its priority agenda. The Colombia effort is most closely associated with Clinton's hard-charging drug-policy "czar," retired Army General Barry R. McCaffrey. Because he was once chief of the U.S. military's Southern Command, then headquartered in Panama, it is perhaps not surprising that McCaffrey would craft a program of in-country interdiction with a heavy military component. Though McCaffrey's Bush-appointed successor at the White House Office of National Drug Control Policy is no less an antidrug hard-liner, it remains to be seen whether he will embrace the Colombia strategy with equal fervor.

With the September 11 terrorist attacks on the World Trade Center and the Pentagon, and the subsequent war in Afghanistan, counterterrorism, not counternarcotics, dominates the national policy discussion. But with trafficker and armed political groups in Colombia employing terroristic tactics to achieve their ends, and with some here arguing that the drug traffic itself is a form of terrorism, Plan Colombia could become defined as a component of the "war on terrorism" now being actively waged.

Plan Colombia is a generator of major headlines below the U.S. border—especially in Colombia, needless to say, where the aerial fumigation of coca and poppy crops is highly controversial, and in neighboring countries. "Our worry," Ecuadorian Foreign Minister Heinz Moeller has complained, "is that the removal of this cancerous tumor will cause it to metastasize into Ecuador," which thus far has succeeded in remaining largely unscathed by the violent and lucrative drug trade. Even if U.S. military aid succeeds in enabling Colombian troops to root out coca and opium poppy growers in southern Colombia, Moeller and his colleagues worry, what is to keep the peasant farmers and their guerrilla protectors from simply picking up and moving to greener fields in neighboring nations? The cautionary model, not surprisingly, is "Vietnamization" of the conflict in Colombia. The long U.S. counterinsurgency war in Indochina eventually spilled over into Laos and Cambodia, with dire consequences for both nations. Might not an American-funded drug war in Colombia similarly destabilize that country's neighbors?

"Rather than reducing coca cultivation and calming Colombia," Bruce Bagley, a professor of international studies at the University of Miami, has predicted, "this is going to unleash Armageddon."

But "this is not Vietnam," Clinton explicitly stated during his eight-hour visit to Cartagena. American advocates of Plan Colombia hasten to note that Washington contemplates nothing on the scale of its intervention in Indochina. Indeed, given post-Vietnam sentiment in the U.S., the Pentagon is not likely to mount that sort of campaign anywhere ever again. At the same time, with the chief rebel group having declared in a communiqué that "all Colombian or foreign military personnel in combat zones will be a military target," the prospect of the U.S. presence escalating simply to defend the original mission cannot be ruled out.

AP/WIDE WORLD PHOTOS

BARRY McCAFFREY, *U.S. drug czar under President Bill Clinton, visits with military and antidrug police at Barranco, a base in the southwestern province of Guaviare, after meeting with Colombia's president, October 21, 1997.*

As already noted, Congress has repeatedly endorsed a limit on the number of troops authorized for use in Colombia. But just as Bush's father bequeathed a sticky military situation to his successor, Clinton, by sending U.S. troops into the chaos of Somalia, so too might Clinton have handed off a troublesome imbroglio in South America to President Bush.

"Plan Colombia probably has one more year to prove itself before it's curtains," Representative Robert Wexler (D-Fla.), a supporter of the effort, said during debate on the plan last summer. "It's just too much American money being spent without results." Moreover, as Wexler pointed out, Colombian President Pastrana, the plan's political parent, must stand down when his term in office ends in 2002, and what deluge might follow him is hard to predict. This is thus sure to be a crucial year for U.S. involvement in the long-running drug war in Colombia.

Few viable alternatives

Given the typically chaotic state of affairs in Colombia, officials there point to their shortage of viable alternatives to the course laid out in Plan Colombia. "This is a peace plan, not a war plan," Foreign Minister Guillermo Fernandez de Soto assures his fellow citizens and Colombia's neighbors. By eliminating coca production in Putumayo and Caquetá, Colombian officials calculate, the leftist rebels will be denied essential revenues and will thus be forced to lay down their arms.

"There will be peace, but first there will be war," General Fernando Tapias, the Colombian chief of staff, has asserted. "With or without Plan Colombia, things are going to get worse."

Things are already pretty bad. Backing up a decade, to events just preceding the senior President Bush's visit to Colombia, Escobar, the leading element of the then dominant Medellín-based cocaine-exporting cartel, was so bold as to order the murder of a prominent candidate for president. That audacity prompted then President Virgilio Barco to announce a campaign against traffickers and the extradition to the U.S. of those for whom Washington had issued arrest warrants.

Barco's government followed up with massive seizures of drug-cartel property. Over 10,000 suspects were detained for questioning. And, as has been their wont, state security forces engaged in such extralegal tactics as summary executions of detainees and committed murders completely unrelated to the drug war. Some 5,700 Colombians died in politically related violence in 1989, an estimated 70% of those killings committed by the army or the police.

The drug gangsters were no less bloodthirsty. That year, a bus packed with half a ton of high explosives detonated in front of the Colombian federal police headquarters, killing 80 people and injuring another 700. A truck bomb destroyed a newspaper's offices, and its crusading editor was gunned down. Uncorrupted police officers and judges were similarly murdered. A commercial airliner was bombed, killing another 107 people.

The threatened extraditions to U.S. prisons never happened. (In fact, only in 2001 did the Colombian judiciary approve the extradition to the U.S. of Fabio Ochoa, a once-prominent member of the Medellín cartel.) In 1993, however, a fugitive Escobar was shot dead by government forces. And over that time, the Medellín cartel was largely dismantled with the vital assistance of the rival Cali cartel, which fed intelligence to the government and mounted its own campaign of assassinations.

All too predictably, the Cali traffickers simply stepped into their defeated predecessors' shoes. Cocaine shipments to the U.S. soared, and the price of the drug in America actually fell following Escobar's killing. Prosecutor General Gustavo de Greiff had predicted precisely this outcome in an interview with an American reporter a few years before. With Escobar out of the picture, he had forecast, "nothing will happen. There is so much appetite in your country for drugs, the killing of Escobar will not be a solution."

Just how much weight the Cali cartel carried became apparent in the wake of the 1994 presidential election, when evidence came to light that the campaign waged by the victor, President Ernesto Samper, had been heavily financed by the drug traffickers. Washington responded by "decertifying"—issuing a formal reprimand to—Colombia for not doing enough to fight drug trafficking. Unless it did more, Uncle Sam threatened, Colombia faced a cutoff in aid, as well as trade sanctions. With 40% of Colombian exports going to the U.S., Samper was pretty much compelled to launch a new campaign against the Cali cartel.

APWIDE WORLD PHOTOS

GENERAL ROSSO JOSÉ SERRANO, *former director of the Colombian National Police, directs his men in a poppy field in the southern state of Huila, February 2000.*

"The cost of the drug war has been staggering," former Colombian minister of defense Rafael Pardo recalled in a recent issue of *Foreign Affairs.* "In the last 15 years, 200 bombs (half of them as large as the one used in Oklahoma City) have blown up in Colombia's cities; an entire democratic leftist political party was eliminated by right-wing paramilitaries; 4 presidential candidates, 200 judges and investigators, half the Supreme Court's justices, 1,200 police officers, 151 journalists, and more than 300,000 ordinary Colombians have been murdered."

By 1996, most of the major Cali operators were dead or in jail. Still, the Clinton Administration never eased the pressure on Samper and he left office two years later still under a cloud. Not surprisingly, Pastrana, Samper's successor, made bringing peace to Colombia the central plank of his campaign. And so was born Plan Colombia.

Amidst all of this bloodshed and drama, the business of producing and shipping vast quantities of cocaine continued apace. The quite ambitious 50% reduction in coca cultivation envisioned under Plan Colombia, after all, would only return us to the 1996 potential production level, which at 300 metric tons was hardly insignificant. (For more on Colombian drug production, see page 50.)

Consider, too, the course of events following President Bush's triumphal visit to Cartagena 10 years ago. At that time, Peru and Bolivia were major coca-cultivating countries. In the years since then, Peruvian and Bolivian coca production has diminished dramatically (by 66% and 55%, respectively), thanks to both plant disease and political pressure. But Colombia's output of coca leaf has increased no less dramatically, to the extent that it now supplies about 70% of the world's raw cocaine and perhaps 90% of the finished product.

Meanwhile, the now-defunct Medellín and Cali cartels have been succeeded by an unruly scramble of several hundred loosely affiliated or directly competing entrepreneurial outfits who continue to ensure that the estimated 768 tons of cocaine produced in South America gets out to its world market. (Though a significant amount, variously estimated at from as little as 10% to as much as almost a half, is seized by authorities before it reaches the consumer.)

"It is a whole new generation of traffickers who have carefully studied and learned from the mistakes of the groups that went before them," General Rosso José Serrano, former director of the Colombian National Police, recently said. "They maintain an extremely low profile, they mix their licit and illicit businesses, they don't carry out terrorist acts and they operate in small, autonomous cells. They are much harder to fight than previous groups because they are much harder to find."

This new class of cocaine criminal has improved both the quality of the coca grown in Colombia (compared to the Bolivian and Peruvian product) and the refining process, significantly boosting the yield in finished product for the same weight of leaf entering the refining process.

Nor has the ingenuity and enterprise traditionally exhibited by smugglers diminished in this new era. The bulk of Colombia's cocaine, of necessity, travels through Mexico, sowing widespread corruption and violence in its wake. When the U.S. cracked down on air and sea smuggling through the Caribbean, however, the traffickers switched to the Pacific route, which is more difficult to patrol. In 2000, the U.S. Coast Guard seized more than 60 tons of cocaine (of the 125 tons it seized that year) from ships in the Pacific. Colombian authorities recently impounded a small submarine designed to deliver 200 tons of cocaine per trip to American shores.

Though the drug sub is an idea whose time has probably not yet come, however the white powder washes over U.S. borders, the scale of the seizures these days is staggering. In just six days late last winter, the Coast Guard captured almost 29 tons of cocaine, including 9 tons confiscated from a rusty fishing boat intercepted off Mexico's Pacific coast. A few months earlier, Arkansas State Police had seized 10 tons of cocaine from a truck hauling cantaloupes.

The Colombian traffickers have also finally succeeded in reaching beyond their traditional North American market. Compared to the roughly 330 tons of cocaine shipped into the U.S. in 2000, roughly 220 tons flowed into Europe, double the amount in 1996. Colombian cocaine is also increasingly available in Australia and Japan, as well as in South Africa and other countries where heretofore it was seldom seen or too expensive to be much of a draw.

The Colombian traffickers, too, are constantly looking for new markets. In the 1970s, Colombian-grown marijuana was a big seller in the U.S. These days, the bulk of American cannabis is grown domestically, either indoors or on covert rural farms, and the Colombian pot market has fallen off. But it has been replaced by a new market in opiates.

AP/WIDE WORLD PHOTOS

DRUG TRAFFICKERS *find increasingly innovative ways to move product to market. Here, Colombian police inspect a submarine being outfitted to carry as much as 200 tons of cocaine below the ocean's surface.*

Ten years ago, Mexico was the only cultivator of illicit opium poppies and producer of heroin in the Western Hemisphere, an impurity-ridden but potent form of the drug known as "black tar." Since then, the Colombian traffickers have taken to poppy cultivation and now supply most of the heroin used on the U.S. East Coast. Not only is this heroin cheaper than ever, it is refined white heroin similar to the "China White" produced in Southeast Asia and thus considered by addicts to be vastly superior to the Mexican product.

The considerable flexibility and adaptability exhibited by the Colombian export market highlights perhaps the most daunting aspect of drug-supply crackdowns: as long as there is demand, someone, somewhere will contrive to generate supply. History suggests, therefore, that barring some major change in American and European drug-use patterns, even if, by some miracle, *all* drug production in Colombia was eliminated completely, that would hardly put an end to illicit drug use in America.

Opium for heroin, of course, can be—and is—grown almost anywhere on the planet, including in the U.S. But even coca, historically associated with the Andean highlands, has in the past been successfully cultivated in lands such as Sri Lanka, Java and Taiwan. As long as there is a market for these substances (the U.S. being merely the largest and richest of those markets) the world will provide the peasants to grow the drugs and the "businessmen" to market them. ■

Colombia's political/ drug problems

COLOMBIA, it must be conceded, boasts an exceedingly violent political culture, even by the rather grim Latin American standards. Perhaps a quarter of a million citizens died, for example, during La Violencia, the Colombian term for a dispute that divided the two leading political parties in the 1950s. In important respects, The Violence has never really ended. Moreover, it is increasingly difficult to disentangle Colombia's political problems from its

THE COCA BUSH—source of cocaine hydrochloride, the highly stimulating and habituating white crystalline powder that so drives the U.S. drug war—was avidly and successfully cultivated by colonial authorities in Java, Sri Lanka and Formosa (Taiwan) early in the last century. But coca originated in the Andean mountain region of South America—which today serves once again as the sole source for tons of cocaine that flood the world market every year.

Traditionally, the bulk of South America's illicit raw coca leaf was grown and harvested by peasants in Bolivia and, especially, Peru. The dried leaves or, preferably, a bulk paste of more easily transported, crudely refined cocaine, was then typically smuggled into Colombia. There it was further refined into pure cocaine hydrochloride and then covertly transshipped, often by the ton, to consumer countries, mainly the U.S.

The numbers here, drawn from an annual narcotics intelligence report compiled by the U.S. State Department, illustrate a striking shift in this historical pattern over the last decade. Increasingly, civil war-torn Colombia is not only the world's chief exporter of finished cocaine, it is also by far the largest cultivator of coca leaves—generating almost three quarters of the total crop by the year 2000.

This evolution can be attributed to a number of factors. In the early 1990s, a fungus devastated much of the crop in Peru, formerly the top coca producer. Enhanced interdiction efforts—such as the U.S.-Peruvian joint effort to shoot down cocaine-transport aircraft that led to the unintentional and fatal downing of a small craft carrying U.S. missionaries in early 2001—have badly degraded the "air bridge" that once linked coca producers in Bolivia and Peru to cocaine refiners in Colombia.

This historic shift to an all-Colombian cocaine operation was also generated by "successes" in the drug war. The many smaller Colombian export groups that arose after the large Medellín and Cali cartels were broken up did not boast the logistical resources needed to sponsor large-scale imports of raw cocaine from neighboring nations. As a result, these smaller operators sought out domestic sources of production nearer at hand. Finally, thanks to Colombia's civil war, large areas of that country are increasingly under the sovereignty of rebel or paramilitary groups, both of which encourage drug farming for the purposes of taxation (and, increasingly it seems, as a source of direct profit).

SUCCESS OF AERIAL ERADICATION

Under the auspices of Plan Colombia, U.S. contract employees have vastly stepped up the aerial eradication of coca plantations with herbicides, especially in rebel-controlled provinces. Time will tell what the final cultivation estimates for 2001 will say about the success of that effort. Preliminary reports from the ground, however, suggest that cultivation is spreading to neighboring provinces less likely to be attacked by crop dusters. Similarly, recent history implies that if the cost of growing coca in Colombia grows too great, the exporter groups could once again fund production in Bolivia and Peru—or even in countries not previously associated with the drug trade, such as Ecuador and Venezuela.

The U.S.-compiled numbers shown here suggest a small decrease in total coca cultivation over the past half decade. Bear in mind, however, that the 185,000 hectares of coca plants estimated to have been grown in 2000 potentially yield more than 650,000 metric tons of leaf, which in turn could be refined into 768 tons of finished cocaine. The United Nations has estimated that roughly

MULES CARRY GASOLINE *to the village of Penas Colorados in southern Colombia, August 2000. The gasoline is used in the refining process to turn coca into coca paste.*

40% of all cocaine hydrochloride is seized by authorities while in transit, but that still leaves 400-plus tons of the drug that actually reaches consumers.

NET CULTIVATION OF COCAINE (in thousands of hectares)

	1993	1994	1995	1996	1997	1998	1999	2000
COLOMBIA	39.7	45.0	50.9	67.2	79.5	101.8	122.5	136.2
PERU	108.8	108.6	115.3	94.4	68.8	51.0	38.7	34.2
BOLIVIA	47.2	48.1	48.6	48.1	45.8	38.0	21.8	14.6
TOTAL	195.7	201.7	214.8	209.7	194.1	190.8	183.0	185.0

If the Western Hemisphere produces all (and consumes much of) the world's cocaine, it is a comparatively minor player in the global market for heroin, which is refined from the opium poppy. With a combined total of an estimated 200,000 hectares of land under poppy cultivation in 2000, Southeast Asia (Burma, Laos, Vietnam and Thailand) and Southwest Asia (Afghanistan and Pakistan) boasted a collective potential to generate 475 metric tons of heroin.

Mexico and Colombia, by contrast, likely did not produce more than 9 tons of heroin that year. The key distinction for Washington is that while the vast bulk of Southwest Asian heroin feeds the European market, this "New World heroin" is destined solely for the streets of the U.S. Mexico has been a source of comparatively crude brown and "black tar" heroin for the American Southwest and Pacific states at least since the fighting in World War II cut off the drug flow from Asia. The most striking development in the opiate trade over the past half decade is the remarkable rise of Colombia as the chief supplier of highly refined "white heroin" to the large addict population on the East Coast of the U.S.

Capitalizing on many of the same channels developed for the cocaine trade, Colombian traffickers have encouraged the peasantry to grow poppies and harvest the opium. They recruited chemists from Southeast Asia for lessons in producing clean, white "No. 4" heroin in Colombian labs. And, with a competitive pricing campaign starting in the mid-1990s, the Colombian drug exporters rapidly succeeded in largely unseating the Southeast Asian producers and traffickers from their former dominance over the lucrative opiate market in the American East.

NET CULTIVATION OF OPIUM POPPIES (in thousands of hectares)

	1993	1994	1995	1996	1997	1998	1999	2000
COLOMBIA			6.54	6.3	6.6	6.1	7.5	6.6
MEXICO	3.96	5.795	5.05	5.1	4.0	5.5	3.6	1.9
TOTAL	3.96	5.795	11.59	11.4	10.6	11.6	11.1	8.5

drug problems, as the two elements tend to feed off one another.

The largest of the currently operating guerrilla groups, the Revolutionary Armed Forces of Colombia, or FARC in the Spanish acronym, began as a rural protection force in the wake of The Violence. FARC coalesced as a rebel army in 1964—the year from which the current troubles are typically dated—not assuming a more formal Marxist coloration until years later when urban intellectuals joined what had until then been strictly a rural, peasant movement.

Currently numbering some 18,000 soldiers, the FARC reaps at least $400 million annually by protecting the burgeoning cocaine trade in its zones of control. In a 1998 bid to open cease-fire and peace negotiations, Pastrana formally ceded to the FARC temporary control of an area in southeast Colombia the size of Switzerland, jokingly termed "FARClandia."

The National Liberation Army, or ELN, started up about the same time as the FARC, but was always smaller and more rigorously Marxist. Today, it boasts a shrinking strength of about 5,000 soldiers, but is most active in Antioquia, which is one of Colombia's more heavily populated provinces, where it regularly orchestrates kidnappings and launches attacks on the power grid. Pastrana's plans to withdraw security forces from a Rhode Island–sized swath of a southern province to create an ELN zone of control preparatory to peace talks, similar to the deal accorded the FARC, foundered when paramilitary forces allied with the Colombian military refused to cooperate.

Arrayed against these two guerrilla groups is the United Self-Defense Forces of Colombia, or AUC, which formally came together in the 1997 as a collection of regional armed outfits created to protect drug lords and small towns from guerrilla attack. More recently, under commander Carlos Castaño, the AUC has become an extremely violent anti-Communist movement that seeks to push Colombia's rural peasantry into the urban centers it controls.

Castaño claims that his movement has no contact with the cocaine industry, save collecting "taxes" on drug movements in the areas he controls, to the tune of $2 million a year. U.S. and Colombian authorities dispute that assertion, claiming that the AUC is heavily involved with cocaine production and movement, generating far more than $2 million annually.

None of these groups has a particularly savory human-rights reputation, a caveat that holds equally true for the military and police organs of the Colombian government itself. Though the U.S. only recently added the AUC to a formal list of terrorist organizations, one that has included the FARC and ELN for years, international groups deem the AUC to be Colombia's most persistent human-rights violator. Colombian officials say that the AUC assasinated almost 800 persons in 2000, and Castaño faces more than 20 arrest warrants on charges of having murdered human-rights workers.

For its part, a leading Colombian human-rights group found that the FARC murdered close to 500 civilians in 2000 after accusing them of being paramilitary or government sympathizers. In a letter last July to FARC leader Manuel Marulanda, Human Rights Watch accused the group of responsibility for disappearances, poor treatment of prisoners and extralegal executions.

AP/WIDE WORLD PHOTOS

PART OF THE MILITARY PRONG *of Plan Colombia, these Black Hawk helicopters transport troops during an offensive against leftist rebels in Guaviare, August 2001.*

Reports of massacres in rural Colombia constantly crop up in the newspapers. Last April, in southern Colombia, for example, right-wing paramilitaries used machetes, chain saws and guns to kill at least 40 civilians. The following month, in northern Colombia, the FARC was held responsible for the murder by machete of at least two dozen civilians.

Not surprisingly, such bloodbaths do little to dampen the human-rights concerns surrounding Plan Colombia. In order to secure U.S. financial support for his plan, Pastrana had to make human-rights pledges to Washington he realistically had little likelihood of being able to carry out—especially considering that the government doesn't even control all of Colombia's territory.

In a fall 2001 report, Human Rights Watch was particularly critical of open cooperation between the paramilitary AUC and official Colombian forces. "Even as President Pastrana publicly deplores successive atrocities, each seemingly more gruesome than the last," the report said, "high-ranking officers he commands fail to take the obvious critical steps necessary to prevent future killings."

Colombia's interior minister responded to the report by condemning any AUC paramilitary/military collaboration. And in November, Colombia's highest court ordered the retrial of an army officer implicated in a 1997 massacre, whose previous conviction on charges of "dereliction of duty" human-rights groups had considered overly lenient.

In a repeat of the one-step-forward, one-step-back pattern, Pastrana signed legislation last August giving the military greater powers to wage war within Colombia and with even less scrutiny—most notably by giving government human-rights investigators only two months, rather than the previous span of a year, to conclude a finding against accused officers. "This will permit even greater impunity for soldiers and police who violate human rights," Gustavo Gallón, director of Colombia's Commission of Jurists, observed. U.S. lawmakers have suggested that this measure could also imperil future U.S. aid packages.

Washington's concern is not really that the FARC somehow threatens U.S. national security. Rather, Washington is pursuing in Colombia, first and foremost, a war against the drug traffic. Pastrana's chief motivation in pursuing Plan Colombia, however, is not so much to stem the flow of drugs, though the traffic in itself is destabilizing to Colombian society, as to force a truce with the leftist guerrillas who have been insurgent for almost 40 years now.

Though Bogotá and Washington are arm-in-arm over Plan Colombia today, the fundamental difference in the motivation of the two countries could lead to some embarrassment for the U.S. Should the FARC eventually come to the peace table, for instance, Washington might find itself allied with a government negotiating the terms of coexistence with "narco-terrorists," an instance which would surely antagonize many in the U.S. Congress.

The two goals inevitably became blurred. Several years ago, the U.S. began supplying the Colombian military with aerial intelligence on the movement of guerrilla forces through drug zones. In a recent interview with *The Los Angles Times*, a Colombian general pointed to a sheaf of these satellite photos. "I'm fighting the guerrillas," he said. "Politically, it's better to say we're fighting narco-traffickers. But really, we're fighting our war. The best is to say what people want to hear."

This internal contradiction is only sharpened by mounting allegations that the FARC is directly involved with trafficking cocaine, not merely with collecting "taxes" in its zones of control. Last August, for instance, a FARC envoy was arrested in Mexico while negotiating what Mexican prosecutors charged was a possible cocaine-for-guns deal with the notorious Arellano Felix drug cartel.

The official State Department position is that U.S. aid is solely for waging war on narcotics, and the Drug Enforcement Administration so far has been reluctant to accuse the FARC of operating like a cartel. For those seeking to avoid a Vietnam-style quagmire in Colombia, which includes pretty much everyone in Washington, there is good reason for this caution. "If you reach the conclusion that [the rebels] are a cartel like any other," former U.S. ambassador to Colombia Myles Frechette observes, "then you back yourself into supporting all-out war with the guerrillas." ■

Repercussions of Plan Colombia

THE MOST VOLATILE debate about Plan Colombia is unfolding inside Colombia itself. Clinton's visit to Cartagena two years ago was greeted by 32 distinct attacks by rebel forces in 13 of Colombia's 22 provinces. Since then, a coalition of more than 100 NGOs in Colombia have banded together in opposition to Plan Colombia. "This plan is just going to make the war worse," Diego Perez, who heads a Catholic human-rights organization, has charged.

Aside from the actual guerrilla war, fervent controversy is aroused by the aerial fumigation of the coca and poppy fields with herbicides. DynCorp, a Virginia-based military contractor, is set up in Colombia with 335 civilian employees (about one third of them American) under a five-year, $170 million contract to fly crop dusters over the drug fields and spray them with poisons. In recent years, two pilots have been shot down on such flights, both of them Colombians. Three Americans have been killed in crashes.

Not surprisingly, the flights are especially controversial among those farmers whose crops are being exterminated. Such spraying is not new in Colombia, though the scope of the effort under Plan Colombia is. The governors of the four southern provinces most affected by the spraying of 70,000 acres of fields early in 2001 complained jointly that half of the acreage hit contained legal food crops, not the poppy and coca crops that are supposed to be the target.

U.S. officials insist that the chemical being used, glyphosate, marketed by Monsanto as Roundup, is harmless to humans and animals and promptly and safely dissipates into the environment. But last summer, a British chemical company stopped supplying an additive used with the glyphosate, stating that the use of the two chemicals together had not been adequately tested. And Colombian critics note that Roundup marketed in the U.S. bears a warning not to let animals into treated fields until two weeks after application. Such precautions are not really feasible under conditions in Colombia, and the protesting southern governors offered videotapes showing dead animals and babies with rashes.

In turn, Colombia's top narcotics officer, General Gustavo Socha, charges that the drug producers are generating propaganda against the spraying campaign. "What I have seen is a plot against fumigations," Socha told reporters. "The drug traffickers are generating false information and forcing people to disseminate it." (Meanwhile, the U.S. is working to develop "myco-herbicides," fungal "biological control agents" that could be developed to specifically attack and kill, say, coca plants.)

It certainly bears noting that cocaine production does the environment few favors. As one researcher who studied coca-growing methods has noted, "there is no agricultural extension service for coca." Peasant growers typically overuse pesticides in plots too close to their homes and without wearing enough protective gear. Similarly, cocaine refiners, who usually operate in jungles and other remote areas, use and dump large quantities of toxic chemicals, such as kerosene and hydrochloric acid.

Last summer, a Colombian judge ordered a temporary halt to the fumigations in Amazonian Indian lands in response to a complaint filed by Indian communities in southeastern Colombia. Because the eradication effort lies at the heart of U.S. reasons for operating in Colombia in the first place, Washington's response to the spraying halt was chilly, to say the least. The U.S. ambassador to Colombia warned that a permanent halt to spraying could jeopardize U.S. aid, and the injunction was promptly lifted.

"Our assistance is a three-legged stool," an anonymous U.S. official explained at the time. "We do not believe that if you pull out any of the legs, the whole thing can stand."

To avoid involuntary aerial fumigation, farmers must join a formal eradication program, whereby they uproot their own drug crops in favor of legal, alternative plantings. The problem is that these alternative development programs are unfolding much more slowly than the fumigation effort, so the peasants are being caught betwixt and between. In any event, these small farmers typically have little experience producing licit cash crops. Coca and opium also pay much better than any conceivable legal crop and pose fewer marketing problems to growers in remote areas, since the traffickers typically come around to collect the harvest. Finally, coca strips the soil of nutrients, leaving a poor legacy for licit plant life.

Unquestionably, the fumigations of the past year have sparked an increase of perhaps as much as 30% in Colombia in the price per kilogram of refined cocaine. But that is likely a transient side effect of the highly publicized eradication campaign. Costs per gram in the U.S. market have not yet gone up, and really need not since the price markup is already so exaggerated once the drug is smuggled over the U.S. border.

In any event, a Colombian news magazine has argued in a lengthy article that with coca acreage beginning to increase again in Bolivia and Peru, the real fiscal crisis the illegal industry faces is not fumigation but overproduction. Even if Colombia lost half its production capability, the *Cambio* article noted, "it is very likely that the market would have readjusted itself, and supply and demand would have remained balanced.... That is to say, if Colombia had achieved its eradication goals in 2000, it would have done a grand favor to the narco-traffickers by ordering the market."

AP/WIDE WORLD PHOTOS

COLOMBIA PRESIDENT *Andrés Pastrana shakes hands with children in the town of Villa Garzón in the province of Putumayo, in southwestern Colombia, May 17, 2001. Putumayo and neighboring Caquetá are the central areas for cultivation of coca.*

ARCADIO, CARTOONISTS & WRITERS SYNDICATE/cartoonweb.com

Spillover in Andean region

Potential geopolitical "spillover" from Colombia's travails also ranks high as a source of worry in the Andes region. At an unprecedented meeting of South American heads of state, staged in Brasília, Brazil's capital, during the summer of 2000, the cross-border implications of Colombia's woes and how they might only increase under Plan Colombia loomed high on the agenda. "We support the Colombian government," Brazilian President Fernando Henrique Cardoso stated at a news conference there. "But Brazil has to take into account the consequences of the Colombia Plan. We have to protect our borders. That's our problem, not Colombia's problem."

On every side, Colombia's problem is already generating regional problems as its drug traffickers and guerrillas spill across international borders. Panama, which has not supported a formal army since Washington's invasion of that nation in 1989, is shifting hundreds of police officers to its short-but-rugged frontier with Colombia. The Panamanian government is also seeking $30 million in U.S. aid to assist further in defending its southern borders.

Brazil, which shares 1,600 kilometers of porous frontier with Colombia, as well as an ever-mounting domestic cocaine-abuse problem, has launched "Operation Cobra," a $10 million effort to bolster that line of control. It has dispatched 6,000 troops to the border, a number that is in the process of doubling. Brazil also plans to purchase four French Cougar AS-532 military helicopters to boost the mobility of its border force.

Having agreed to let the U.S. operate a drug-trafficking surveillance facility out of the port town of Manta, Ecuador is understandably worried by pronouncements from the FARC that the new base constitutes a "declaration of war." Anticipating a surge in the flow of Colombian refugees already crossing the 590-kilometer-long border, Ecuador is also planning five camps that could hold up to 5,000 displaced persons, an effort for which Washington has offered that country $15 million in aid.

Ecuadorian President Gustavo Noboa has also recently asked Pastrana to be kept closely informed on Colombian military actions near their common border, so that his own military could prepare to deal with the growers, guerrillas and civilians fleeing the disarray of Colombia. Already, Ecuadorian soldiers have found and eliminated at least four small Colombian-run cocaine-processing facilities located on their side of the border.

"If Colombia is going to be another Vietnam, as everyone keeps saying, then Ecuador is going to become the Cambodia of this war," says the mayor of an Ecuadorian border town that in December 2000 alone saw 15 dead in clashes among Colombians and another five killed when an oil pipeline was bombed. "We are not ready for this war, we don't want to be a part of it, but we are being dragged into the conflict against our will."

Peru, which shares an even longer border with Colombia and has only recently emerged from a bloody civil conflict of its own, nurtures similar concerns. A year ago, Peruvian intelligence officials announced that they had broken an international arms-trafficking ring that had purchased 10,000 Russian assault rifles in Jordan, moved them through Peru and on into Colombia. Among those arrested were two Peruvian military officers. "We're concerned," then Peruvian President Alberto K. Fujimori said at the time, "that these FARC arms shipments are meant to counteract the military support the U.S. is now giving Colombia."

Finally, there is Venezuela. Boasting the longest stretch of common frontier with Colombia of any of its neighbors, Venezuela's chief concern is the mounting influx of Colombian refugees. In just one recent instance, 500 Colombians fled into Venezuela following an attack by right-wing paramilitaries. An estimated 80% of the 100,000 residents of the Venezuelan border town of Machiques, to cite another indicator, are immigrants from Colombia. And when Colombians migrate, so do Colombian politics and criminal behavior. With Colombian kidnapping rings increasingly preying on Venezuelan landowners, "For Sale" signs are mushrooming along the frontier as Venezuelans move out of the border area. Moving in are Venezuelan border guards, which currently number about 25,000 troops. ■

Prognosis for Plan Colombia

"THIS IS A LONG-TERM PLAN, maybe 15 to 20 years," Pastrana asserted in a speech promoting Plan Colombia during his visit here last year. It seems highly unlikely, though, that the plan has anything like that span of time in which to prove itself. Pastrana himself will be out of office by the end of 2002 when his one permitted four-year term expires. Whatever personal charm and credibility Pastrana has brought to the campaign will soon no longer be available to promote a policy initiative increasingly viewed as troubled.

"The total cost and activities required to meet the plan's goals remain unknown," the Congress's General Accounting Office noted in a recent assessment, "and it will take years before drug activities are significantly reduced."

A viable candidate from Pastrana's Conservative party has yet to emerge. The strongest of the three opposition figures who have staked a claim to Pastrana's job is Alvaro Uribe Velez of the Liberal party's conservative wing. Tied by the Colombian media to the right-wing paramilitaries, and boasting a tough law-and-order aura, Uribe could prove to be a difficult horse for Washington to back, given the already-heightened concern over human rights in Colombia and American implication in any abuses.

Even more complicating is how the U.S. and Colombian governments have essentially different primary goals in their joint campaign and the question of how long it will be before any contradictions between those goals render the current close alliance all but impossible to sustain.

In a startling editorial in *The Guardian* last summer, former British ambassador to Colombia Keith Morris termed the drug war in Colombia unwinnable and offered a peek at the resentment and frustration simmering beneath the surface in Colombian governing circles. "Colombia has now been involved in antinarcotics efforts under U.S. pressure for 30 years.... And for the past 12 years there has been intense international cooperation," Morris wrote. "But as General Serrano, the highly respected former commander of the Colombian police told me in March, in spite of all that, the flow of drugs has increased. The cost: tens of thousands dead, more than a million displaced people, political and economic stability undermined and the country's image ruined."

Especially frustrating for Colombians, as for the residents of other drug-source countries, is what they see as Washington's tendency to blame them for what they view as a U.S. problem: the American populace's seemingly insatiable desire for illicit chemical mood enhancement. When U.S. courts recently handed down only a five-month sentence to a U.S. Army officer—who had concealed the money earned by his wife by trafficking in heroin while he was filling an antidrug position at the U.S. embassy in Bogotá—public reaction in Colombia was outrage at the leniency shown.

On the American side, frustration with Colombia's entrenched corruption (inevitable, perhaps, in a nation whose largest source of foreign earnings happens to be illegal) and resentment of its inability to come to grips with the forces that foster continuing soaring levels of drug exports make for a highly fragile alliance of interests.

The quandary for U.S. policymakers is that Colombia's narcotics trade could actually get a lot worse before it gets better. As Washington discovered under the Samper government in the mid-1990s, punishing weak Colombian regimes tends to make the drug situation worse rather than better. But if a future Colombian government felt compelled to arrive at some variety of open accommodation with drug traffickers—not an impossibility given how intermingled all of these elements have become there—it might be hard to avoid a break between Washington and Bogotá.

With Plan Colombia currently seen as facing a rocky road ahead, the best hope for those who would want to sustain a high level of U.S. involvement in the Colombian counternarcotics campaign may be to piggyback on the cause of the moment, and likely that of the next several years at least: counterterrorism.

In the wake of the 9/11 attacks on New York and Washington, and the U.S. declaration of war on terrorism that followed, Plan Colombia's advocates have already hastened to cast Colombia's chaos as a facet of the international terrorist threat. The recent arrest in Colombia of three Irish Republican Army members, visiting "FARClandia" to advise the rebels on the ins and outs of waging urban warfare, certainly facilitates this use of the terrorist bandwagon. As does the fact that the FARC, the ELN and the AUC constitute 10% of the 29 groups on the State Department's "major terrorist organization" list.

"Members of Congress at a senior level are making the link between drugs and terrorism," a Republican Senate staffer told *The Baltimore Sun.* "As we focus our policy on Colombia, that is going to become a very important part of our debate." Given the horrors that were unleashed at the World Trade Center and the Pentagon last September, this strikes some critics of U.S. policy in Colombia as a bit of a stretch.

Whether terrorism as an ingredient will actually whet and sustain Congress and the public's appetite for continued or increased intervention in Colombia's messy and dismaying internal affairs remains to be seen, but the richest irony of American involvement there thus far is that the U.S. finds itself, in one way or another, supporting both sides of the Colombian civil war.

IN MAY 2001 U.S. CUSTOMS *Officers seized 1,195 pounds of cocaine hidden in a 40-foot cargo container that was supposed to hold building material*

On the one hand, American drug users purchase mind-numbing quantities of Colombian cocaine and heroin, indirectly supporting armed groups on the left and the right who feed off the trade. On the other hand, direct U.S. assistance to Colombia makes it the world's third-largest recipient of American aid, after Israel and Egypt. That elements of the Colombian military and their paramilitary allies directly profit from both the drug trade *and* U.S. government counternarcotics aid, only intensifies the irony.

U.S. policy options

❑ **1. The U.S. should construe Colombia's current problems as basic evidence of terrorism calling for counterterrorist action.**

Pro: As the former head of the Colombian police said about the war on drugs, "the flow of drugs has increased,...tens of thousands [are] dead...[and there are] more than a million displaced people."

Con: According to Colombian President Pastrana, Plan Colombia "is a long-term plan, maybe 15 to 20 years." And many Colombians see American's insatiable desire for illicit drugs as a major problem to be addressed.

❑ **2. The U.S. should continue to provide antinarcotics assistance to Colombia, the third-largest recipient of American aid after Israel and Egypt.**

Pro: The three-pronged military effort being financed by the U.S. will pay for counterdrug operations in southern Colombia, buy sophisticated military items to interdict drug shipments and support eradication efforts.

Con: The U.S. may be stepping into a Vietnam-like foreign intervention and may become associated with the abuses of Colombia's corrupt armed forces, which also feed off the illicit drug trade.

❑ **3. The "spillover" of Colombia's problems into neighboring Andean countries should be a strong concern of the U.S. government in the interest of keeping regional peace.**

Pro: The Administration should make every effort to assure that its assistance to Colombia at least keeps that country's problems from becoming the problems of bordering nations.

Con: The U.S. cannot be responsible for financially or militarily keeping drug-trafficking operations, guerilla activities or displaced persons within Colombia's borders. ■

OPINION BALLOTS are on pages 43–44

DISCUSSION QUESTIONS

1. South American commentators frequently argue that the bigger problem is not the supply of drugs south of the U.S. border, but American demand north of that border. Which do you think is probably the dominant factor: supply or demand?

2. What validity do you give to critics' worries that U.S. involvement in the counternarcotics and counterinsurgency campaign in Colombia threatens to escalate into "another Vietnam"?

3. Does U.S. assistance to the Colombian government make the American people complicit in any human-rights abuses committed by that government's forces or their allies?

4. By the same token, does the use of Colombian-grown cocaine or heroin by individual Americans make them complicit in any atrocities committed by that nation's traffickers or the rebel and paramilitary groups that live off the illicit drug traffic?

5. Congress has insisted that no more than 800 military and civilian advisers or technicians can be operating in-country under Plan Colombia at any time. Does this strike you as a reasonable precaution against escalation of the U.S. presence? Or is this unnecessary and obstructive micromanagement?

6. Is the aerial spraying of drug crops with herbicides by crop dusters a legitimate tactic in the drug war? Discuss the impact this technique might have on the attitudes and loyalties of local farmers, as well as on the regional supply of cocaine.

READINGS AND RESOURCES

Clawson, Patrick L., and Lee, Rensselaer W. III, **The Andean Cocaine Industry,** New York, St. Martin's Press, 1998. 282 pp. $16.95. Crafted by an acknowledged expert on the drug issue (Lee) and another on international development (Clawson), this analysis focuses strictly on the South American dimension of the Western Hemisphere's drug dilemma.

Malamud-Goti, Jaime E., **Smoke and Mirrors: The Paradox of the Drug Wars,** Boulder, Colo., Westview, 1992. 117 pp. $33.00. Written by a former state secretary and human-rights adviser to the post-junta Argentine government, this slim and eloquent book suggests that the chief paradox afflicting the U.S. antidrug effort in Latin America is that drug enforcement "actually enhances and perpetuates the cocaine trade."

Menzel, Sewall H., **Cocaine Quagmire: Implementing the U.S. Anti-Drug Policy in the North Andes-Colombia,** New York, University Press of America, 1997. 232 pp. $36.50. A former U.S. Army "foreign area specialist" on Latin America, and academic expert on political violence and drug trafficking in that region, Menzel has significant experience in this area of interest.

Rabasa, Angel, and Chalk, Peter, **Colombian Labyrinth: The Synergy of Drugs and Insurgency and Its Implications for Regional Stability,** Santa Monica, Calif., RAND, 2001. 113 pp. $15.00. While U.S. policy in Colombia has been driven by the antidrug campaign, the evolving situation in the Andes region poses as much of a national security threat as it does a domestic drug problem, or so argue these two think-tank analysts. This monograph can be accessed for free, or ordered as a book, at **www.rand.org/publications/MR/MR1339/**

U.S. General Accounting Office, **Drug Control: U.S. Assistance to Colombia Will Take Years to Produce Results,** Washington, GAO, Oct. 2000. 13 pp. "Although U.S.-provided assistance has enhanced Colombia's counternarcotics capabilities," this study by Congress's research arm finds, "its usefulness has sometimes been limited because of longstanding problems in planning and implementation." This report can be accessed or ordered in hard copy (first copy free) on **www.gao.gov** and searching for the report coded "GAO-01-26." Or call (202) 512-6000 and order by that code number.

DRUG REFORM COORDINATION NETWORK, 2000 P St. NW # 210, Washington, DC 20036; (202) 293-8340; Fax (202) 293-8344. **www.drcnet.org.** ■ An information and advocacy group committed to changing U.S. drug control laws. It publishes a free weekly online report covering national and international events in this area.

DRUG ENFORCEMENT ADMINISTRATION, 2401 Jefferson Davis Hwy., Alexandria, VA 22301; (202) 307-4778; Fax (202) 307-4778. **www.usdoj.gov/dea/index.htm.** ■ A division of the Justice Department, the DEA is a sort of narco-FBI, dedicated to illicit drug control. Any research on this topic can only benefit from a visit to the DEA's website. Among other items of information, it contains the full text of many of the narcotics trafficking intelligence reports that the agency assembles every year.

UN OFFICE FOR DRUG CONTROL AND CRIME PREVENTION, Vienna International Centre, P.O. Box 500, A-1400 Vienna, Austria; Phone +43 1 26060 0; Fax +43 1 26060 5866; **www.undcp.org/index.html.** ■ This UN body is charged with international coordination of member nations' antidrug efforts. Not only is its website a handy source of information, but the ODCCP also publishes the useful "World Drug Report 2000." That report is available on the website, or can be ordered by calling the UN Publications Office at (800) 253-9646.

LEARN MORE ABOUT THIS TOPIC AT *www.greatdecisions.org*

Access links to online resources • Order the recommended readings • Take the GD Quiz • Find maps in the online atlas • Submit your opinion ballots • Read the latest National Opinion Ballot Report • and more ...

India today: a rising democracy

As the world's two largest democracies seek more cooperative ties, Americans need greater understanding of how India is evolving politically and economically.

by Dennis Kux

APWIDE WORLD PHOTOS

A STREET IN THE OLD SECTION OF NEW DELHI, *March 2001, when India's population passed 1.02 billion. In the past decade, India grew by over 180 million people, more than the total population of Brazil.*

INDIA HAS NEVER BEEN easy for Americans to understand. In earlier years, there were contradictory images of fabulously rich maharajas and impoverished beggars, of erudite civil servants and illiterate peasants, and of Mahatma Gandhi's call for nonviolence and the chilling violence of Hindu-Muslim communal riots. A half century after gaining its independence, India has consolidated its democracy, is making economic progress and is moving gradually toward great-power status. Although major hurdles must still be overcome before India achieves middle-income status, it has taken significant strides forward in recent years. But contradictions remain. India has tested nuclear weapons, boasts some of the world's finest computer minds and has a burgeoning information-technology industry. Yet more than a third of its one billion people are illiterate and 40% of all humans below the poverty line lives in India.

In the international arena, the U.S. and India found themselves estranged during the cold war (1947–89) even though the two countries shared democratic political values. In the past few years, relations have improved substantially. President Bill Clinton paid a highly successful visit to India in 2000 and President George W. Bush wants to firm up friendlier ties. India also has been eager for better relations with America. Two significant signs of the altered relationship were India's positive response to the Bush Administration's controversial missile-defense initiative and its prompt and unqualified support for the war against terrorism after the tragic events of September 11, 2001.

As the world's two largest democracies seek more cooperative ties, Americans need greater understanding of how India is evolving politically and economically, of how its foreign and defense policies are developing, and of the major issues that confront Washington policymakers as they deal with New Delhi, India's teeming capital of over 10 million.

DENNIS KUX *is a retired State Department South Asia specialist and the author of* India and the United States, 1941–1991, Estranged Democracies *(1993) and the recently published* The United States and Pakistan, 1947–2000, Disenchanted Allies. *He is currently a Senior Scholar at the Woodrow Wilson Center in Washington, D.C.*

Democratic success story

Despite India's traumatic birth in 1947 when the British Indian Empire split into two countries presaging the tumultuous influx and exodus of some 12 million Hindu and Muslim refugees, the subsequent three-plus wars with Pakistan, the bewildering array of internal regional differences including some 18 official languages, the complexities of the Hindu caste system and the staggering problems of trying to overcome mass poverty and illiteracy, representative government has taken firm root during the past half century. Among the new nations of Asia and Africa, India stands out as a success story for democracy.

Why has India succeeded where so many other new nations have failed? First, India was fortunate that its major nationalist movement, the Indian National Congress (later the Congress party), was a well-established political organization long before 1947 and not just an independence movement lacking other programmatic goals. Moreover, unlike many nationalist movements that relied on violence in seeking independence, the Congress struggle against the British was one of nonviolent protest.

Second, India was lucky that it possessed a pool of competent political leaders whose mettle had been tested in the freedom struggle against the British. Although the most revered figure, Mahatma Gandhi, was assassinated in January 1948, his political heir, Jawaharlal Nehru, served as prime minister for 17 years before his death in 1964. A devoted democrat and eloquent communicator, Nehru dominated the political scene but followed democratic rules and parliamentary procedures.

Third, India enjoyed two decades of political stability after independence thanks to Nehru's leadership and the sweeping victories of the Congress party in the first three national elections—1952, 1957 and 1962. This gave India time to consolidate as a nation-state. In 1950, a democratic constitution was adopted, establishing a federal parliamentary system. The central government redrew the administrative boundaries left by the British to form more linguistically homogenous states and to integrate large areas formerly ruled by Indian princes. Unlike in neighboring Pakistan, the primacy of democratically elected political leaders over the military and the civil service was firmly established. Finally, India stressed the concept that it was a secular state in which the Hindu majority (some 80% of the population) shows tolerance for the rights of the 20% non-Hindu minority (roughly 14% Muslim, 2% Christian, 2% Sikh and 2% other).

When Nehru passed away in 1964, the smooth transition to his successor, Lal Bahadur Shastri, and then, after Shastri died suddenly in January 1966, to Indira Gandhi, Nehru's daughter, tested the strength of India's young democracy. Although initially unsure of herself, Mrs. Gandhi developed into a tough but adept leader. After splitting the Congress party to ensure her dominance, she won an overwhelming election victory in 1971 on a populist program of "eliminating poverty." Mrs. Gandhi reached the peak of her popularity after the 1971 India-Pakistan war led to the splitting of Pakistan and the independence of Bangladesh, the former East Pakistan.

More authoritarian than her father, she did not shrink from invoking the emergency powers of the constitution in June 1975 in the face of rising political opposition and a legal challenge to her election to parliament. For nearly two years, India became just another Third World dictatorship with its press muzzled and opposition leaders jailed. But concerned about her legitimacy, Indira Gandhi held free elections in March 1977 and, to her surprise, suffered a stunning defeat. The Janata (People's) party, a heterogeneous coalition, including many former Congress party leaders, took power. India was once more a democracy and for the first time ruled by a non-Congress government. Mrs. Gandhi, however, was able to stage a comeback, winning election in January 1980 after the Janata coalition collapsed from internal dissension.

Political unrest

The decade of the 1980s proved a time of political troubles and unrest. Intent on concentrating power in her own hands, Mrs. Gandhi intervened at the state level to sideline local leaders who showed signs of seeking independence. In the prosperous Punjab province, homeland of the Sikh community, her tactics misfired and helped spark a full-scale insurgency. Militant and armed Sikhs demanded an independent country and seized the Golden Temple of Amritsar, the Sikh religion's holiest place. When the Indian army ousted the insurgents, the bloody battle badly damaged the temple and further alienated the Sikh community.

In October 1984, Sikh bodyguards assassinated the prime minister near her residence in New Delhi. A shaken Congress, which had, in effect, become a Nehru-Gandhi family fiefdom, turned to her son Rajiv Gandhi to lead the country. A mild-mannered former airline pilot, Rajiv had become his mother's close aide after the death of his elder brother Sanjay Gandhi in a plane accident in 1980. Although the youthful Rajiv gained an overwhelming victory in the 1984 elections, he proved a lackluster leader. After charges of corruption in the procurement of antiaircraft guns tarnished his image, an anti-Congress coalition won narrowly in the 1989 general elections. Ending four decades of nearly unbroken rule by the Nehru-Gandhi family, the 1989 elections underscored the gradual decline of the Congress and the rise of other political parties, especially the Hindu nationalist Bharatiya Janata party (BJP) on the right and regional parties limited to single states in many parts of India.

Like its predecessor a decade earlier, the coalition that took power in 1989 proved an unstable and short-lived affair. It collapsed a little more than a year later after the BJP quit in opposition to proposed special treatment for middle- and lower-caste groups. (Those at the bottom of the caste ladder—the untouchables—already received favored treatment under long-standing affirmative-action programs.) The BJP sought broader popular support for making Hindu values, not secularism, India's national ethos by launching an emotionally charged campaign to remove a mosque in Ayodhya in Uttar Pradesh that the Mughal Emperor Babar had built in 1528 on the site of a Hindu temple. According to legend, the temple marked the birthplace of Lord Ram, one of the leading Hindu deities.

During the ensuing 1991 election, a reinvigorated Rajiv Gandhi was barnstorming in the southern Indian state of Tamil Nadu when he was assassinated by a suicide bomber, a female Tamil terrorist from neighboring Sri Lanka. Rajiv had angered Tamil extremists by deploying Indian troops to Sri Lanka in 1987 to help the Colombo government combat the Tamil insurgency. The Congress chose as its new leader a veteran south Indian politician, P.V. Narasimha Rao. The septuagenarian Rao, who eked out a narrow election victory, was able to form a minority government and surprised observers by serving a full five-year term. Although he successfully launched the reforms that replaced Nehruvian socialism with free-market and private-sector economic policies, Rao's tenure was marred by his inability to prevent BJP extremists from destroying the mosque in Ayodhya on December 6, 1992. The tumultuous incident sparked the most serious Hindu-Muslim communal riots since independence, taking about 2,000 lives before order was restored.

In the 1996 elections, the BJP moved past the Congress to become the largest party in the Lok Sabha (People's Assembly, one of two houses of Parliament). After it failed to gain a parliamentary majority, however, an anti-BJP coalition formed a government with the backing of the Congress. Within two years and two prime ministers, the fractious coalition fell apart. In March 1998, India went to the polls once more. This time, after cobbling together a coalition with smaller parties called the National Democratic Alliance (NDA), the BJP won a narrow victory that enabled its leader Atal Bihari Vajpayee to become prime minister. The 74-year-old Vajpayee, who had served for nearly half a century in Parliament, presented the moderate face of the BJP. The No. 2 man in the government, Home Minister L.K. Advani, spoke for party hard-liners and their supporters in the Rashtriya

AP/WIDE WORLD PHOTOS

ON THE EVE OF ELECTIONS, *October 1999, an artisan chisels a pillar with images of Hindu gods and goddesses at Ayodhya. The pillar will be one of the main entrance columns of a proposed temple to be built at the site of a demolished mosque.*

1948–91: Nehru-Gandhi Decades

INDIA'S INDEPENDENCE LEADER, *Mahatma Gandhi, sits with his political heir, Jawaharlal Nehru (left), who was prime minister until 1964; Nehru's daughter, Indira Gandhi, who followed in her father's footsteps in 1966, is seen at a nuclear site in 1974; Indira's son, Rajiv, was elected prime minister after his mother's assassination in 1984, seen here preparing her ashes for distribution to 22 Indian states.*

Swayamsevak Sangh (RSS or National Volunteer Corps), which provided the BJP with its core cadres. Founded in the 1920s on the model of Mussolini's Black Shirts (party militants), the RSS remains a strong influence on the BJP government.

To appease its coalition partners, the BJP downplayed the more controversial parts of its platform, such as the call to build a Hindu temple on the site of the destroyed mosque in Ayodhya. However, Vajpayee quickly proceeded to conduct nuclear-weapons tests in mid-May 1998, a step long urged by the hawkish BJP. Although the step was enormously popular among the Indian elite who saw the tests as a sign of India's attaining great-power status, the BJP-led coalition proved unsteady. In early 1999, Vajpayee lost a vote of confidence in Parliament by a single vote. India went to the polls again.

This time, in the third national election in three years, Indian voters returned the BJP and its coalition supporters with a comfortable 30-vote majority in the Lok Sabha. In the contest between Vajpayee, who had become India's most respected and popular leader, and Sonia Gandhi, the inexperienced widow of Rajiv Gandhi, to whom the Congress reverting to its dynastic tradition had turned, Vajpayee won hands down. The fact that Mrs. Gandhi was foreign-born and had only become an Indian citizen in 1983 and a Hindu only a few years earlier became an election issue that significantly hurt the Congress.

The 1999 election results appeared to offer India political stability for the first time in nearly a decade. With a working parliamentary majority, the prime minister appeared eager to press ahead with economic reforms to accelerate growth. Finance Minister Yashwant Sinha unveiled an ambitious and widely applauded budget in February 2001 that included a number of additional reform measures. Almost before the applause subsided, however, the NDA coalition faced a crisis of confidence that tarnished its image for cleaner and less corrupt governance than the Congress had provided. A sting operation by journalists to probe corruption in defense procurement snared senior coalition leaders. Posing as arms salesmen, the journalists videotaped BJP President Bangaru Laxman and Jaya Jaitley, the president of Defense Minister George Fernandes's Samata party, taking bribes. When television news beamed footage of the BJP leader receiving a satchel full of rupees ($2,175), a tremendous upsurge of public opinion forced Vajpayee to fire Laxman and accept the resignation of his defense minister, who was recently reappointed.

Just as the BJP-led coalition was beginning to recover, scandals in the financial markets and a poor showing in several state elections shook the government once more. An additional blow came from the collapse of the July 2001

summit with Pakistan's president and military dictator, General Pervez Musharraf. The meeting that Vajpayee had initiated failed to reduce tensions between the quarreling neighbors or to make progress toward ending the bloody decade-long insurgency in Kashmir.

As the year 2002 begins, the Vajpayee government faces an important political test in local elections in Uttar Pradesh, India's most populous state. Should the BJP lose power, the ruling coalition in New Delhi would be further weakened, although few expect that it will collapse. Indeed, the government's greatest strength may well lie in the failure of Sonia Gandhi and the Congress party to offer a plausible alternative.

Summing up politically

The Congress party's rule of India for four decades—except for the Janata government between 1977 and 1980—lent unusual stability to the country's political life. Since the1989 election, however, instability has been the rule. Neither the BJP nor the Congress has been able to muster support throughout the country. Even though the BJP has eclipsed the Congress in the past three elections, it seems unlikely to win enough seats to take power on its own and will need the help of smaller and often difficult coalition partners. Barring a major political shift, unsteady coalition governments seem in prospect for the foreseeable future. In contrast, at the state level, two-party systems prevail in most of India. In some states, the BJP and the Congress battle for power. In others, one or both of the parties are groups whose support is limited to a single state. Election results in recent years have also reflected a major social development: the success of lower-caste groups in exploiting their numbers at the ballot box to gain greater political power.

In the U.S., the public tends to vote its pocketbook in national elections. In India, the impact of economics seems less important than caste and religious community considerations. Election success or failure often turns on parties picking candidates who appeal to the major local caste or religious groups, or "vote banks," as they are popularly called. Thus, the upcoming state election in Uttar Pradesh pits three caste-related groups against each other. The BJP has the backing of upper castes. The Samajwadi (Socialist) party is supported by lower castes and Muslims, while the Dalits (as untouchables are now called) at the bottom of the caste hierarchy give their vote to the Bahujan Samaj party (Majority Community party).

Over the years, India's judicial system and the media have gained in importance and strength. Although justice is often slow, the courts are widely respected and not considered the handmaiden of the executive. As literacy has increased, newspaper circulation has gradually risen. A half dozen flourishing English-language dailies form the apex of a burgeoning press that includes thousands of newspapers in Hindi and the regional languages. Television has also blossomed spectacularly during the past decade. Previously India had a single channel of government-run television that offered dull fare and pro-government news coverage. Today, thanks to cable linkups and satellite technology, viewers can choose from dozens of channels, including several that beam independent news on a 24-hour basis. The latter had a tremendous impact on public opinion during last year's arms-procurement scandal.

REUTERS/JAYANTA SHAW/GETTY IMAGES

A CHILD LABORER *carries bricks to a kiln at a brick factory in Raichak, December 27, 2000. Though literacy has increased and India has a burgeoning information-technology industry, Indian authorities estimate that about 18 million children work instead of go to school.*

The sting affair pointed up the malady of widespread corruption in Indian politics. With the idealism of the early years of independence long gone, politicians at all levels and many civil servants are considered open to bribery. Although corruption badly upsets the educated classes, the man in the street seems to accept it as a part of life. Thus, in state elections in Tamil Nadu in 2001 and in Bihar the year before, movie star-turned-politician Jayalalitha and peasant caste leader Laloo Prasad Yadav emerged victorious even though both were badly tarnished with the brush of corruption.

Except for rigged elections in the disputed state of Kashmir, voting in India has been fair, if at times unruly, especially in the northern states of Bihar and Uttar Pradesh, where serious law-and-order problems have plagued politics. Despite the need to have three national elections in 1996, 1998 and 1999, voter participation has remained relatively high and stable with 58% to 62% of the eligible casting their ballots. Interestingly, public opinion surveys reveal that the poor and illiterate place greater value on their vote than the well-educated.

A half century after independence, democracy is thriving and vibrant in India. This would be an impressive achievement anywhere, but it is especially so in a country as large, as populous and as diverse as India. Even though India has faced an extraordinary range of complex and demanding internal problems since gaining independence, it has remained true to the democratic aspirations of its founding fathers. ■

Economic policy: from state control to the free market

A LITTLE MORE THAN a decade ago, in January 1991, India faced severe economic difficulties. A sudden rise in the oil import bill after the Persian Gulf war caused a balance-of-payments crisis and near bankruptcy. In order to provide collateral for an emergency loan from the International Monetary Fund (IMF), New Delhi secretly transferred part of the country's dwindling gold reserves to London. The crisis underscored the failure of the system of state controls and public-sector enterprises that Prime Minister Nehru had put in place in the 1950s. Despite important successes, such as the green revolution which enabled the country to feed itself, India's overall growth rate remained well below that of the booming economies of China and East Asia. Nehruvian socialism had condemned India to what *The Economist* (London) described as "the Hindu rate of growth": 3.5% of gross domestic product (GDP) a year. This barely kept pace with the population that doubled from 439 million in 1961 to 844 million in 1991. Although during the 1980s, Prime Ministers Indira and Rajiv Gandhi had made tentative moves to liberalize the economy which was growing at a considerably faster annual rate of 5.6% of GDP, they did not dismantle the "license raj," the system of comprehensive government controls that throttled India's private sector and contributed to widespread corruption. Nor did they significantly reduce the barriers to foreign trade and investment.

Rather than muddling through with stopgap measures, Prime Minister Rao responded to the 1991 crisis by launching major reforms that amounted to a revolution in Indian economic policy. Despite Rao's reputation for caution, he supported Finance Minister Manmohan Singh's introduction of sweeping administrative actions to make the free market and the private sector rather than the government the primary economic driver and to open India's formerly closed economy to the rest of world. Singh devalued the Indian rupee by 20%, slashed export subsidies, cut import duties, reduced foreign-exchange controls, largely eliminated licenses and controls on industrial production and greatly reduced restrictions on foreign investment.

The Indian economy responded with a burst of vigor that resolved the balance-of-payments crisis and attained an annual growth rate of 7.5% of GDP in 1996 when Rao's term as prime minister ended. Successor governments have continued the reform program, but, of late, governmental action has fallen short of official rhetoric. A consensus has developed in favor of the free market to replace the Nehruvian socialism as India's economic-policy model. The consensus has, however, yet to embrace the hard tasks of ending politically popular subsidies, permitting sick industries to close down and selling off public-sector enterprises. In the late 1990s, the GDP growth rate gradually slipped back but was still 6% in the year 2000. In the face of the global economic slowdown, however, it had dipped to 4.4% in November 2001.

India's Runaway Population

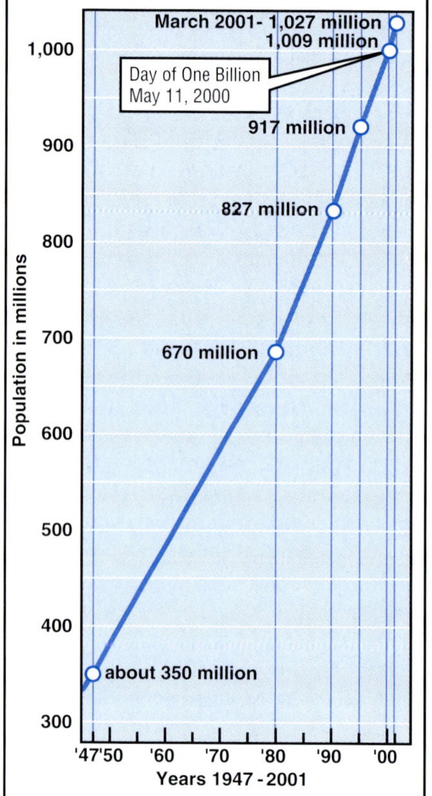

Source: Population Reference Bureau

MICHAEL SAMUEL GRAPHICS

The achievements of the past 10 years have, nonetheless, been significant. During the decade of the 1990s, the GDP rose at a 6.5% annual rate, making India the fastest-growing Asian economy after China. Industrial production grew annually at a 5.7% rate. Exports rose at an impressive 11.3% annually during the 1990s. Foreign direct investment rose from a pitiful $162 million in 1990 to $2.6 billion in 1998. Perhaps most important in human terms, the middle class, according to India's National Council of Applied Economic Research, doubled to 169 million people, or 18% of the population, by the mid-1990s.

Even better than raw statistics, a visit to burgeoning markets and stores in India's major cities vividly tells the story of the change that has occurred. Previously the Indian consumer faced a slim array of shoddy items produced for the protected domestic market. Today, the Indian middle class can choose from a vastly improved selection of imported and domestically produced goods—television sets, refrigerators, washing machines, scooters, cars, cassette players, air conditioners, etc.—including many items made in collaboration with foreign investors.

Information technology (IT) is the sector that has advanced the fastest, and the one that offers the greatest potential. Although the computer industry barely existed in India in 1991, it has enjoyed a phenomenal rise. The volume of IT business reached $8.26 billion in the year 2000–2001, including some $6.2 billion earned in software exports, mainly to the U.S. A number of factors explain IT's rapid growth. First, Nehru's emphasis on scientific and technological education produced a large pool of competent, English-speaking engineers and scientists. Hundreds and then thousands of young Indians found jobs in the U.S. as the demand for computer specialists soared. Indeed, 30% of the programmers in California's

Silicon Valley were said to be of Indian origin. Indian-American entrepreneurs also made their mark. The creator of Hotmail, 31-year-old Sabeer Bhatia, sold his e-mail product to Microsoft for a tidy $400 million in 1998.

Second, the American industry exploited the possibility of outsourcing computer programming and research to India. After Texas Instruments set up shop in Bangalore, the capital of the southern state of Karnataka, in 1985, the city soon developed into India's Silicon Valley. Outsourcing to India made economic sense because of far lower labor costs, fluency in English, high level of technological knowledge and satellite communications that permitted IT companies to vault over India's antiquated telephone system to ensure uninterrupted digital links.

Finally, geography was a significant plus. The fact that India was halfway around the globe from the U.S.—Bangalore, India's chief computer center is 13½ hours ahead of California—enabled software companies to work what amounted to a 24-hour day. As programmers went home in Silicon Valley in the evening, their counterparts in India were arriving at their offices the next morning.

Serious problems remain

Of late, the Indian elephant is moving ahead at a brisker pace, but it has not become an Asian tiger. Despite impressive advances, India seems unlikely to attain Chinese GDP growth rates of 8% to 9% per annum any time soon. India has passed through a first phase of reforms, lifting licenses and government controls and taking other actions that could be accomplished administratively. The road ahead remains full of potholes and political problems. Some of those stem from India's lack of financial resources, while others relate to the difficulties of implementing politically unpopular measures in a democracy.

One of the most significant restraints is poor physical infrastructure. India's teeming cities—some 23, according to the 1991 census, have more than one million people—have little more than rudimentary urban support systems. In most, open sewers and drains continue to spread germs and disease. Pollution from motor vehicles, factories, and power-generating plants has become an increasingly serious health problem.

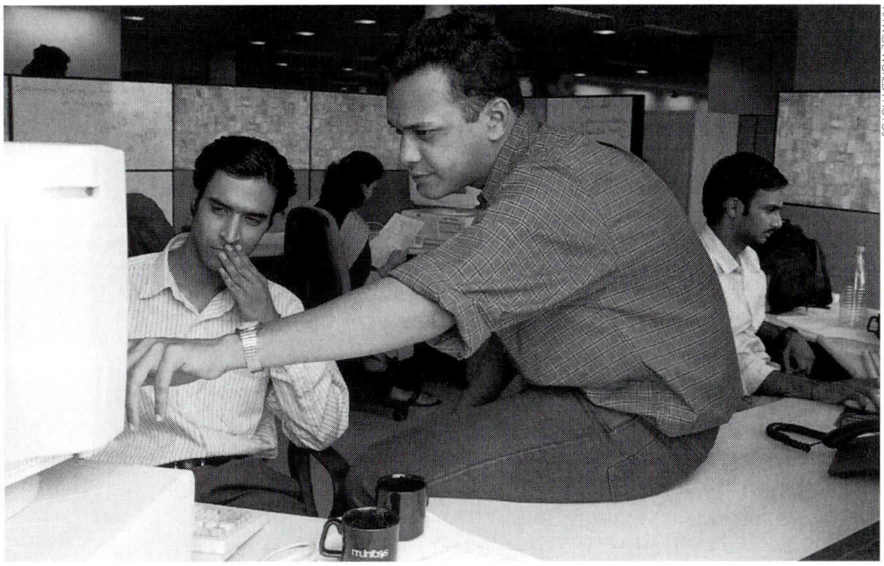
APWIDE WORLD PHOTOS

BANGALORE, INDIA: PROGRAMMERS AT WORK *at Infosys, one of the best known software companies in India's Silicon Valley.*

Lack of electricity is another major restraint on growth. Installed generating capacity is 10% below demand. During periods of peak load, the power deficit can run as high as 20%.

India lacks a modern road transportation system and only now is constructing four-lane highways to link Delhi, Mumbai (formerly Bombay), Chennai (formerly Madras), and Calcutta, the four major cities. The crowded roads are a driver's nightmare as buses jammed full of passengers, overloaded trucks, motorcycles and motor rickshaws, passenger cars and—reminders of a slower past—bullock carts and horse-driven carriages or tongas vie chaotically with each other. The Indian railways, one of the world's largest systems, function reasonably well and provide the mainstay of long-distance passenger transportation. But rail travel is highly subsidized and trains chug along at an average speed of less than 30 miles an hour. An inefficient rail-freight system has been losing ground to the trucking industry despite the poor condition of the roads. And like other public-sector enterprises, the railways are badly overstaffed.

Not only does power generation fall short of demand, but almost all the state electric power systems run annual losses that the government must make up. Poor management, free or subsidized power for agriculture, high line losses from theft (official figures indicate 23%, but experts assume the reality is higher), and inadequate and corrupt bill-collection systems cause the deficit. In 2001, this amounted to $5.1 billion. The Vajpayee government has made power-sector reform a top priority, proposing to separate electricity boards into independent production, distribution and sales units that would function as businesses. New Delhi has offered to cover the existing debt burden so that the new entities can start with a clean balance sheet. It remains to be seen how successful Vajpayee will be. State-level politicians, civil servants and consumers, who enjoy free or subsidized power or line their pockets with bribes, are reluctant to discard the present system.

There are also human infrastructure problems. One has been failure to make more progress toward wiping out illiteracy and promoting rural education, especially for women. India has paid considerable attention to college and university-level education but has neglected primary and secondary schooling, especially in the countryside where two thirds of the country's one billion people still live. The 2001 census revealed that 36%, or about 350 million Indians, remain illiterate, with the figure far higher among females.

As literacy increased and family-planning programs gained ground, the annual rate of population increase dropped from 2.5% in 1981 to 1.8% in 2000. But like economic development, progress has been uneven. In some parts of India, for example, in the southern states of Kerala and Tamil Nadu, growth has almost declined to replacement level. In other regions, especially in economically backward states such as Uttar Pradesh and Bihar, the birthrate continues to gallop.

The high fiscal deficit that the central and state governments run, now estimated at 10% of GDP, poses a further brake on the economy. There is no secret about the causes: subsidies for farmers in the form of above-market procurement prices for food grains, subsidized or free fertilizer and irrigation water, losses sustained by public-sector enterprises and deficits run up by state electricity boards. Solving the problem means confronting politically strong interest groups, an action no government as yet has been willing to take.

The slow pace of disinvestment and privatization of public-sector enterprises has been another problem. Most of these entities, which were a centerpiece of Nehruvian socialist policies, are chronic money losers and, in effect, subsidized by the Indian public since the central and state governments must cover the deficits. Although rhetorically, privatization stands high on the reform agenda, the current BJP government and its predecessors have not made significant progress. Governments in New Delhi and state capitals have been unwilling to alienate politically powerful labor unions who vehemently oppose the inevitable employment cutbacks that private-sector management would impose. Ideological opponents of privatization on the left have also been joined by voices from the nationalist right in arguing against dismantling India's public sector, especially the sale of units to foreigners.

Foreign investment slows

Given these difficulties and India's lethargic and often corrupt bureaucracy, foreign investment has fallen off after an initial burst of enthusiasm following the start of reforms. Even though India is receiving about $2.5 billion a year, vastly more than during the 1980s, the inflow is less than one third of what the government had hoped to attract from abroad. In theory, the door is wide open to foreign investors. In practice, India still lags behind other Asian countries in terms of investor friendliness. As the extreme left and right of the political spectrum continue to stir up antiforeign attitudes, criticism of globalization and of multinational corporations has resonated, further dampening the investment climate. During the 1990s, the U.S. emerged as the largest foreign investor. By the end of the decade, investment was flowing in at an annual rate of about $250 million. This was a giant leap forward compared with minuscule inflows to India in the 1980s, but less than U.S. investment in Thailand. One recent development that has damaged India's image has been the ongoing dispute between the consortium led by Enron, the Houston, Texas, energy company, and the Maharashtra State Electricity Board over a power plant constructed at Dabhol, south of Mumbai. Once seen as a flagship for American investment, the $2.9 billion Dabhol venture has become a nightmare.

The sole customer for the plant's electricity, the Maharashtra State Electricity Board, can no longer afford the high rates fixed by the contract and has stopped paying. When Enron invoked an arbitration clause, the electricity board countered by fining the company for being in technical violation of the contract. The government of India, which backed the contract with a sovereign guarantee, insists that it will honor this if Maharashtra loses the commercial dispute. All concerned, including consortium led by Enron, the now bankrupt Texas energy company, claim they want a solution but this will not be easy to attain, given the complexity of the situation.

In short, India's current economic picture is mixed even if the longer-term outlook remains positive. After lumbering along at a 3.5% growth rate, India has started moving ahead at a snappier pace since it shifted from a state-regulated economy to a more market-led system in the 1990s. Prudent fiscal management has also enabled India to avoid the boom-or-bust experience of the Southeast Asian tigers and has kept inflation within reasonable bounds. Considering the enormous increase in population, from 350 million at the time of independence to over one billion 55 years later, India has not done that badly, especially during the past 20 years. It is, however, as Stephen Philip Cohen has aptly written, India's "(very) gradual economic revolution." ■

Foreign and security policies

Jawaharlal Nehru, who served as his own foreign minister, kept India aloof from the rival camps of the cold war and pursued a policy of neutralism and nonalignment. After the U.S. became a military ally of Pakistan in 1954, India moved closer to the Soviet Union even though New Delhi continued to emphasize its nonaligned status. Although India played a major international role in the days of Nehru, his successors have had more modest ambitions and focused their attention mainly on India's immediate neighbors, especially its difficult relations with Pakistan. While Indian foreign policymakers still would like a seat at the great-power table, there is growing recognition that India must develop its economic capabilities further to make this aspiration a reality.

Since the end of the cold war, nonalignment has lost much of its meaning. India has been trying to adjust its policies in the new global environment by broadening relations with countries of East Asia, the Middle East, Europe and especially the U.S. Even so, India remains uncomfortable with having a single superpower, the U.S., dominate the international scene and would prefer a multipolar world, one in which India would be one of the poles as well as a permanent member of the UN Security Council.

Defense capabilities

Heir to the proud military traditions of the British Raj, India has the world's third-largest army, a well-trained and highly professional force numbering 1.1 million soldiers. In addition, a roughly equal number serve in a wide variety of paramilitary organizations, such as the Border Security Force. The air force boasts some 770 combat aircraft. The small navy is slowly developing the capability to police India's long coastline and adjacent Indian Ocean sea-lanes. Until the frontier war with China in Oct.–Nov. 1962, Nehru kept defense spending down in line with his desire to give highest priority to economic development. India's defeat, however, resulted in a substantial military buildup to enable the armed forces to fight a two-front conflict—one against Pakistan in the west and the other against China in the Himalayas.

In recent years, the demands of internal security and counterinsurgency have increasingly occupied regular army units. Several hundred thousand soldiers have been tied down in Kashmir fighting the anti-India insurgency. Significant military forces are also deployed against less publicized but long-lived insurgencies in India's northeastern corner. Over the years, spending on defense has fluctuated between 2.5% and 3% of GDP.

Nuclear-weapons policy

Although the 1998 nuclear tests took the world by surprise, India has had a long-established nuclear effort. In the late 1940s, Prime Minister Nehru endorsed an ambitious civil program although he strongly opposed India's acquiring nuclear weapons. His daughter Indira Gandhi was more ambiguous and refused to sign the 1968 Nuclear Non-Proliferation Treaty. Even though India detonated an underground nuclear device in 1974, it moved hesitantly toward developing a weapons capability. Prime Minister Rajiv Gandhi gave the green light for India's nuclear scientists to develop the bomb only in the late 1980s after New Delhi realized Pakistan had attained this capability or was close to it. When the nationalist BJP, which had long advocated India's becoming a nuclear-weapons state, gained office in 1998, it promptly conducted a series of tests.

The future specifics of India's weapons program remain unclear. Apart from a pledge against first use, India has not formally adopted a nuclear strategy. New Delhi speaks of developing a "minimum deterrence," which in practical terms means using aircraft and short-range missiles to target Pakistan and developing longer-range missile systems capable of reaching the heartland of China. Competing demands for India's limited budget resources have been a major restraint in the past and will continue to be so. Another restraint has been the international nonproliferation restrictions barring help from abroad that have made the nuclear and missile programs entirely indigenous affairs.

For its part, India has said that it will not test again except in extremis and has pledged to impose strict controls on sensitive nuclear exports. Now that India has tested, the policy challenge the U.S. faces is how to fit India (and Pakistan) in the global nuclear system without upsetting the nonproliferation regime.

Pakistan and Kashmir

Relations with Pakistan and the problem of Kashmir are deeply rooted in the bitter preindependence struggle between the Muslim League and the Indian National Congress over the future of British India. The dispute began in October 1947 after Pakistani irregulars tried to seize the princely state with a Muslim majority population but a Hindu ruler. The Maharaja of Kashmir, who had been wavering over the state's future, then officially joined India. New Delhi was able to rush in troops to maintain physical control of the beautiful Srinagar Valley, the heart of the state, and to repel the intruders from Pakistan.

In April 1948, the UN Security Council called for a plebiscite to settle the state's future (a step Nehru himself had recommended), but India and Pakistan were unable to agree on the modalities. Even so, fighting stopped in January 1949 after a UN-brokered cease-fire went into effect. This left the western one third of Kashmir under Pakistani control, the so-called Azad (Free) Kashmir area and the small mountainous principalities of Gilgit and Hunza. The rest of the state stayed with India—the southern and mainly Hindu Jammu area, the largely Muslim Srinigar Valley and the Buddhist-majority Ladakh region in the far north.

AP/WIDE WORLD PHOTOS

SRINAGAR, INDIA: *Hazratbal shrine reflected in Dal Lake in the Kashmir Valley where, when night falls, one tends to think of the possibility that "terrorists" in this dangerous area may set the stage for the first nuclear war.*

Fifty-three years later, India and Pakistan remain at odds over Kashmir. The cease-fire line, now called the line of actual control, has become a de facto, if disputed, border. The two countries fought a brief but fierce war over Kashmir in 1965, sparred indecisively there when they fought over East Pakistan in 1971, and during the past decade have engaged in an undeclared proxy war in which several hundred thousand Indian troops have battled an insurgency by disgruntled Kashmiri Muslim youth supported by Pakistan-based insurgents. In the process, thousands have died and the Kashmir economy lies in shambles.

During the 1950s and 1960s, the UN and the U.S. attempted a number of times to settle the Kashmir problem, without success. The difficulty, veteran U.S. diplomat W. Averell Harriman told President John F. Kennedy in December 1962, was that any solution India was willing to accept was unacceptable to Pakistan. At that time, India was prepared to agree to the status quo with minor adjustments to the cease-fire line. Pakistan wanted a plebiscite to permit Kashmiris the right of self-determination, at least in the Srinagar Valley. Four decades later these positions re-

AP/WIDE WORLD PHOTOS

NEW DELHI, OCT. 17: SECRETARY OF STATE COLIN POWELL *paid a visit to Indian Prime Minister Atal Bihari Vajpayee and Foreign Minister Jaswant Singh (right) to reassure them that America's growing ties with Pakistan would not come at India's expense. "The U.S. and India are united against terrorism and that includes the terrorism that has been directed against India," said Powell.*

main unchanged although, after the decade-long insurgency, attitudes, if anything, have hardened in both countries.

Hopes for reduced tensions between India and Pakistan have risen and fallen in recent years. They rose when Prime Minister Vajpayee visited Lahore, Pakistan, in February 1999, but plummeted in midyear 1999 following a rash Pakistani attempt to seize strategic heights across the line of control in northern Kashmir. President Clinton personally intervened to pressure Pakistan to withdraw its forces. In late 2000, India announced a cease-fire, which it canceled in May 2001 after the insurgency failed to abate. Vajpayee coupled this action with an invitation to Pakistan's President General Musharraf for a summit in the historic city of Agra, the site of the fabled Taj Mahal. The gathering ended in failure when the two leaders were unable to agree on a statement dealing with Kashmir.

What makes the long-festering dispute far more dangerous is the fact that both countries are now declared nuclear-weapons states. The U.S. worries that if tensions in Kashmir escalate into another India-Pakistan war, the conflict could involve the first use of nuclear weapons since the U.S. dropped atomic bombs to destroy the Japanese cities of Hiroshima and Nagasaki in August 1945.

China and other South Asian neighbors

Because of its size, population and economic strength, India dominates its neighbors in South Asia other than Pakistan. India "guides" little Bhutan's foreign policy and exerts great influence over Nepal. Bangladesh gained its independence after the Indian military defeated the Pakistan army in the 1971 war. Grievances of the Tamil minority have led to the bloody and protracted insurgency in Sri Lanka. In dealing with its neighbors, India has at times played the role of a regional hegemon, pressuring the smaller countries when they fail to follow Delhi's wishes. At other times, the Indians have adopted a friendlier policy, recognizing the sensitivities of the smaller neighbors. For example, in 1996, India and Bangladesh settled a long-standing and politically sensitive dispute over sharing the waters of the Ganges and Brahmaputra rivers.

India's largest and most populous neighbor, China, poses a different and strategically far more complex problem. The two countries brush up against each other along the 3,400-kilometer-long, largely unpopulated and undemarcated border along the crest of the world's highest mountain chain, the Himalayas. When the Communist victors in China's civil war reasserted political control over Tibet in 1950, Prime Minister Nehru relinquished privileges that India had inherited from the British Raj as part of his policy of seeking friendly relations with Beijing, popularly called Hindi-Chini Bahai-Bahai (India and China are brothers). After negotiations failed to fix the frontier in the Himalayas and India welcomed thousands of Tibetan refugees in 1959, including the Dalai Lama, a brief conflict in Oct./Nov. 1962 saw the Chinese humiliate poorly equipped Indian troops.

The defeat was a tremendous psychological shock that is still felt 40 years later. Although, in recent years, the Indians and the Chinese have made progress toward more normalized relations, India still regards China warily and considers it a long-term rival. China's close and long-standing security ties with Pakistan continue to upset New Delhi, particularly Beijing's help for Pakistan's nuclear-weapons and missile programs.

The U.S.S.R., then Russia

India and the Soviet Union established close ties after Washington had forged a security alliance with India's enemy, Pakistan, in the mid-1950s. In time, the Soviets became India's main supplier of sophisticated military hardware. The Soviets also backed the Indian position on Kashmir, wielding their veto to block UN Security resolutions that India disliked. In turn, New Delhi adopted an understanding attitude toward Soviet actions that stirred international opposition, such as Moscow's intervention in Hungary in 1956, in Czechoslovakia in 1968, and in Afghanistan in 1979.

Although communism, as such, had limited appeal in India (Communist parties were strong only in the states of West Bengal and Kerala), Indians regarded the Soviet Union as a reliable friend. The end of the cold war and the disintegration of the Soviet Union were thus a shock to India's foreign policy and political elite. Russia, the successor state, has continued to provide military equipment—for payment in dollars not rupees—and to offer political support. Still, New Delhi recognizes that Moscow possesses only a shadow of its former power and influence.

After the breakup of the Soviet Union, India had high hopes for establishing close economic ties with the new countries of Central Asia. However, the chronic instability in

Afghanistan and tensions with Pakistan have frustrated these prospects. In the case of Afghanistan, India strongly opposed the Taliban both because of their Islamic fundamentalism and of their willingness to provide training bases and other facilities for insurgents fighting against India in Kashmir.

Relations with the U.S.

The cold-war years saw India and the U.S. at odds much of the time, especially after Washington established a military security relationship with Pakistan in 1954. When the Nixon Administration "tilted" against India during the 1971 India-Pakistan war, bilateral links reached their nadir. They remained essentially estranged until the cold war ended.

This development and the rupture in 1990 of U.S.-Pakistan security links, because of Islamabad's nuclear program, removed two major barriers to better relations. After launching economic reforms in 1991, India expanded commercial links with the U.S., which became New Delhi's largest trading partner and source of foreign investment. The emergence of the 1.7 million strong Indian-American ethnic community also became a positive factor in promoting better relations. The 130-member India caucus in the House of Representatives reflects the growing political influence of Indian-Americans.

Yet memories of past frictions continued and bilateral ties unraveled once more after the 1998 nuclear tests and the imposition of sanctions by the U.S. They, however, gradually improved as a result of talks between India's minister of external affairs, Jaswant Singh, and U.S. Deputy Secretary of State Strobe Talbott. Although these discussions initially focused on nuclear matters, they eventually embraced a far wider range of issues. They became the most sustained Indo-U.S. dialogue in several decades. The result was greater mutual understanding between New Delhi and Washington and a feeling in India that the U.S. was at last willing to take it seriously as a dialogue partner.

In mid-1999, Indians reacted positively when the Clinton Administration pressured Pakistan to pull back its forces after the rash attempt to seize strategic heights across the Kashmir line of control. For the first time in many years, New Delhi felt that Washington had sided with India and not Pakistan over Kashmir. A further boost came as a result of the highly successful March 2000 visit by President Clinton, the first chief executive to travel to India in two decades, and the good return visit by Prime Minister Vajpayee to the U.S. later in the year. Clinton not only charmed the Indian public, but also impressed the policymaking elite when he urged Pakistan to solve the Kashmir problem peacefully.

The Bush Administration wants to advance the process of improved relations that Clinton began. When Singh visited Washington in April 2001, the new Administration rolled out the red carpet. Since then, the two countries have continued to expand the scope of their bilateral dialogue. For its part, India was one of the few countries to react positively to the Bush Administration's controversial missile-defense initiative. New Delhi also promptly offered the U.S. its full support after the September 11 terrorist attacks on the World Trade Center and the Pentagon. President Bush welcomed Vajpayee to the White House in November 2001—the first time a prime minister had visited Washington two years in a row.

In sum, there has been a gradual but substantial change in U.S. and Indian attitudes. The relationship between the world's two largest democracies has moved from estrangement to engagement. Even though differences continue, the two countries have drawn closer together than at almost any time since India became independent. Looking ahead, the course of events in the "war against terrorism" will have an inevitable major impact. With the U.S. reestablishing closer relations with Pakistan, India is concerned about the scope and nature of these ties. In Indian eyes, moreover, Pakistani-supported attacks in Kashmir are "terrorism." The manner in which the U.S. deals with this issue will greatly influence Delhi's attitudes toward Washington and the course of the relationship.

U.S. policy options

❑ **1. Washington should continue its policy of offering no help for any Indian nuclear activities.**

Pro: Continue current policy because a changed approach could weaken the international nonproliferation regime.

Con: While India's testing was undesirable, it is a reality. Cooperation, especially in the field of nuclear power and safety, could encourage New Delhi to adopt a more restrained nuclear posture.

❑ **2. The U.S. should adopt a more active stance in trying to get India and Pakistan to resolve the Kashmir dispute.**

Pro: The danger of nuclear conflict makes it essential that the U.S. intervene forcefully to seek reduced tensions and hopefully a Kashmir settlement.

Con: The two countries remain so far apart that outside intervention has little or no prospect of success.

❑ **3. As the U.S. improves relations with India, it should pay close attention to the impact this has on Pakistan.**

Pro: Washington needs to balance relations with the two countries. As the recent terrorist attacks have shown, Pakistan remains a country important to U.S. interests. Gains from better relations with India are not likely to offset the potential losses from worse relations with Pakistan.

Con: Bilateral U.S. links with India and Pakistan should run on their own separate tracks. It is not in the U.S. interest to try for balanced relations as Washington has often attempted to do in the past. Quite apart from the short-term but key interests that the U.S. has in obtaining Pakistan's cooperation in dealing with Osama bin Laden and the Taliban in Afghanistan, Washington should not ignore that Pakistan has been using what amounts to terrorism to promote its cause in Kashmir.

❑ **4. The U.S. should back India's quest for a permanent seat on the UN Security Council.**

Pro: India's size, population and growing international economic and political importance warrant a Security Council seat. Security Council membership should reflect the realities of the year 2002, not of 1945.

Con: Supporting India will badly strain U.S.-Pakistan relations while the Kashmir dispute remains unsettled. In addition, given past difficulties with India in the international arena, there appears little advantage for U.S. interests were India to acquire the Security Council seat. ■

OPINION BALLOTS
are on pages 69–70

DISCUSSION QUESTIONS

1. Now that India has exploded a nuclear device, should the U.S. continue its past restrictive nonproliferation policies or try to find some way to accommodate India within the nuclear club? Can this be done without undermining nuclear nonproliferation policies?

2. India and Pakistan remain at odds over Kashmir, territory they have disputed since 1947. Since 1989, opponents of Indian rule have mounted a serious and bloody insurgency, supported by Pakistan. The situation has been made more dangerous by the fact that both countries have now tested nuclear weapons. Should the U.S. adopt a more active role in trying to resolve this longstanding dispute or should it continue to work quietly through diplomatic channels?

3. U.S.-India relations have warmed in recent years after decades of estrangement. How far do you think that the U.S. can or should go in pressing for closer and friendlier ties with India? What will the impact of friendlier U.S. relations with India be on U.S. ties with Pakistan, which has once more become important for U.S. interests as a key player in the war against terrorism in Afghanistan?

4. India hopes to become a member of the UN Security Council. In the past, the U.S. has been unwilling to support India's wish for membership. Should this position be maintained?

5. India has been developing at a faster pace during the past decade. Do you think it will be able to maintain the forward movement? What are the major problems that India faces in maintaining the process of economic reform initiated in 1991?

6. India and China are Asia's two largest countries. In the past, their relations have been difficult, although in recent years they have downplayed their differences somewhat. As these two giant countries move ahead in the 21st century, will they become rival power poles or will they be able to establish more cooperative ties?

7. India is a leader of the developing world and the U.S. leads developed nations. On world economic issues, the two countries have frequently adopted conflicting trade and environmental policy positions. Do you think New Delhi and Washington can reconcile their differences?

8. India has been a rare political success story, one of the few Third World countries that has been able to establish and maintain democracy. What have been the major strengths and weaknesses of the Indian system in the past, and what do you think of future prospects?

READINGS AND RESOURCES

Cohen, Stephen Philip, **India: Emerging Power.** Washington, DC, Brookings Institution Press, 2001. 280 pp. $28.95. A leading South Asia analyst provides a readable and comprehensive assessment of India's foreign and defense policies and New Delhi's prospects for attaining great-power status.

Crossette, Barbara, "India: Old Civilization in a New World." **Headline Series** No. 320. New York, Foreign Policy Association, 2000. 78 pp. $5.95. A former **New York Times** correspondent in India presents a sweeping overview of India's past and present.

Das, Gurcharan, **India Unbound.** New York, Knopf, 2001. 406 pp. $27.50. Former Indian business executive discusses his career to illuminate policy problems that throttled India's economic development before 1991 economic reforms.

Hardgrave, Robert L., and Kochanek, Stanley A., **India: Government and Politics in a Developing Nation.** 6th ed. New York, Wadsworth Publishing, 2000. 536 pp. $45.95. Two leading South Asia academic specialists offer a broad introduction and overview of India's domestic, political, social and governmental scene.

Harrison, Selig S., Kreisberg, Paul H., and, Kux, Dennis, eds., **India and Pakistan: The First Fifty Years.** New York, Cambridge University Press and Washington, D.C., Woodrow Wilson Center Press, 1998. 200 pp. $17.95. Separate chapters by leading American scholars assess India's (and Pakistan's) political, social and economic development and the course of foreign policy and relations with the U.S. during the first half century of independence.

Kux, Dennis, **India and the United States, 1941–1991, Estranged Democracies.** Washington, NDU Press, 1993. A comprehensive account of U.S.-India relations during the cold-war years.

ASIA SOCIETY, 725 Park Ave., New York, NY 10021; (212) 288-6400; Fax (212) 517-8315. **www.asiasociety.org** ■ This site provides information about current issues in Asia and focuses on developing a greater understanding between Asians and Americans. The society publishes the **Asian Update Series** as well as country briefings. It also maintains the information website **www.asiasource.com.**

EMBASSY OF INDIA, 2107 Massachusetts Ave., NW, Washington, DC 20008; (202) 939-7000; Fax (212) 265-4351. **www.indianembassy.org** ■ A source of information on India including press releases, policy statements and links to official Indian government offices, organizations and agencies.

NATIONAL BUREAU OF ASIAN RESEARCH (NBR), 4518 University Way, NE, Suite 300, Seattle, WA 98105; (206) 632-7370; Fax (206) 632-7487. **www.nbr.org** ■ Site contains information on and analysis of current Asian issues; links to hundreds of websites about Asia, including several on India.

U.S. STATE DEPARTMENT ■ Background notes, including information about the history and political conditions of India as well as many other countries, may be found at the department's website, **www.state.gov/r/pa/bgn.**

OPINION BALLOTS

Please submit only one ballot per person, per topic. *Ballots must be received by June 30, 2002.*
Vote online at ***www.greatdecisions.org*** *(code: gd2002fpa) or mail ballots to:*

FOREIGN POLICY ASSOCIATION, 470 PARK AVENUE SOUTH, NEW YORK, NY 10016-6819

TOPIC 5 India today

ISSUE A. Do you agree or disagree with the following statements?

	AGREE	DISAGREE
1. Since India is now a nuclear power, the U.S. should help it with its nuclear program.	❑	❑
2. The U.S. should support India's quest for a permanent seat on the UN Security Council.	❑	❑
3. The U.S. should seek closer ties with India—a democratic success story—even if that means straining U.S. ties with Pakistan—a key ally in the war on terrorism.	❑	❑

Comment: ______________________________

Your zip code: ___ ___ ___ ___ ___

Date: / /2002 *Ballot continues on reverse side...*

TOPIC 5 India today

ISSUE A. Do you agree or disagree with the following statements?

	AGREE	DISAGREE
1. Since India is now a nuclear power, the U.S. should help it with its nuclear program.	❑	❑
2. The U.S. should support India's quest for a permanent seat on the UN Security Council.	❑	❑
3. The U.S. should seek closer ties with India—a democratic success story—even if that means straining U.S. ties with Pakistan—a key ally in the war on terrorism.	❑	❑

Comment: ______________________________

Your zip code: ___ ___ ___ ___ ___

Date: / /2002 *Ballot continues on reverse side...*

TOPIC 6 AIDS in Africa

ISSUE A. Do you agree or disagree with the following statements?

	AGREE	DISAGREE
1. The global AIDS pandemic is a security threat to the U.S.	❑	❑
2. The U.S. should commit at least $3 billion a year to the Global Health Fund to fight AIDS.	❑	❑
3. The U.S. should support cancellation of most foreign debts owed by African countries.	❑	❑

Comment: ______________________________

Your zip code: ___ ___ ___ ___ ___

Date: / /2002 *Ballot continues on reverse side...*

TOPIC 6 AIDS in Africa

ISSUE A. Do you agree or disagree with the following statements?

	AGREE	DISAGREE
1. The global AIDS pandemic is a security threat to the U.S.	❑	❑
2. The U.S. should commit at least $3 billion a year to the Global Health Fund to fight AIDS.	❑	❑
3. The U.S. should support cancellation of most foreign debts owed by African countries.	❑	❑

Comment: ______________________________

Your zip code: ___ ___ ___ ___ ___

Date: / /2002 *Ballot continues on reverse side...*

ISSUE B. Regarding the long-standing dispute between India and Pakistan over Kashmir, the U.S. should (choose one):

___ **1.** Take a more active role in resolving that dispute

___ **2.** Work quietly through diplomatic channels

Comment: ______________________________

ISSUE C. Do you think that in the future, India and China are more likely to become (choose one):

___ **1.** Major adversaries

___ **2.** Close allies

Comment: ______________________________

ISSUE D. How would you rate the prospects that the U.S. and India will reconcile their differences over world economic issues (choose one):

___ **1.** High

___ **2.** So so

___ **3.** Low

Comment: ______________________________

ISSUE B. Regarding the long-standing dispute between India and Pakistan over Kashmir, the U.S. should (choose one):

___ **1.** Take a more active role in resolving that dispute

___ **2.** Work quietly through diplomatic channels

Comment: ______________________________

ISSUE C. Do you think that in the future, India and China are more likely to become (choose one):

___ **1.** Major adversaries

___ **2.** Close allies

Comment: ______________________________

ISSUE D. How would you rate the prospects that the U.S. and India will reconcile their differences over world economic issues (choose one):

___ **1.** High

___ **2.** So so

___ **3.** Low

Comment: ______________________________

ISSUE B. In its fight against the global AIDS pandemic, should the U.S. focus more on treatment or more on prevention? (choose one)

___ **1.** Treatment

___ **2.** Prevention

Comment: ______________________________

ISSUE C. Concerning the availability of drugs against AIDS, the U.S. should (choose one):

___ **1.** Defend the patent rights of U.S. drug companies

___ **2.** Make exceptions for countries unable to afford brand-name drugs

Comment: ______________________________

ISSUE D. In its economic policy toward African countries, the U.S. should give the stronger emphasis to (choose one):

___ **1.** Trade liberalization

___ **2.** Public investment in health, education and infrastructure

Comment: ______________________________

ISSUE B. In its fight against the global AIDS pandemic, should the U.S. focus more on treatment or more on prevention? (choose one)

___ **1.** Treatment

___ **2.** Prevention

Comment: ______________________________

ISSUE C. Concerning the availability of drugs against AIDS, the U.S. should (choose one):

___ **1.** Defend the patent rights of U.S. drug companies

___ **2.** Make exceptions for countries unable to afford brand-name drugs

Comment: ______________________________

ISSUE D. In its economic policy toward African countries, the U.S. should give the stronger emphasis to (choose one):

___ **1.** Trade liberalization

___ **2.** Public investment in health, education and infrastructure

Comment: ______________________________

AIDS in Africa: is the world concerned enough?

If African countries are left to confront the HIV/AIDS pandemic with the small level of outside support they have received to date, few are likely to succeed and the spread of instability will heighten global insecurity.

by Salih Booker and William Minter

APWIDE WORLD PHOTOS

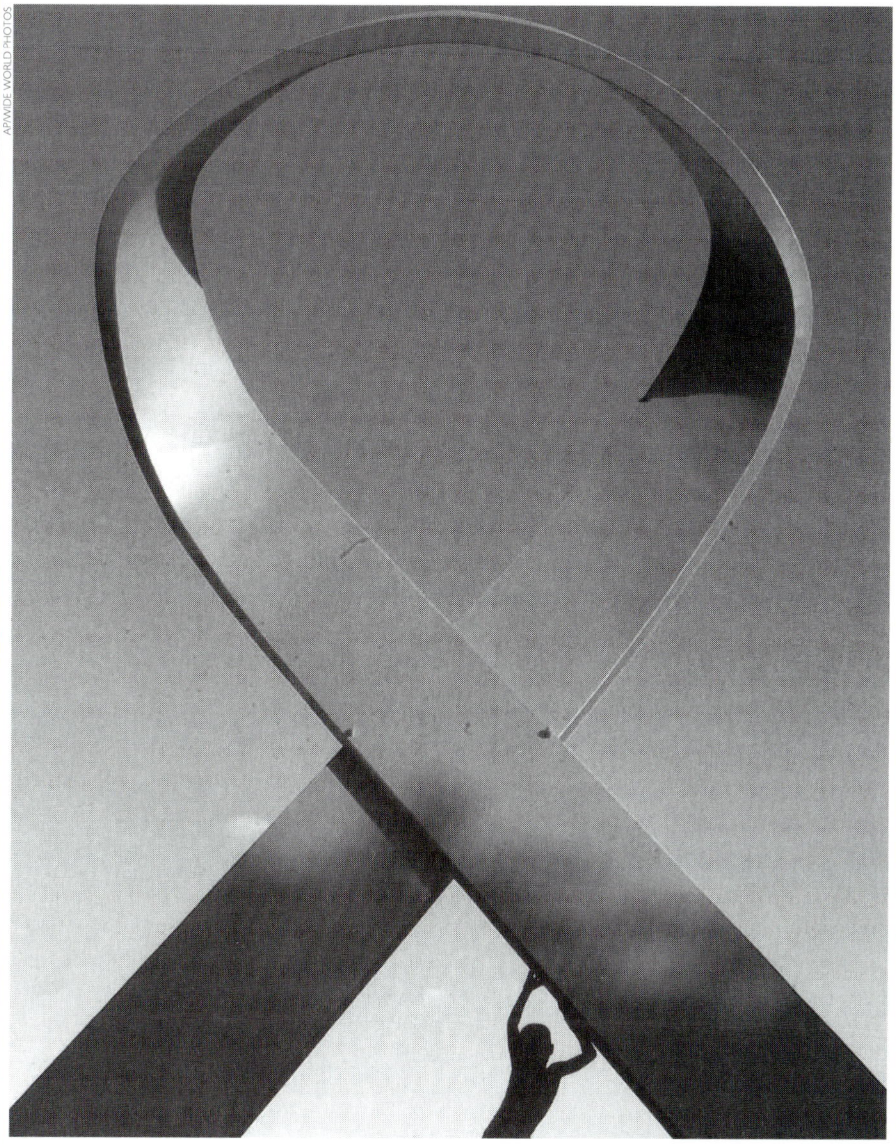

AIDS RIBBON MONUMENT *was unveiled by South Africa's deputy president, Jacob Zuma, to mark the opening of the 13th world AIDS conference in Durban, South Africa, July 2000.*

IN 2001, AN ESTIMATED 3 million people died in the global AIDS pandemic. Of those deaths, 77% were in sub-Saharan Africa, home to just over 10% of the world's population. Of 40 million people living with HIV/AIDS in December 2001, 28.1 million were in sub-Saharan Africa.

Since it began two decades ago, the pandemic has taken more than 22 million lives, more than 17 million of them in sub-Saharan Africa. In comparison, approximately 450,000 have died of AIDS in the U.S. during the same period; the total population of the U.S. is half that of sub-Saharan Africa. There are estimated to be more than 13 million orphans who have lost their mothers or both parents to AIDS, 12 million of them in sub-Saharan Africa.

In the U.S. and other developed countries, the death trend from AIDS has been declining since the introduction of life-prolonging drugs in 1996. In Africa, however, it is still rising rapidly and, unless it is reversed, AIDS may kill as many as one in every three young adults in a number of countries. Estimates of the likely economic impact differ in detail, but there is a growing consensus among international agencies, insurance companies and business analysts that for many countries it will be catastrophic. Health services are already being overwhelmed by AIDS patients in many countries, and deaths among teachers are devastating educational systems. Mining and manufacturing companies see the death rate among skilled workers as a significant disincentive for investment and as a threat to profits. AIDS poses the greatest single hindrance to economic development in the world's poorest region and will dramatically increase global economic disparities with destabilizing consequences for the entire world.

By January 2000, a U.S. National Intelligence Estimate had identified global infectious diseases, including HIV/AIDS, as a major threat to national security. Despite this formal recognition, the warning failed to evoke a sense of national urgency, just as was the case be-

SALIH BOOKER *is executive director and* **WILLIAM MINTER** *is senior research fellow at Africa Action, the oldest U.S.-based Africa advocacy group. Africa Action is currently engaged in a campaign for Africa's right to health.*

AP/WIDE WORLD PHOTOS

THOUSANDS OF PROTESTERS *demand affordable access to AIDS drugs at a march during the international AIDS conference in South Africa in 2000.*

fore September 11 in response to official warnings of the possibility of terrorism inside the U.S. In the wake of the September 11 attacks, the AIDS pandemic remains a critical test of whether policymakers can be farsighted enough to pay attention to a wider range of global threats.

In every country, rich or poor, denial has crippled the response to AIDS. But poverty increases the risks and reduces the capacity to respond. For two decades, the pandemic has raced ahead of the global response. While the HIV virus affects people of all races and income levels, both men and women, most of those now dying of AIDS are black, poor and female. As the president of Botswana recently remarked, the survival of entire nations is at risk. AIDS has already become the worst plague in human history. The world's persistent failure to respond raises fundamental questions of global human rights and international economic policy, as well as more specific issues of U.S. bilateral relations with Africa, priorities for assistance programs, and U.S. obligations for global public investment.

In 1987, when the first anti-AIDS drug began to slow the death rate in the U.S., 10 times as many people were dying of AIDS in Africa as in the U.S. But it was not until July 2000, when Durban, South Africa, hosted the first global AIDS conference to be held in Africa, that the world began to pay attention. Since then, protests against pharmaceutical companies and emerging competition from generic drug producers in developing countries have resulted in somewhat reduced drug prices. The lowering of costs has meant that policymakers could begin to conceive of ways to actually defeat the pandemic in Africa, by investing massively in treatment efforts and new prevention programs that together could turn the tide. An unprecedented UN special session in June 2001 produced new pledges to act. Yet, in late 2001, UN Secretary General Kofi Annan's new Global Health Fund had received much less than 10% of the estimated $10 billion a year needed to cope with the global health emergency. And only a minuscule fraction of those with AIDS in Africa had gained access to anti-AIDS drug therapy.

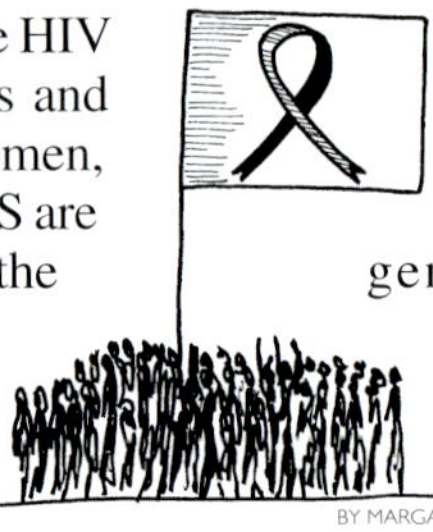

BY MARGARET SCOTT

U.S. policymakers must consider the following questions:

- At a time when the U.S. has a renewed appreciation for the vulnerability of all life and the need for international cooperation to defeat global threats, can Washington afford to ignore this growing danger to human security? With HIV infection still spreading worldwide, with no cure yet in sight, what will happen if the U.S. continues to treat the international HIV/AIDS pandemic as a relatively low priority?
- How can the U.S. address factors that block a priority response to the pandemic, such as stigma, discrimination and the assumption that black lives are expendable?
- What are the most effective combinations of prevention, treatment and research to combat HIV/AIDS and cope with its disastrous consequences for individuals, families and communities?
- Can international responsibility for this global pandemic be satisfied by those resources wealthy countries are willing to make available as development assistance, or does the U.S. share a universal obligation to protect the global right to health? And does the U.S. have a national security interest in doing so?
- Are economic policies imposed by international financial institutions and demands for repayment of foreign debt, even at the expense of resources for health and education, among the causes of the growth of the pandemic?
- Should the high cost of AIDS drugs be protected by patent rights for large pharmaceutical companies, or should governments and the World Trade Organization (WTO) give priority to public health in such an emergency and override patent rights, if necessary, to ensure the cheapest production of essential medicines? ■

From disease to pandemic

AIDS (acquired immunodeficiency syndrome) was first identified as a medical condition in 1981 and named in 1982. It is not a single disease but rather a weakening of the body's immune system so it loses its normal capacity to defend against infections. The diseases that take advantage of this weakness are called "opportunistic" infections. AIDS cases are tracked either by tests that measure the level of certain types of infection-fighting cells (T4 lymphocytes) or by the presence of the most distinctive opportunistic infections.

HIV (human immunodeficiency virus) was identified in 1983 as the cause of AIDS. It is transmitted by sexual contact, by the use of infected blood, or from mother to infant during pregnancy, delivery or breast-feeding. Both the chances of transmission in a given contact, and how rapidly the virus produces symptoms of AIDS, are highly affected by general health conditions and other factors. The median time lag between infection by HIV and the onset of AIDS is estimated at 10 years.

Although drugs are available to treat the most common opportunistic infections, no cure or vaccine has yet been discovered. Since 1996, HAART (highly active antiretroviral treatment) has been available to slow the effects of HIV on the body's immune system.

The long time between infection and visible disease syndrome, in addition to the complexity of the virus itself, has complicated research on the origin and spread of AIDS, as well as the search for a cure. Together with reluctance to speak openly about sexually transmitted diseases and the stigmatization of people living with HIV/AIDS, this delayed-action characteristic of AIDS has encouraged denial and contributed to slowness in responding to the pandemic.

The first AIDS cases in Africa were identified less than two years after the first cases in the U.S., and HIV/AIDS spread there far more rapidly than in the U.S. Yet research and public attention until very recently was almost entirely determined by the pattern in North American nations and other highly industrialized countries. In particular, AIDS has been identified as afflicting "high-risk" groups such as gay men, intravenous drug users, and hemophiliacs or others coming into contact with infected blood. Some scientists at first refused to accept that HIV could be transmitted by heterosexual intercourse. At one point, Haitians in the U.S. were the focus of attention and stigmatization, while scientists speculated that HIV might have reached the U.S. from Haiti. In fact, researchers later concluded that HIV had most likely been carried to Haiti by tourists from the U.S.

Despite a few dissenters, almost all researchers now accept that HIV produces AIDS. There is also consensus on the principal means of transmission, and therefore on the general strategy for prevention. But there is little consensus on which factors are most important in determining the speed with which it spreads.

Virus transmission from one person to another depends both on the characteristics of the virus and on a wide variety of risk factors, some open to individual choice and others not. Most significantly, social factors decisively influence the "acceleration" of transmission which makes a disease "epidemic" (widespread) or "pandemic" (reaching national or global proportions).

Social and economic conditions, as well as levels of access to health services of all kinds, are primary determinants of who lives and who dies as a result of the AIDS pandemic. Both the internal vulnerabilities of Africa's societies and their marginalization within the current world order are reflected in the catastrophic course of HIV/AIDS on the continent. The same factors are at work elsewhere: the Caribbean is the second-most-affected region worldwide, in the U.S. AIDS is increasingly concentrated in minority communities, and the poverty-stricken South Asian subcontinent will possibly be the next region to experience explosive growth rates in infection.

HIV/AIDS in Africa

The most striking feature of HIV/AIDS in Africa, as compared with the pattern in developed countries, is that from the start it has not been concentrated in narrowly defined high-risk groups (such as gay men), but rather has spread in all population categories. Most significantly, in Africa more women than men are infected with HIV. As many as one quarter of those dead of AIDS have been children infected through mother-to-child transmission. While African societies have a strong tradition of caring for orphans through extended families and community efforts, both are being overwhelmed by the millions now orphaned by AIDS.

In wealthier countries, transmission through infected blood was quickly addressed through heightened security in blood banks and medical facilities. In the U.S., debates over how to prevent infection through contaminated needles focus on users of illegal drugs. In contrast, in many African countries the infection has probably been spread by impoverished health services, through inadequately screened blood and insufficiently sterilized needles that are reused in injecting medicines or vaccines. This was particularly the case in the decisive early stages before much was known about HIV; due to lack of

MICHAEL SAMUEL GRAPHICS

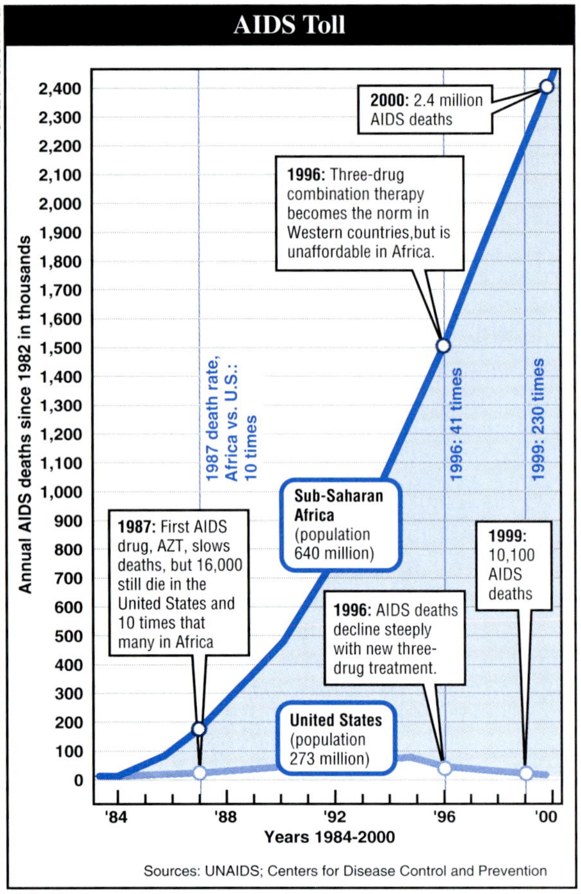

MICHAEL SAMUEL GRAPHICS

resources, it is still happening today.

The years of delay between infection and disease appearance meant that the pandemic had a massive head start before it was even detected. Any sexually active adult was at risk, most often without knowing it, as was anyone inadvertently exposed to infected blood. A few African countries responded quickly and urgently to the threat; most did not. In any case, the problem was soon so massive as to be beyond most countries' capacity to respond alone.

There were many reasons for denial, in addition to the aversion to frank talk about sex that Africans shared with most in the developed world as well. For many Africans, AIDS was simply one more threat to survival, and not the most immediately visible, as compared to war, drought, violent crime, impoverishment, or other endemic killer diseases such as malaria. The image of AIDS in the popular global media and in medical circles as well was of a disease of gay white men. When international attention did begin to focus on AIDS in Africa, it also came with unfounded speculation about African "promiscuity" that aroused resentment and distrust rather than reinforcing joint efforts to combat the pandemic.

In Africa as elsewhere, HIV does spread more rapidly within high-risk groups such as prostitutes and people who have multiple sexual partners. Patterns of sexual contact—influenced by such factors as wars, refugee movement and migrant labor, as well as culture and religion—influence how the virus spreads. But it is the broader societal context, including weak health services, poverty, and especially the subordinate position of women, that provides the most powerful determinants of disease spread. Indeed, in Africa a far wider and more diverse range of people could be considered high risk simply because of the hardships of life that most Africans face.

The effects of weak or absent health services play out in many ways. The chances of transmission of the virus in a single sexual encounter are much greater when there are other untreated sexually transmitted infections. Yet treatment for such diseases is not widely available. Prevention campaigns require encouraging people with no symptoms to be tested for HIV, but facilities for testing are in short supply. And when there is no chance of access to treatment, there is scant incentive to be tested. Without adequately screened blood supplies, a surgeon may have no choice but to weigh saving a life with a transfusion against the chance of infection. Hospitals unable to provide good nutrition or sanitation may themselves spread disease.

Research also indicates that immune systems in Africa are more vulnerable, probably because they are exposed to stress from more diverse disease threats. Once infected with HIV, a person is more vulnerable to any other infections present in the environment. Notably, tuberculosis is among the most frequent opportunistic infections associated with AIDS in Africa. The dominant types of HIV found in Africa are more virulent than the dominant type in North America. For many reasons, death comes more rapidly to AIDS patients in Africa.

Poverty, in more general terms, also has profound effects in spreading the pandemic. Throughout Africa, cities are growing rapidly. More than one third of Africans now live in cities, and there are more than 30 cities with populations above one million. Yet these cities, which continue to draw people fleeing war or poverty in the countryside, do not provide adequate housing, sanitation or jobs. Most significantly, families must often split themselves between city and countryside to put together enough income to survive. Both the lack of stable family life in the city and the visits by men to their families in the rural areas help promote the spread of AIDS.

Vulnerability of women

The effect of poverty is multiplied by the vulnerable position of women, who face both subtle and violent subjugation and exploitation in many African societies. Some may seek survival through commercial sex or through marriage relationships they would not otherwise choose. Even when knowledge levels and awareness about HIV/AIDS are very high (as is now the case in many African countries), and when condoms are available, male resistance severely limits the options for a woman to insist on use of a condom. This is particularly hard within marriage, since consistently using condoms implies a decision not to have children.

Tragically, just as the pandemic was taking off in the 1980s, the World Bank and the rich-country bilateral creditors that hold Africa's foreign debt were insisting on austerity policies that further weakened health services and accentuated poverty. Many countries were forced to cut health budgets and impose user fees for services that were previously free, which reduced access by the poor to health services and consequently increased sexually transmitted infections. Paying off foreign debts was given higher priority than long-term investment in health and education.

There are of course pronounced differences within the continent, which is more than three times the size of the U.S. There is almost no data available on the pattern of AIDS in Africa north of the Sahara Desert, but prevalence is thought to be low there. Within sub-Saharan Africa, regional differences are significant. So far, most West African countries are less affected than those in Central, East and Southern Africa. In East and Central Africa, regional wars and the movement of soldiers and refugees were one of the major forces propelling the pandemic in the 1980s and 1990s. In addition to deliberate rapes by some forces, such as those who carried out the genocide in Rwanda in 1994, war anywhere in the world has always been accompanied by sexual violence, prostitution and other social dislocation which facilitates disease spread.

Southern Africa also suffered war. During the final years of apartheid in the 1980s, South Africa's efforts to defend white-minority rule brought devastation to its neighbors. In this region, it was primarily in the 1990s that the pandemic exploded. The accelerants included good transport networks linking South Africa and its neighbors, the pull of South Africa's more advanced economy, and the migrant-labor system inherited from the apartheid era. In addition, the HIV subtype predominant in Southern Africa is the most virulent and easily spread. Cruelly, the pandemic was taking off just as the whole world celebrated with Nelson Mandela the South African victory over apartheid.■

How four African countries cope

THE PATTERN of HIV/AIDS and the response to it vary significantly by country as well as by region. Uganda in East Africa and Senegal in West Africa are two examples of relative "success" in coping with the pandemic. Botswana and South Africa, neighbors in Southern Africa, are both among the most gravely affected countries in the world. Currently Botswana is among the pioneers in fighting back against HIV/AIDS; the South African response has so far been profoundly ambivalent.

UGANDA

Uganda was one of the earliest countries to be devastated by HIV/AIDS, beginning in the early 1980s when it spread in the aftermath of the war that overthrew the repressive regime of Idi Amin. Uganda has also long been cited as a model of how to respond since by the mid-1980s, the government had become strongly engaged in reinforcing early responses by the health sector and community groups. President Yoweri Museveni and other officials spoke openly about HIV/AIDS and the government also initiated a multisectoral approach to confront the pandemic and encourage collaboration with nongovernmental initiatives.

By 2001, an estimated 2.2 million (nearly 10% of Uganda's total population of 24 million) were estimated to have been infected with HIV; approximately 800,000 of them were estimated to have already died of AIDS. Almost every Ugandan family has been affected. In 1999, the AIDS death toll was approximately 110,000, about 75 times as great on a per capita basis as in the U.S.

By extraordinary efforts of public education, testing, condom distribution and other prevention measures, with religious groups as well as government and other civic groups joining in, Uganda began to reverse the rate of HIV infection in the 1990s. At the end of the decade, the rate had declined from as high as 15% of adults in the early 1990s to 8% at the end of 1999.

Even so, UNAIDS estimated that as many as 770,000 adults and 53,000 children were living with HIV/AIDS at the end of 1999. In 2001, stigmatization of people with HIV/AIDS was still a powerful reality in Uganda. Only a small fraction of Ugandan AIDS patients had access to antiretroviral treatment; a program for all HIV-positive pregnant women to prevent mother-to-child transmission was only launched in late 2001. Despite Uganda's reputation compared with other countries, AIDS activists sharply criticized the lack of consistent government efforts to step up the campaign against the pandemic.

SENEGAL

At the end of 1999, Senegal, with a population of some 10 million people, had an HIV-prevalence rate of less than 2% of the adult population, one of the lowest in sub-Saharan Africa. Senegal's success to date in avoiding a wider epidemic is apparently due to multiple factors: (1) universal prevalence of circumcision, which decreases the risk of virus transmission, in this predominantly Muslim country; (2) low and still-decreasing rates of premarital and extramarital sex; (3) early and strong engagement of Muslim and Christian religious leaders, as well as government and community groups, in promoting the use of condoms in any extramarital sex, as well as delay for youth in beginning sexual relations; (4) strong and long-established government health programs to treat sexually transmitted diseases and provide other primary health-care services; and (5) explicit concentration of prevention and health measures on sex workers, a policy made possible by the early legalization of prostitution in 1969.

BOTSWANA

A relatively prosperous and well-governed African country adjoining South Africa, with about 1.6 million people, Botswana is nevertheless one of the countries worst affected by AIDS. It has served as a source of migrant labor for South Africa's mines, and as a land-transport route linking South Africa with countries to the north. Before the 1990s, HIV prevalence was less than

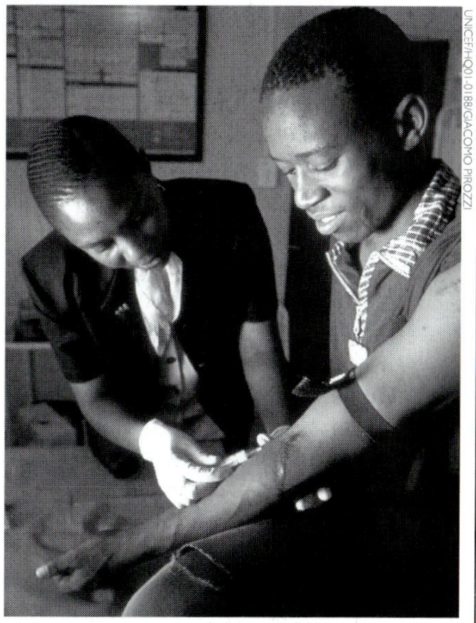
UNICEF/HQ01-0188/GIACOMO PIROZZI

IN GABORONE, BOTSWANA, *a nurse draws blood during a medical examination at a UNICEF-supported clinic that provides free health services, including information, voluntary testing and counseling for HIV and other sexually transmitted diseases.*

JOÃO SILVA/THE NEW YORK TIMES

TO CURB THE SPREAD OF HIV *in Swaziland, King Mswati III issued the controversial decree that young women must stop having sex for the next five years and must wear brightly colored tassels (umcwasho) to indicate their celibacy. Lungile Ndlovu, regally appointed leader of the maidens, believes it will be no problem, but many Swazis disagree.*

10%. But rates shot up in the 1990s, to the current estimate of some 36% of the adult population. Life expectancy, which had risen to 67 in the mid-1990s, was projected at less than 50 by the end of the decade. While health authorities were alarmed, other government officials and society at large were slow to realize the scale of the catastrophe.

Now, however, Botswana is fighting back. Prevention campaigns have gone into high gear. The government plans universal coverage of drugs to prevent mother-to-child transmission for the 24,000 HIV-positive women giving birth each year. The national diamond company, half-owned by the government, is paying for treatment for workers who need it, and officials are committed to providing access to all citizens. Botswana is collaborating with Harvard University and others on a high-tech laboratory for research particularly targeted at HIV/AIDS in Southern Africa.

SOUTH AFRICA

According to estimates for the year 2000, almost 4.2 million of some 43 million South Africans were infected with HIV, the largest number of any country in the world. Although it is the African country best prepared in economic and political terms to cope, according to *The Washington Post,* it has "proven among the least capable of overcoming economic inequality, bitter distrust and social barriers" that fuel the pandemic.

The combination of low levels of social cohesion inherited from the apartheid era, combined with relatively high incomes and population mobility, provided an ideal environment for the epidemic to spread, according to Alan Whiteside, one of South Africa's leading researchers on AIDS. While South Africa's political transition to democracy in the 1990s was rightly applauded around the world, the economic and social patterns of racial division and inequality were more resistant to change. In fact, despite advances for many black South Africans, poverty, social disruption and criminal violence continue to grow as a result of earlier socioeconomic divisions and current economic policies that put market stability for investors at the top of government priorities.

The response to the pandemic by South African government officials has been beset by denial and ambivalence, and has lacked internal coherence. At the same time, AIDS activists and health professionals in South Africa—including many in the government—have actively taken practical initiatives at many levels, and have taken the lead in working for national and global action to lower drug prices, combat stigma and confront the overwhelming impact of AIDS on African countries.

Initially ambivalence was fueled by the stereotype of AIDS as a gay white men's disease—the pattern among white South Africans and the one most widely publicized until the mid-1990s. The pandemic also hit South Africa relatively late. Given the lag between infection and the onset of AIDS, and the stigma-based reluctance to identify AIDS as the cause of death, AIDS only ranked 12th in statistics on the causes of death as late as 1995. Top South African leaders, preoccupied with the transition to democracy in the mid-1990s and with a host of issues after the democratically elected government took power, failed to take AIDS seriously enough.

South African President Thabo M. Mbeki, who succeeded Mandela in 1999, bears much of the responsibility for the continuing failure. While AIDS activists and medical professionals agree that President Mbeki is correct in pointing to the close links between poverty and AIDS, they reject his doubts about the connection between HIV and AIDS, his use of outdated statistics, and his government's refusal to maximize use of AIDS drugs to stop mother-to-child transmission and to prolong the lives of those living with AIDS.

Nevertheless, it was the 13th international conference on AIDS, hosted by South Africa in July 2000, that marked the beginning of world attention to AIDS in Africa. In the year that followed that conference, AIDS activists and the South African government joined in defense against a pharmaceutical company lawsuit that had challenged a South African law making it easier to obtain AIDS drugs more cheaply. In response to worldwide media attention and activist support, the companies withdrew the suit.

FOREIGN POLICY ASSOCIATION

THABO M. MBEKI, *thought by many to be slow in recognizing the seriousness of AIDS, speaks to a Foreign Policy Association World Leadership Forum, September 2000.*

The debate in the South African government and wider society about what to do remains intense. Medical professionals both within and outside the government warn of the dangers of continued ambivalence. Church and trade union leaders have joined AIDS activists in demanding action, comparing the crisis to a new apartheid. But the outcome is uncertain. ■

Overcoming a global challenge

If African countries are left to confront the HIV/AIDS pandemic with the small level of outside support they have received to date, few are likely to succeed in checking or reducing the pandemic. And success in any one country can easily be reversed due to the spread of AIDS among neighboring countries. No state is an island when it comes to AIDS, and there are no national fire walls. At an African summit on HIV/AIDS in April 2001, government leaders pledged to try to increase their health budgets to some 15% of expenditures. But they will have little chance of meeting this pledge unless foreign debts are cancelled or substantially reduced and unless economic growth and capital inflow expand far more rapidly than anyone predicts. Even if such budget commitments are achieved, they would fall far short of meeting the challenge.

The U.S., with less than 20,000 people a year dying of AIDS, spends almost $11 billion on HIV/AIDS. Less than 5% of this amount goes for efforts to combat the pandemic internationally, where AIDS kills 3 million people a year. At the special session of the UN General Assembly on HIV/AIDS held in New York in June 2001, the world's nations affirmed that AIDS is a global threat and that fighting the pandemic is a global responsibility. They also pledged to support UN Secretary General Annan's target of $10 billion a year for a global health fund. The sum is very modest in comparison with developed countries' budgets and economies, but the question for the U.S. and other wealthy countries remains whether they will ante up.

Prevention, treatment, research

At the UN special session in June 2001, the world's governments agreed that treatment and prevention were both essential, and that research must give greater attention to the search for a vaccine, particularly for strains of HIV in the most affected regions. Despite such general agreement, however, disagreements in practice on priorities still have profound implications. In 2001, for example, investment in research on a vaccine for AIDS still accounted for less than 1% of health research and development worldwide. U.S. officials still refused to acknowledge the urgent need for access to antiretroviral treatment for Africans.

Until 2000, few questioned the fact that Africans had little or no access to antiretroviral drugs that in 1996 had begun to slow the death toll from AIDS in the U.S. and other developed countries. AIDS activists protesting against artificially high drug prices and the worldwide attention that followed the Durban conference in July 2000 led to a dramatic shift in world opinion. The case of Brazil's successful government program, which supplies low-cost treatment to all who need it, showed that treatment not only prolongs lives but also provides an incentive for people to be tested. In countries that offer no hope of treatment, the odds are stacked against persuading those infected to be tested and join prevention efforts. The consensus grew that treatment and prevention are both essential and intrinsically interrelated.

The U.S. government, despite signing on to the conference consensus, continued to deny funding and to lobby against including antiretroviral treatment in multilateral programs for poor countries. USAID (U.S. Agency for International Development) administrator Andrew Natsios touched off a furor of protest when in an interview with the *The Boston Globe,* June 7, 2001, he claimed Africans could not follow instructions for taking AIDS medicines because they "don't know what Western time is....Many people in Africa have never seen a clock or a watch their entire lives." AIDS protesters and medical professionals attacked Natsios's statement as reflecting both racist indifference to African lives and ignorance of the medical facts about AIDS treatment. U.S. officials have acknowledged that Natsios's statement may have been insensitive, but he has issued no retraction and the U.S. has not abandoned its opposition to making antiretroviral treatment widely available in Africa.

The issue of patents

Lack of access to antiretrovirals is linked to many factors, but above all to cost. In the U.S. a full course of "triple therapy" costs between $10,000 and $15,000 a year. Manufacturing costs represent much less than 5% of that price: indeed, Indian generic drug manufacturer Cipla offers the combination drug at $350 a year. The high prices result from drug-company patents giving monopoly pricing power to the original manufacturers, protected by vigorous lobbying against use of generics on the part of drug companies and their home governments, particularly the U.S.

In fact these patents are determined by national laws and do not yet apply in many countries, including India and many African nations. International trade rules also explicitly provide for the right of countries to take such measures as granting "compulsory licenses" to meet urgent public health needs. Brazil, for one, has aggressively taken advantage of its rights to pressure drug companies for lower prices and to defend the right to manufacture its own generic varieties of the drugs. Most African countries, however, have lacked the will or capacity to challenge the drug companies.

Ironically, the drug companies helped fuel an international campaign against their pricing policies by bringing a suit in 1998 against Mandela to block new legislation that would give South Africa greater flexibility in purchasing and manufacturing medicines. The suit delayed implementation of the law by at least three years. But by the time it was due to come to trial in March 2001, South Africa's Treatment Action Campaign (TAC) had been joined by supporters worldwide, including groups

AP/WIDE WORLD PHOTOS

UN SECRETARY GENERAL *Kofi Annan, background second from left, and others unfurl an AIDS memorial quilt at the opening of a three-day session on AIDS, June 25, 2001.*

such as Doctors without Borders, Oxfam, ACT-UP and Africa Action, to mobilize against it. These protests—and widespread media coverage—resulted in the companies dropping the suit. The U.S. government also moderated its stance.

Some African governments, including Nigeria and Kenya, made plans to import generic antiretrovirals from India. Drug companies reacting to public exposure and to competition began to lower their own prices, and even offered some products free to developing countries. But the companies continued to argue that they needed strong patent protection and high prices to provide capital for research and development of new drugs. Critics responded that the drug companies had among the highest profit rates of any industry and that much of the research on drugs was in any case funded by the public sector.

In 2001, the debate on affordable drugs for AIDS continued in two major arenas: criteria for drug purchases by international agencies and international trade rules. In both, the U.S. government joined with the pharmaceutical companies in opposing greater flexibility. Advocates of affordable medicines argued that international health agencies should create a database of available drugs and pricing, and that the new Global Health Fund and other buyers should be able to choose the best quality and lowest-cost alternatives, including generic products. The developing-countries group, with the support of international nongovernmental organizations, successfully pushed for explicit statements within the context of WTO talks that trade rules, including the agreement on Trade-Related Intellectual Property Rights (TRIPS), should not be used to hamper countries' efforts to make drugs affordable.

In contrast, U.S. officials argued that voluntary price discounts by drug companies were adequate and that strong patents were vital to preserving incentives for research on new drugs. They also contended that the existing TRIPS agreement provided all the flexibility countries needed to manage their health policies, and that no clarification was needed.

Public investment issue

Cost estimates for HIV/AIDS prevention, treatment and support in low- and middle-income countries worldwide run between $7 billion and $10 billion a year, as much as five times current levels. These estimates do not include funds for research, for general health infrastructure, or for alleviating the economic impact from the loss of human resources. The poignant questions are: Who will pay? And what are the consequences if no one does?

The sums are in fact very small compared with government budgets or national economies in the well-endowed countries. A U.S. commitment of some $3 billion a year, a sum appropriate to the U.S. share in the world economy, would be equivalent, for example, to only 1% of the U.S. defense budget, less than one tenth of the tax rebate sent to U.S. taxpayers in 2001, and only 50% more than the cost of one B-2 bomber.

African countries must also shift their own budget priorities, but many are still paying more each year in debt service to international financial institutions than they spend on health: Sub-Saharan African countries spend about $13.5 billion a year to service their foreign debt. Since 1996, the World Bank and the International Monetary Fund (IMF), together with bilateral creditors, have managed a program for debt reduction for heavily indebted poor countries (HIPC). Even World Bank analysts agree that implementation of this has been slow and that today the remaining debt burden of most countries is still unsustainable. Almost all of the remaining debt is owed to the international financial institutions themselves, the result of perpetual recycling of earlier debt with new loans being used to pay off old ones rather than to service new productive investment.

Even before recent attention to the HIV/AIDS pandemic, African countries and international campaigners for debt relief or cancellation argued that more drastic action was needed to erase unpayable debts. Not only is the debt unsustainable and a primary obstacle to new development efforts, but much of it was also illegitimate in the first place, incurred to bolster undemocratic regimes such as Mobutu Sese Seko in the Congo and the apartheid regime in South Africa. Even conservative business analysts have concurred there is no point to pretending the loans can be paid and that there should be an international equivalent to domestic bankruptcy procedures for individuals and businesses. UN Secretary General Annan has proposed temporary suspension of debt payments from the most indebted countries, along with a new international commission to find a sustainable solution, including debtors as well as creditors, in contrast to the creditor-dominated HIPC process.

Ironically, in 2001, the World Bank's own new initiatives on HIV/AIDS were still in the form of loans, increasing African indebtedness, despite critics (including the incoming U.S. secretary of the treasury) who argued that it was better to acknowledge from the start that grants rather than loans were needed. Some countries, like Malawi, have turned down offers of loans for AIDS programs because they would only increase indebtedness that already undermines the health-care system.

The Global Health Fund launched by Annan, with the target of raising $7 billion to $10 billion a year, was projected to be operational by the beginning of 2002. In late 2001, however, pledges still fell far short of the goal—only $1.5 billion—much of it for multiyear periods.

The U.S. had promised only $200 million for its initial contribution to the Global Health Fund. In the aftermath of the UN special session, some members of Congress had proposed larger sums, but these became even more marginalized after 9/11.

Continued failure to match the scale of the pandemic with adequate responses to combat it will impose massive costs on the U.S. as well as African countries. The loss of human lives, the collapse of economies, and the spread of instability will heighten global insecurity in both predictable and unpredictable ways. The cost of new humanitarian and security requirements will, within 10 years or less, far exceed the cost of "scaling up" action now. The question remains: Will the U.S. and other developed countries have the vision to join Africa now in confronting the pandemic or will the failure of imagination and solidarity persist?

U.S. policy options

❑ **1. The U.S. government should commit at least $3 billion a year to the Global Health Fund and other channels for combating the HIV/AIDS pandemic and the wider health emergency it represents. Both moral obligation and national security require the U.S. to give priority to global health.**

Pro: There are many reasons that the U.S. should contribute to combating HIV/AIDS in proportion to its share in the world economy and its role in global leadership. In addition to the moral obligation to defend the global right to health, the consequences of continued failure to establish a base level of human security against disease will damage not only Africa but also the U.S. If nations collapse, they will provide ongoing reservoirs for the worldwide export of humanitarian crises and terrorism.

Con: Granted, the U.S. government could do more, but there are many higher priorities for official U.S. resources, both domestic and international. The U.S. is already the largest bilateral donor to international AIDS efforts and filling the gap should be left to private foundations, businesses and other nongovernmental initiatives, including faith-based programs.

❑ **2. The U.S. should support cancellation of unpayable debts owed by African and other developing countries to the World Bank and the IMF. Access to new grants and loans should be linked to the capacity to implement effective development programs, including combating disease and promoting public health.**

Pro: Most African countries are still paying out unsustainable amounts to the international institutions that are supposed to be promoting development. The chances for scaling up national investment in health care, including specific measures against HIV/AIDS, are slim without significant debt cancellation.

Con: Canceling debt would erode the future creditworthiness of African countries and would not provide significant new resources for other purposes. The HIPC debt-reduction programs should be continued and expanded.

❑ **3. In both bilateral programs and support for multilateral efforts, the U.S. government should follow a balanced approach to combating HIV/AIDS. It should put equal emphasis on prevention and treatment and place a high priority on the search for a vaccine.**

Pro: Providing treatment as well as prevention is not only a moral imperative: In the U.S., even with the high cost of drugs, it has lowered total health costs by keeping more patients out of hospitals; Brazil has had even greater success along these lines and has reduced AIDS-related deaths by 50%. In Africa, prolonging life and enabling more people to remain productive members of society is also essential for reducing the loss of skilled professionals and workers, and enabling more parents to raise their children. In the long run, greater investment in the search for a vaccine is the only hope for victory over AIDS.

Con: Those arguments might be convincing if there were enough money to go around. Prevention is still more cost-effective in terms of future lives saved than treatment to prolong the lives of people who are doomed anyway.

❑ **4. The U.S. should endorse the developing countries' position explicitly stating that nothing in current or future trade agreements should be interpreted to "curtail the ability of developing and least-developed-country members to avail themselves of every possible policy option to protect and promote public health."**

Pro: Patents are a temporary monopoly and both national and international law have recognized that exceptions can be made to defend the public interest. The U.S. should join in unequivocally affirming the priority of public health over the most expansive interpretations of patent rights.

Con: There is ample flexibility in current regulations for countries to take the actions they need to get essential drugs for their citizens. The problem is not trade rules but lack of policy consistency and adequate financing. Announcing greater flexibility would encourage abuse by generic drug manufacturers, at the expense of U.S. companies.

❑ **5. Both in bilateral relations with African countries and in the policies it advocates for multilateral financial institutions, the U.S. should stop promoting a one-sided economic agenda that advances trade liberalization and budget cutting, at the expense of productive public investment in health, education and infrastructure. Instead, it should work with African governments, civil society and development specialists to implement balanced development policies that can address the structural roots of Africa's marginalization in today's world economy.**

Pro: The standard package of economic policies promoted by the U.S. and the World Bank should include adequate investment in health, education and all kinds of infrastructure. In the long-term, "free-market fundamentalism" is bad economics. African countries will never be able to have self-sustaining economies unless both African governments and their partners make adequate investments in human resources.

Con: Health, education and other such investments are important. But African countries must first get their economies straightened out so that they can generate enough resources to make these investments. The best way to do that is to open their economies to the world market, attract foreign investment and increase exports. ■

OPINION BALLOTS are on pages 69–70

DISCUSSION QUESTIONS

1. Imagine you are a participant in a cabinet meeting in an African country, considering the national response to a commission reporting that one third of your citizens is likely to die of AIDS. What would you say if you were the minister of health? The minister of finance? The foreign minister?

2. Just before the world AIDS conference in South Africa in July 2000, UNAIDS director Peter Piot commented on the world's failure to respond to the worst pandemic in human history. "If this had happened with white people," he said, "the reaction would have been different." Many AIDS activists charge that the world's response to the pandemic reflects an international "double standard" in which black lives are valued less than white lives. Do you agree? Why, or why not?

3. The constitution of the World Health Organization, adopted in 1946, says "The enjoyment of the highest attainable standard of health is one of the fundamental rights of every human being without distinction of race, religion, political belief and economic or social condition." The U.S. government opposes any "rights-based" approach to HIV/AIDS and other health or socio-economic problems, saying that this might create legal obligations that governments are unwilling or unable to fulfill. Do you agree? Why, or why not?

4. In your opinion, under what circumstances should patent protection for a drug be suspended in the public interest? What do you think is the most effective way to encourage research in the interest of global public health?

5. What is the relationship between investment in public health and economic growth? Discuss to what extent public health advances are results of economic growth, and to what extent they are requirements for economic growth. What are the likely results, for Africa and the world, of failure to control the AIDS pandemic?

READINGS AND RESOURCES

Baylies, Carolyn, and Bujra, Janet, **Aids, Sexuality and Gender in Africa: Collective Strategies and Struggles in Tanzania and Zambia.** New York, Taylor and Francis, 2001. 256 pp. $25.95 (paper). Essays by African scholars.

Farmer, Paul, **Infections and Inequalities: The Modern Plagues.** Berkeley and Los Angeles, University of California Press, 2001. 389 pp. $17.95 (paper). Essential book on the connection between disease and poverty by a physician with extensive personal experience in Haiti.

Garbus, Lisa, "Sub-Saharan Africa: Profile." AIDS Reseach Institute, University of California, San Francisco, May 2001. **http://hivinsite.ucsf.edu/InSite.jsp?page=cr-02-01**

Garrett, Laurie, **The Coming Plague: Newly Emerging Diseases in a World Out of Balance.** New York, Viking Penguin, 1995. 730 pp. $15.95 (paper). Chapter 11 of this book provides a well-informed account of the first decade of HIV/AIDS in both North America and Africa.

Rosenberg, Tina, "Look at Brazil," **The New York Times Magazine**, January 28, 2001, p. 26+. **www.nytimes.com/library/magazine/home/20010128mag-aids**

Whiteside, Alan, and Sunter, Clem, **AIDS: The Challenge for South Africa.** Cape Town, Human & Rousseau, 2001. 180 pp. $10.95 (paper). Written for South Africans, this book summarizes the facts about the pandemic and its impact, and calls for national action against it on many fronts.

AFRICA ACTION, 110 Maryland Ave., NE, #508, Washington, DC 20002; (202) 546-7961; Fax (202) 546-1545. **www.africapolicy.org.** ▪ Information and advocacy group on African issues, with a current focus on "Africa's Right to Health."

CENTERS FOR DISEASE CONTROL AND PREVENTION (CDC), 1600 Clifton Rd., Atlanta, GA 30333; (404) 639-3534; (800) 311-3435. **www.cdc.gov** ▪ U.S. government agency conducts programs aimed at understanding infectious diseases and creating practical strategies to fight epidemics.

GLOBAL TREATMENT ACCESS CAMPAIGN. www.globaltreatmentaccess.org. ▪ Coalition of groups working for affordable AIDS drugs and essential medicines. Website has current news and action alerts.

THE HENRY J. KAISER FAMILY FOUNDATION, 2400 Sand Hill Road, Menlo Park, CA 94025; (650) 854-9400; Fax: (650) 854-4800. **www.kff.org.** ▪ Website provides background publications, statistics, and access to a daily news service on HIV/AIDS-related issues.

JOINT UNITED NATIONS PROGRAM ON HIV/AIDS (UNAIDS), 20 Avenue Appia, CH-1211 Geneva 27, Switzerland; (41-22) 791-36-66; Fax (41-22) 791-4187. **www.unaids.org** ▪ UNAIDS is the coordinating agency for UN action on HIV/AIDS. Its website has documents and links with the most recent and comprehensive reports and conference proceedings.

TREATMENT ACTION CAMPAIGN (TAC), PO Box 31104, Braamfontein, 2017, South Africa; (27-11) 403-7021 or (27-21) 403-0390; Fax (27-11) 403-2106. **www. tac.org.za.** ▪ TAC is a leading AIDS activists group in South Africa.

WORLD HEALTH ORGANIZATION (WHO), Avenue Appia 20, 1211 Geneva 27, Switzerland; (41-22) 791-2111; Fax (41-22) 791-3111. **www.who.org** ▪ UN's chief health organization provides up-to-date information on current health concerns.

LEARN MORE ABOUT THIS TOPIC AT *www.greatdecisions.org*

Access links to online resources • Order the recommended readings • Take the GD Quiz • Find maps in the online atlas • Submit your opinion ballots • Read the latest National Opinion Ballot Report • and more ...

Russia reexamined: new politics and economy

Recent events necessitate a reexamination of Russia's political and economic systems and a reassessment of its relationship with the U.S.

by Allen Lynch

AFP PHOTO/ANATOLY MALTSEV

MOSCOW STREET VENDOR *opens matrioska doll portraying President Vladimir Putin, with former President Boris Yeltsin doll underneath.*

THE TERRORIST ATTACKS on the U.S. on September 11, 2001, have helped redefine U.S.-Russian relations. For most of the 1990s, Russia was predominantly an object of and/or an obstacle to U.S. policies: U.S. attention focused primarily on Russia's domestic transition away from communism and its efforts to establish elements of a market economy and a representative democracy. The U.S. expended considerable resources in an attempt to remake Russia along Western political and economic lines, as well as to help reduce and protect Russia's extensive military and civilian nuclear-materials stockpiles. Russia had frequently been seen as an impediment to U.S. foreign policy objectives, whether it was Russian resistance to admitting former Soviet satellite states to the North Atlantic Treaty Organization (NATO), its sponsorship of Serbian President Slobodan Milosevic, the cultivation of a special relationship focused on nuclear reactors with Iran, or Russian resistance to the economic embargo of Iraq.

The events of September 11 changed this. Almost immediately, Russia became a valued partner of the U.S. as it sought to cement the broadest possible international coalition against international terrorism. Within days of the attacks, the U.S. stopped criticizing Russian military operations in Chechnya, which were often fairly characterized as terroristic themselves, and linked its campaign against Osama bin Laden with Moscow's campaign to crush Chechen armed resistance to Russian rule. Russian President Vladimir Putin's public support of the U.S. position on terrorism was quickly followed by increased Russian arms deliveries to Afghanistan's Northern Alliance. Long embittered by what Russia's ruling elite saw as the U.S. belittlement of Moscow's international role—epitomized by NATO's bombing of Russian ally Serbia in spring 1999—the Russian government has jumped at the opportunity to play the role of American ally and interlocutor. Be-

ALLEN LYNCH *is professor of government and foreign affairs at the University of Virginia and is the director of the university's Center for Russian and East European Studies. He has written numerous articles for the Foreign Policy Association.*

MICHAEL SAMUEL GRAPHICS

cause of its cooperation in securing maximum U.S. access to Afghanistan, Russia will now likely receive U.S. support for establishing a solid sphere of influence in the vast and fragile Central Asian regions of the former Soviet Union. In short, the traumatic atrocities of September 11 have shifted the focus of U.S.-Russian relations from Russia's internal affairs to the intersection between its international interests and those of the U.S.

In 1999, President Putin consolidated his political authority following a series of (allegedly Chechen) terrorist attacks on Russian apartment buildings that resulted in the loss of nearly 300 lives. This shifted domestic priorities from democratization to establishing a state that has the capacity to rule. Russia may now count upon the U.S. to reinforce President Putin's domestic position.

Be that as it may, the fact remains that Russia is still a weak government at home and a weak state abroad. What kind of partner may the U.S. expect Russia to be in the years ahead? What does the condition of Russia's economy and the evolution of the Russian political system portend for Russia's place in the international order? Finally, what are the prospects for Russian-American relations? ■

Russia's continuing (and hidden) economic crisis

HAVING EXPERIENCED a probably unprecedented economic decline throughout the 1990s, the Russian economy finished the decade with unexpectedly good news. After the 70% drop in the ruble's value in August 1998, Russian domestic production picked up. The rise in world oil prices—between January 1999 and summer 2000 the price of oil increased from $9 to $35 per barrel—has filled official Russian coffers, enabling the state to finance the war in Chechnya and still meet its external debt-servicing obligations as well as wages and pension arrears at home. Russian gross domestic product (GDP) was up approximately 8.3% in 2000, versus 1998 when it fell by 4.8%. It was projected to rise by 4% to 5% in 2001. Exports in this period grew by 46% and real income by 9%. Russia now has a budget surplus of 90 billion rubles (about $3.2 billion) and a positive balance of trade. Thus, the short-term picture is rosier than many anticipated in the aftermath of the Russian financial crash.

Yet, the structural fundamentals of the Russian economy are hardly as strong as the recent data would appear to suggest. Russia's dollarized GDP i half that of the Netherlands and its foreign trade turnover is similar to Denmark's. Its exports are dominated by oil and gas and are virtually nonexistent in other, value-added sectors.

The consequences of Russia's decade-long economic decline have been dramatic, not only for Russia's internal condition but also for its international standing. By the end of the 1990s China, which had more than doubled its national income in the 1980s and again in the 1990s, was beginning to approach and perhaps even to exceed Russia in

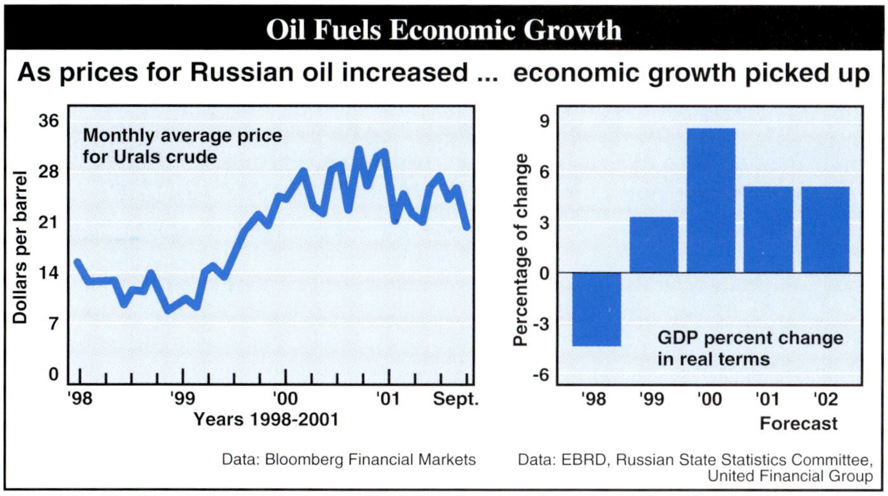

MICHAEL SAMUEL GRAPHICS

several indicators of economic development.

This represents one of the most astounding changes in the economic balance of power ever to have taken place between two major countries in such a short period of time.

Russia's increasingly obsolete capital stock requires annual investment of some $50 billion per year over the next decade. If Russia is to prosper it must inject massive amounts of capital to repair, maintain and develop the country's industrial, transportation and communications infrastructure. Without such investment, Russian Prime Minister Mikhail Kasyanov has stated, Russia "will remain in the backyard of the world economy." Yet capital investment in Russia in the late 1990s was less than a fifth of the 1990 level. As a result, the capital stock of the country is rapidly wearing out.

Breaking down Russia's investment requirements by sector provides a better sense of the urgency and scale of the problem. Much of the Russian railway system, which accounts for 73% of all freight moved in Russia, is considered by Western observers to be in "very poor repair." On the highways, "poor road quality" means lower truck speeds and thus higher transport costs. Forty percent of Russia's villages cannot be reached on tarmac roads, and there are no Western-type highways in the whole country. Russia's ports are generally in a "poor state of repair," according to the Economist Intelligence Unit, while its maritime fleet is the oldest in the world. Fully half of Russia's electricity generation and distribution network, as well as the industry's fixed assets, are past their intended productive lives, the consequence being, *The Economist* (London) says, that "Russia could face serious supply squeezes by the middle of the decade."

Even in the critical oil and gas sector, which typically earns half of Russia's hard-currency export receipts and accounts for as much as 40% of the federal government's budget revenues, exploratory drilling in 1999 was about one fifth what it had been in 1990, a figure that corresponds to the depreciation of Russian capital stock across sectors. As existing oil fields are depleted and fewer new ones are coming into production, Russian oil output continues to decline. Annual investment of $10 billion to $11 billion over the next 20 years will be required in the oil sector alone. Meanwhile, Russian oil companies have been quite active in Western investment markets. Lukoil, for example, has opened 1,300 gas stations in the U.S. under the "Getty" name.

In these circumstances, Russia's short- to medium-term economic prospects are highly constrained. A decade or more of neglect of infrastructure cannot be made up easily. For example, in 2000, in response to the rise in world oil prices, Russian producers decided to increase production significantly. Yet they could at most squeeze out an extra 20 million tons (about 7% of total production), mainly by opening old wells that had been mothballed.

Unified Energy Systems, the state electricity monopoly, requires $30 billion to $50 billion in capital investment over the next decade, but currently has no plans for investing in generating equipment in 2001. Some of the consequences may be seen in the widespread collapse of the power infrastructure in Arctic Russia and the Far East where, in mid-January 2001, with temperatures of -4°F, there were daily 15-hour power cuts. Anatoly Chubais, head of the Unified Energy System, explained that the municipal energy system had been destroyed. "Locking attachments and materials of nonferrous metals have been stolen. The pipelines are run down. They have been hit by the freezing temperatures. The heating units lack essential parts. The basements in buildings are partially flooded."

The telecommunications industry requires approximately $40 billion in capital investment over the next decade. Comparable sums would have to be invested in the railroad system, the ports, the oil and gas complex, highways, etc.

Why is getting capital investment such a daunting task in Russia? In general, production costs in Russia—especially for large-scale, outdoor infrastructure—tend to be quite high. The severity of Russia's climate, the vast-

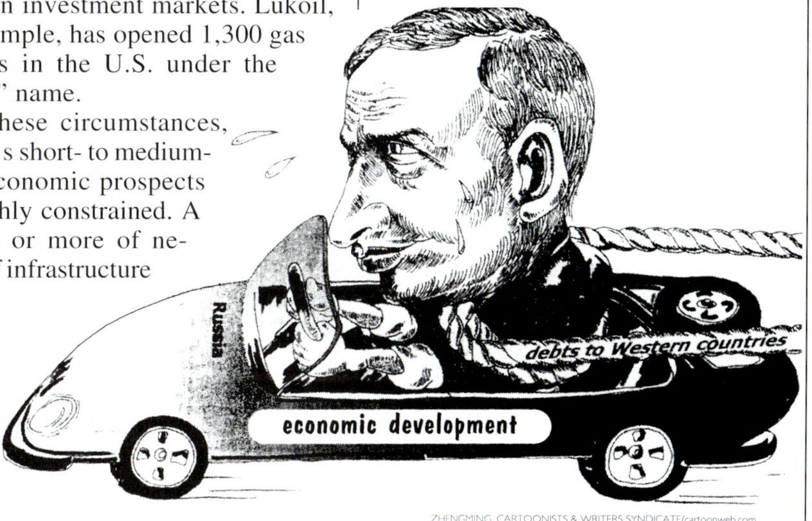

ZHENGMING, CARTOONISTS & WRITERS SYNDICATE/cartoonweb.com

AP/WIDE WORLD PHOTOS

A HEAVY ROLLER *crushes computer discs containing pirated software into the ground at the Khmetyevo dump site near Moscow. Pirated software accounts for more than 90% of the Russian computer-software market according to official estimates.*

ness of the Russian space and a reliance on land transport instead of cheaper sea transport mean that in most areas of the Russian economy infrastructure and production costs are two to three times as much as almost anywhere else in the world. Because private investors will turn to the world's more attractive investment possibilities, it is questionable whether Russia can develop under predominantly liberal-market auspices. An economy that protects Russian industry and directs resources from profitable (mainly natural resource based) sectors to unprofitable but vital sectors and regions is essential to the country's welfare.

What conclusions may be drawn? First, on strictly liberal-market grounds, most of the Russian economy should be declared bankrupt. As Columbia University economist Richard Ericson has observed, "A large proportion of [Russian] firms in any industry, and all firms in some basic processing industries, are nonviable in the most basic sense—they can never produce goods that could sell for more than the cost of production." By 1998, nearly 49% of Russian enterprises were operating in the red (under admittedly opaque Russian accounting practices).

Second, taking geography seriously underscores that there is an enormous difference between resources that exist and those that are economically viable to extract. The huge initial costs of development associated with Siberian investment, particularly at a time of political and legal uncertainties, have deterred foreign and Russian investors from paying for new systems of production. The physical inaccessibility of much of Russia's oil and gas reserves means that they are, in the words of one Russian economist, "no more accessible than methane from Jupiter." Climate and geographical factors apply much less, if at all, in indoor industries. There, legal and administrative uncertainties present an obstacle, as do other barriers specific to certain businesses. For example, there is no intrinsic reason why Russia should not be a worldwide software leader. But the inability of the Russian state to contain software piracy places it at a clear competitive disadvantage when compared with India, which also has even lower labor costs, more widespread use of English and the aid of the government.

Third, under these circumstances, it is clear that liberal economic premises apply far less to Russia than the famous "Washington consensus" of the 1990s presumed. Russia as a whole cannot be developed economically without the state. The Russian economy experienced the fastest growth rate in the world in the several decades before 1914 and modernized sufficiently, if brutally, to survive the Nazi onslaught and harass the U.S. for nearly half a century. Russia has thus modernized when it has been open to the West and when it has been closed to it; it has also modernized in the presence of the market and without it. Yet in each of these cases, the Russian state played a decisive role. Russia has never developed under conditions of free movement of capital and possibly cannot do so.

This does not mean there is no place for the market in the Russian economy. But in a liberal world economic order, why should capital flow to a Russia whose costs of development are typically two to three times higher than almost anywhere else in the world, even with cheap and relatively skilled labor? The corrupt and criminalized state that prevails today is a further deterrent to investment. As Thane Gustafson has observed, "The quasi-stabilization we see in Russia today, founded on what remains of the Soviet inheritance, is not viable over the longer run, because it cannot generate growth and prosperity." Russia desperately needs a state structure and state policies to compensate for the many inherent disadvantages that the country faces as a result of its economic geography. There is plenty of room to debate the kinds of state policies and their relationship to the market economy—for example, the degree of tariff protection; the most beneficial currency valuation, industrial policy, redistribution of wealth; the degree of free movement of goods and capital; the relative importance of state and private ownership and so on. But holders of capital, whatever their nationality, can no longer be coerced into financing Russian development. They must be persuaded to do so. At a minimum, some combination of a weak ruble, targeted protectionism, production-sharing agreements for foreign investors and a legal basis for trading in land to stimulate domestic mortgage, loan and insurance markets would seem to be required to encourage substantial direct investment in Russia and the prospects of a sustained recovery. Other tools of persuasion must include clear, stable and enforceable property rights and transparent corporate governance. ■

The evolution of Russia's political system: from Yeltsin to Putin

THE EXTREME CONCENTRATION of political power in the hands of the Russian president was illustrated by the political crisis of March 1998, in which President Boris N. Yeltsin sacked Viktor Chernomyrdin, his prime minister of more than five-years' standing and appointed a virtual unknown, the young Sergei Kiriyenko, in his stead. According to the Russian Constitution, the president may submit a candidate to the Duma three times for approval; if the Duma refuses each time, the president may dissolve the parliament.

What Yeltsin did in the spring of 1998 demonstrated the extent of presidential contempt for parliamentary prerogatives: He submitted Kiriyenko's name three times to the parliament, in effect daring the parliament to turn his candidate down. On the third vote, the Duma, given Yeltsin's record of violence and the risk of losing a number of valuable privileges attendant upon parliamentary status (including immunity from prosecution, no small thing in today's Russia), gave in and allowed the installment of Kiriyenko as head of government.

This open flaunting of executive power was only the surface of the story. Behind the scenes, in what amounted to Yeltsin's court, key members of what Russians called "the family" were desperately searching for an eventual successor to Yeltsin who could constrain the Communists and extreme nationalists from coming to power and thereby also protect the family from having its newly privatized wealth expropriated and from criminal prosecution.

Increasingly alarmed at the deteriorating state of Yeltsin's health and the Russian economic crash of August 1998, Yeltsin's entourage acceded to the appointment of the parliament's candidate, Yevgeny Primakov, as prime minister in September 1998, only to undermine him as soon as possible. In May 1999, Primakov was replaced by Sergei Stepashin, a career police official, who at the end of August was replaced by Vladimir Putin, a lower-ranking career intelligence officer who had previously been deputy in charge of Kremlin property. The prime criterion in Putin's advancement appears to have been his personal loyalty to Yeltsin and others advancing his career toward the top, as well as an apparent determination to wield power aggressively in light of another war looming in Chechnya. Without Yeltsin's court, and in disregard of Russia's formal constitutional mechanisms, a Putin—a middle-ranking career intelligence officer with no political constituency, a complete unknown upon assuming office in August 1999—could never have come to power. Such was the desiccation of the Russian political system after nearly a decade of political and economic "reform."

Dramatic developments dominated Russian politics at the turn of the century. At the end of December, Yeltsin announced suddenly that he would resign effective January 1, 2000, in favor of Putin. Putin's first act of state as acting president was to sign a decree granting Yeltsin full immunity from prosecution. This seemed to bear out the hopes that the family placed in him. Putin did, however, take actions that forced Boris Berezovsky and other "oligarchs" like Vladimir Gusinsky into foreign exile and even arrest.

According to the Russian Constitution, presidential elections must be held within three months of the sitting president's resignation. When Putin submitted himself to the electorate, he received 53% of the vote in the first round, ensuring his inauguration as president of the Russian Federation in May 2000, for a four-year term.

The confidence that Yeltsin's entourage had in Putin winning the presidential election was based on the remarkable surge of nationalist sentiment in favor of Putin following the government's prosecution of the second war against Chechnya in the 1990s. The public had been skeptical of the government's first war in Chechnya in 1994–96, but a series of five bomb blasts in the first half of September 1999 in Moscow, where nearly 300 people were killed, and southern Russia galvanized public opinion, which saw this war in Chechnya as a defense of the interests of the Russian

AP/WIDE WORLD PHOTOS

CHECHEN CHILDREN *warm themselves at a bonfire in Karabulak refugee camp near the Chechen border, January 2001. More than 200,000 refugees live in poorly heated tents and railway cars in northwest Chechnya and the neighboring Russian republic of Ingushetia.*

APWIDE WORLD PHOTOS

SURVIVORS OF BOMB EXPLOSION *carry their belongings from the site in Moscow, Friday, September 10, 1999. Moscow's Mayor Yuri Luzhkov claimed a bomb planted on the first floor caused the explosion.*

nation, behind the government. Tight media control, the apparent limiting of Russian casualties by massive bombarding of the Chechen capital city of Groznyy (which leveled much of the city) and fear about the spread of Chechen insurgency to neighboring areas of Russia's north Caucasus region, such as Dagestan, united Russian opinion behind the government.

The wave of pro-government political support propelled the pro-Putin Unity party, which had been created in September 1999, receiving 23.9% of party-list votes in the December 19, 1999, parliamentary elections, putting it in second place just behind the Communist party, which got 24.6%. Putin was elected as Russian president at the end of March.

Once again, Russia held national elections on schedule, as it has since 1989. And again, the government showed that it is capable of using the executive power of the state to structure electoral situations so as to strongly favor the government and to insulate the government from serious accountability once it is in power. Most important was not the outright stealing of votes but rather using the executive power of the government to influence the outcome. Thus, the government—and government-controlled and government friendly media, especially television—orchestrated (as it did for Yeltsin in 1996) a blitz of pro-Putin coverage, while excoriating opponents with libelous charges and giving them little or no opportunity to reply. More broadly, the government ably exploited the nationalist sentiments of Russians in the wake of the Moscow apartment bombings and used the second Chechen war to mobilize public opinion behind Putin. Antigovernment views were easily portrayed as antipatriotic, even treasonous. Thus, the one presidential candidate who dared to express even mild dissent from the government line on the Chechen war, Grigory Yavlinsky, saw his public support drop immediately and precipitously. The often wanton brutality displayed by the Russian Army in Chechnya, warranting a rebuke by the UN Commission on Human Rights on April 26, 2000, has had no appreciable effect on Russian public opinion.

Almost immediately upon election as Russian president, Putin began to streamline the operations of Russian government. No doubt, this was aimed at trying to improve the conditions for investment in the Russian economy, reduce the power of regional governors and strengthen the chain of command emanating from the Russian president's office. These measures included:

- reorganizing Russia's 89 regions within the framework of seven new super regions, corresponding to existing military districts and supervised by presidential appointees drawn mainly from the military and intelligence services;
- inducing the Duma to give Putin the authority to dismiss elected regional leaders if a court deemed that they had violated federal law more than once;
- reorganizing the upper house of the federal assembly by making seats subject to presidential appointment, thereby depriving regional leaders of a national forum and input on federal legislation.
- encouraging the merger of Russian political parties into one omnibus pro-government party, as reflected in the decision by Moscow mayor Yuri Luzhkov, once viciously attacked by Putin's supporters, to combine his Fatherland-All Russia party with Putin's Unity party. In the process, the parliament would be rendered even more of a tool of the Russian president.

The question remains, as ever: Is there a sufficient political and social consensus in Russia to allow the country's leader to amass enough political and administrative authority to encourage the influx of capital investment that is vital to Russia's prospects as a state, a nation and a civilization? As *The Economist* has put it, "The presidential administration remains fearsomely powerful. It is very wealthy, having inherited most of the Communist party's vast property holdings..., which provides it with a big sack of carrots. But the Kremlin lacks real administrative power to make things happen regularly and reliably, especially in the far-flung corners of the bureaucracy." ■

Prospects for Russian-American relations

THROUGHOUT MOST OF THE 1990s, the framework for partnership between Russia and the U.S. that had been established before 1989 by Mikhail Gorbachev and U.S. leaders continued to inform the priorities and direction of Russian foreign policy. By then the geopolitical focus and realist assumptions of the early Reagan era were beginning to yield to an increasing preoccupation with the internal consequences of Soviet disintegration and Russian economic and political transformations. Russian policy elites, for their part, welcomed not only the fundamentally warmer diplomatic relationship with the U.S. but the American effort to assist Russia's internal transformation to post-Soviet political and economic systems and to integrate the post-Soviet Russian state into the North Atlantic political economy and security system. By early 1997, however, the integrationist premises of Russian policy toward the U.S. were largely discredited in light of the granting of NATO membership to former Soviet allies in Eastern Europe and the unsatisfactory consequences of Russia's alleged liberal experiment in politics and economics of the previous five years. Any doubts in Russia on this score were removed in the wake of NATO's war in Serbia in the spring of 1999. What explains this apparent sea change in Russian-U.S. relations? How decisive is the break in the pattern of relations established in the late 1980s? What are its implications for the future contours of Moscow's relations with the U.S.?

That Russia and the U.S. are involved in a joint enterprise to advance important common interests and values has been prompted by two factors. These are, first, that each side's vital and primary interests are not at heart incompatible with those of the other. The second, and more novel assumption, presumes that there exists a compatibility of interests and values that can underwrite a relationship that goes beyond a simple détente. U.S. leaders have gone out of their way to demonstrate by word and deed, by acts of commission and omission, that they do not see their own vital or even primary interests threatened by those of the Russian Federation. Russia's vital interests are understood to include:

- the territorial integrity of the Russian Federation;
- the geopolitical primacy of Russia in the region described by the borders of the former Soviet Union;
- the security and stability of Russian nuclear weapons and other weapons of mass destruction;
- Russian economic development;
- Russia's status as a great international power; and
- maximal feasible peerage with the G-7 group of advanced industrial democracies.

By comparison, key U.S. interests with respect to Russia are not in conflict with those Russian interests just enumerated. These include:

- ensuring that no hostile, hegemonic power emerges in Eurasia that could threaten international security throughout Western Europe and the East Asian/Pacific rim;
- maintaining the security and stability of the Russian nuclear arsenal, as well as that of other weapons of mass destruction located across Russian and post-Soviet space;
- believing that conflict and instability throughout Russia's vital post-Soviet "geopolitical space," however troubling, does not warrant the commitment of serious U.S. political-military, economic or even diplomatic resources;
- supporting the continued territorial and political integrity of the Russian Federation, in part in order to assure effective control over weapons of mass destruction; and
- supporting Russian economic "reforms," in the conviction that "liberal" reforms would lay the foundation for long-term harmony in Russian-U.S. relations.

This is not to say that there were not serious conflicts in Russian-American relations throughout the 1990s, but those conflicts that arose tended to occur and to be addressed within a framework of relations in which neither side's vital interests were seen as conflicting with those of the other. A common group of values and interests has enabled each side to see specific conflicts within a broader developmental framework for Russian-American and Russian-Western relations. This shared broader conviction led to the establishment of the "Gore-Chernomyrdin" Commission headed by the U.S. vice-president and the Russian prime minister that addressed emerging conflicts in Russian-American relations. It was just one of several institutionalized arrangements for the transaction of Russian-Western relations in the 1990s. Others included the Contact Group of major powers which has dealt with various Balkan wars since 1994; the "G-7 plus 1" group of economic powers that has

AP/WIDE WORLD PHOTOS

PRESIDENT GEORGE W. BUSH *and Russian President Vladimir Putin walk down the Colonnade at the White House, November 13, 2001, after their Oval Office meeting.*

mollify Russian concerns about its great-power status; the highly structured and professional collaboration between Russian and American militaries in the field of nuclear-weapons dismantlement; and the fateful NATO-Russian Charter of May 1997. At heart, and running through each of these separate bodies, has been the question: To what extent has Russia's institutional participation in international agencies dominated by the West, particularly the U.S., been substantive as opposed to symbolic? More crudely, have Russia and the G-7 nations been able to find a way to transact their business with each other in ways that do not simply reflect the gross imbalance in international power in favor of the latter?

These questions assume greater urgency in the aftermath of the terror bombings in the U.S. and the Bush Administration's interest in leading a broad international alliance against terrorism. The challenge of dealing with international terrorism has underscored several features of the "post-post-cold-war" international order: First, military power, where the U.S. possesses the largest margin of superiority, applies to a very narrow range of cases. Second, in most other contexts, where the cooperation of other states is required, diplomacy and political discretion remain central. While the U.S. does have the power to block international policy initiatives along a broad range of issues, it can achieve little of enduring importance without the voluntary agreement of many states, Russia included, that have a complex set of coincident and divergent interests vis-à-vis the U.S.

Shift in U.S.-Russia relations

In fact, the terrible events of September 11 have propelled a basic shift in U.S.-Russian relations. Now that vital U.S. interests are at stake in an area—combating international terrorism—that requires substantial cooperation with Russia and a number of other states, America has shifted away from concern with the domestic transformation of Russian society. The U.S. government needs the cooperation of Russia in the following areas:

- legitimizing the antiterror campaign through the UN Security Council, where Russia, like Britain, France and China, wields veto power;
- providing U.S. troops with access to Afghanistan from neighboring countries where Russia has significant influence, such as Uzbekistan, Tajikistan and Turkmenistan;
- obtaining cooperation from Russian and other regional intelligence services; and
- delivery of weapons to allies within Afghanistan such as the Northern Alliance who have opposed Afghanistan's Taliban government.

The Russian government has a strong interest in responding positively to U.S. needs in fighting terrorist cells in Afghanistan. For years, Russia has been proclaiming the need to contain what it sees as radical Islamic fundamentalism from penetrating Russian client states in Central Asia and Russia itself, where one seventh of the population is Muslim. Moreover, cooperating with the U.S. in this field entails U.S. recognition of two central Russian foreign policy interests: neutralizing inter-

RUSSIAN SOLDIERS *tending a water-pumping machine used to drain a swampy site near Shchuchye, 975 miles southeast of Moscow, June 2001. The site will house Russia's largest facility to destroy chemical weapons.*

national criticism of the war that Russia is waging in Chechnya and accepting that Russia possesses a sphere of influence in Central Asia comparable to that which the U.S. has historically had in Central America and the Caribbean. From this point of view, it is Russia that will determine which states may involve themselves in this part of the world and under what terms.

More generally, U.S. courting of Russia after September 11 has brought relations with Russia to the forefront of U.S. foreign policy. In the process, the U.S. has tacitly accepted long-standing Russian preferences in the bilateral relationship: the U.S. focus on the intersection of each state's international interests rather than upon Russia's domestic affairs and Russia being an indispensable power in any global security order. Clearly, any eventual establishment of a less hostile government in Afghanistan will require Russian cooperation within the UN Security Council and in the region itself.

APWIDE WORLD PHOTOS

A NORTHERN ALLIANCE FIGHTER *rides a bicycle past a Russian T-55 tank at the last defense line 19 miles north of Kabul, September 2001. Northern opposition forces prefer the Soviet-era weapons they know best.*

Tensions of terrorist crisis

The terrorist crisis besetting the U.S. has thrown into sharp relief the tensions between previous U.S. policies, especially the tendency to resort to unilateral methods in foreign policy and the conditions that would encourage other states to collaborate with the U.S. As far as U.S. policy toward Russia is concerned, this entails:

- the tension between U.S. ideological principles on the one hand (for example human rights and democratization) and pragmatic interstate interests of power;
- the tension between U.S. criticism of Russian military conduct in Chechnya and the requirement of obtaining Russian military and intelligence cooperation on Afghanistan;
- the importance of basing rights in states like Uzbekistan and Tajikistan, against concern over the human-rights records of those states, which the U.S. State Department and the independent organization Freedom House have called among the most repressive governments in the world;
- expansion of the NATO alliance and U.S. plans for a national missile defense—each of which assumes that the U.S. can maximize its security without Russian cooperation—versus the need for such cooperation.

The three-day summit between presidents Bush and Putin in November pointed up both the strengths and limits of the relationship between the two countries. The meeting, held at Bush's Texas ranch, featured apparent camaraderie, jokes, barbecue and a visit to a local high school. Both leaders promised to help bring stability to Afghanistan. But when the meeting ended, they were unable to agree on amending the Anti-Ballistic Missile Treaty of 1972, which Washington seeks to do so it can develop a missile defense system.

In their closing statements, neither Bush nor Putin addressed the Russian economy. But, as has been discussed earlier, this may be an area where the U.S. should change its tack, not by abandoning market principles but by urging Russia to strike a proper balance between state and market in an economy that faces overwhelming obstacles to its integration into the world economy. Liberal economic policies that require unfettered dismantling of Russian trade barriers and an unregulated flow of capital into and out of Russia are difficult to reconcile with the development of Russia as a whole. A reasonably capable and stable Russian state is essential both for Russian economic recovery and international order throughout Eurasia. Just consider the possible consequences for global security if the Russian state, like the Chinese state in the first half of the 20th century, were to decompose:

- Russia's already vulnerable and massive "nuclear archipelago," a by-product of the cold war, would become much more accessible to outside interests; as would its massive stockpiles and expertise in the fields of chemical and biological weapons;
- international ability to combat terrorism in Central Asia would decrease dramatically;
- the ensuing regional anarchy—which would inevitably draw in major powers like China, Turkey, Iran and the U.S.—would vastly complicate the development of Central Asia's vast energy resources.

The events of September 11, 2001, have brought home in the most direct possible way a painful truth about politics, be it domestic or international: Order precedes justice. While a just order is likely to be a more enduring order, without a minimum and antecedent degree of order, justice is impossible to achieve on anything other than an individual or familial basis. The second truth is a more familiar one: Politics makes strange (and sometimes unpleasant) bedfellows. ■

OPINION BALLOTS are on pages 91–92

DISCUSSION QUESTIONS

1. Under what circumstances should the U.S. ignore the human-rights record of governments whose cooperation is useful to it in the short term?

2. How can the state and the market be reconciled to promote sustained economic development in Russian circumstances?

3. How does Russia's internal evolution affect its prospects to be a reliable partner of the U.S.?

4. Would you invest your own money in the Russian economy?

5. What might be done to help ensure that Russia remains a stabilizing factor in world politics for the foreseeable future?

6. Do you see any role for the U.S. and Russia in guaranteeing regional stability vis-à-vis Afghanistan and the projection of international terrorism from that part of the world?

7. Is it necessary to sacrifice important foreign policy interests (e.g., NATO expansion, national missile defense) in order to obtain Russia's cooperation in imposing maximum security on its stockpiles of nuclear, chemical and biological materials left over from the cold war?

READINGS AND RESOURCES

Aron, Leon, and Yeltsin, Boris, **Yeltsin: A Revolutionary Life.** New York, St. Martin's Press, 2000. 934 pp. $35.00. A somewhat positive but nevertheless encyclopedic biography of Russia's first post-Soviet leader.

Colton, Timothy J., and McFaul, Michael, "America's Real Russian Allies." **Foreign Affairs,** Nov./Dec. 2001, pp. 46–59. Examines the attitude of the Russian masses toward democracy and the U.S.

Lynch, Allen C., "The Realism of Russia's Foreign Policy." **Europe-Asia Studies,** January 2001, pp. 7–31. An analysis of the pragmatic tendency of much of current Russian foreign policy.

————, "Russia: Report Card on Survival." **Great Decisions 2000,** pp. 21–30. New York, Foreign Policy Association 2000. Examines the state of the Russian economy 10 years after the collapse of communism.

Putin, Vladimir, **First Person: An Astonishingly Frank Self-Portrait by Russia's President,** trans. by Catherine A. Fitzpatrick. New York, Public Affairs, 2000. 208 pp. $15.00. A series of interviews with the Russian president.

"Putin's Russia." **BusinessWeek,** November 12, 2001, pp. 66–76. Special report examines the changing relationship between the U.S. and Russia from confrontation to cooperation.

"Russia: Ten Years Later." **Current History,** October 2001. Entire issue. Articles by respected academics and observers on all major aspects of Russia today.

"A Survey of Russia." **The Economist** (London), July 21, 2000. A 16-page survey of the Russian political, economic, social and foreign policy scene.

Trenin, Dmitri V., **The End of Eurasia: Russia on the Border Between Geopolitics and Globalization.** Washington, D.C., Carnegie Moscow Center, 2001. 340 pp. $24.95 (paper). A Russian analyst's view of his country's role in world politics.

White, Stephen, **Russia's New Politics: The Management of a Postcommunist Society.** New York, Cambridge University Press, 2000. 300 pp. $19.95 (paper). A comprehensive overview and interpretation of Russia's post-Soviet political, economic and social development.

THE HARRIMAN INSTITUTE, 420 West 118th St., 12th fl., MC 3345, New York, NY 10027; (212) 854-4623; Fax (212) 666-3481. **www.columbia.edu/cu/sipa/regional/hi** ■ The institute specializes in teaching and research on Russia, the Soviet bloc and post-Communist states. It publishes the quarterly **Harriman Review**.

INSTITUTE FOR EASTWEST STUDIES, 700 Broadway, 2nd fl., New York, NY 10003; (212) 824-4100; Fax (212) 824-4149. **www.iews.org** ■ The institute provides information about the potential tensions and conflicts in Russia that threaten stability and promotes the development of democracy.

JOHNSON'S RUSSIA LIST. www.cdi.org/russia/johnson ■ This site provides a daily newsletter that is very informative, comprising articles published on Russia from both inside and outside the country.

KENNAN INSTITUTE FOR ADVANCED RUSSIAN STUDIES (WOODROW WILSON INTERNATIONAL CENTER FOR SCHOLARS), One Woodrow Wilson Plaza, 1300 Pennsylvania Ave., NW, Washington, DC 20004-3027; (202) 691-4100; Fax (202) 691-4247. **http://wwics.si.edu/kennan** ■ Academic center that fosters advanced research on Russia and the former U.S.S.R. by scholars, government officials and the press. Publications include a monthly newsletter and **Occasional Paper Series**.

NATIONAL COUNCIL FOR EURASIAN AND EAST EUROPEAN RESEARCH, 910 17th St., NW, Suite 300, Washington, DC 20006; (202) 822-6950; Fax (202) 822-6955. **www.nceeer.org** ■ The council specializes in research on the economic, political, social and historical development of Russia, Eastern Europe and Eurasia.

LEARN MORE ABOUT THIS TOPIC AT www.greatdecisions.org

Access links to online resources ● Order the recommended readings ● Take the GD Quiz ● Find maps in the online atlas ● Submit your opinion ballots ● Read the latest National Opinion Ballot Report ● and more ...

7/8 OPINION BALLOTS

Please submit only one ballot per person, per topic. *Ballots must be received by June 30, 2002.*
Vote online at ***www.greatdecisions.org*** *(code: gd2002fpa) or mail ballots to:*

FOREIGN POLICY ASSOCIATION, 470 PARK AVENUE SOUTH, NEW YORK, NY 10016-6819

TOPIC 7 Russia reexamined

ISSUE A. What should be the more important focus of U.S. policy toward Russia? (choose one)

___ **1.** Russia's internal development

___ **2.** Shared U.S.-Russian interests in world politics

Comment: ______________________________

ISSUE B. Should the U.S. secure the cooperation of Russia and its Central Asian allies in its fight against international terrorism even if that means ignoring human-rights abuses by those countries? (choose one)

___ **1.** Yes

___ **2.** No

Comment: ______________________________

Your zip code: ___ ___ ___ ___ ___

Date: / /2002 *Ballot continues on reverse side...*

TOPIC 7 Russia reexamined

ISSUE A. What should be the more important focus of U.S. policy toward Russia? (choose one)

___ **1.** Russia's internal development

___ **2.** Shared U.S.-Russian interests in world politics

Comment: ______________________________

ISSUE B. Should the U.S. secure the cooperation of Russia and its Central Asian allies in its fight against international terrorism even if that means ignoring human-rights abuses by those countries? (choose one)

___ **1.** Yes

___ **2.** No

Comment: ______________________________

Your zip code: ___ ___ ___ ___ ___

Date: / /2002 *Ballot continues on reverse side...*

TOPIC 8 Energy and environment

ISSUE A. Do you agree or disagree with the following statements?

	AGREE	DISAGREE
1. The U.S. faces a serious energy crisis.	❑	❑
2. The deregulation of electricity is a good idea.	❑	❑
3. The evidence of global warming is conclusive.	❑	❑

Comment: ______________________________

ISSUE B. Regarding the Kyoto Protocol on global warming, the U.S. should (choose one):

___ **1.** Support the Kyoto Protocol

___ **2.** Seek to renegotiate the Kyoto Protocol

___ **3.** Remain opposed to the Kyoto Protocol

Comment: ______________________________

Your zip code: ___ ___ ___ ___ ___

Date: / /2002 *Ballot continues on reverse side...*

TOPIC 8 Energy and environment

ISSUE A. Do you agree or disagree with the following statements?

	AGREE	DISAGREE
1. The U.S. faces a serious energy crisis.	❑	❑
2. The deregulation of electricity is a good idea.	❑	❑
3. The evidence of global warming is conclusive.	❑	❑

Comment: ______________________________

ISSUE B. Regarding the Kyoto Protocol on global warming, the U.S. should (choose one):

___ **1.** Support the Kyoto Protocol

___ **2.** Seek to renegotiate the Kyoto Protocol

___ **3.** Remain opposed to the Kyoto Protocol

Comment: ______________________________

Your zip code: ___ ___ ___ ___ ___

Date: / /2002 *Ballot continues on reverse side...*

ISSUE C. How important is the role of the Russian state for Russia's economic development? (choose one)

___ **1.** Very important

___ **2.** Somewhat important

___ **3.** Not important

Comment: ______________________________

____

ISSUE D. How much of a stabilizing force is Russia going to be in world politics in the foreseeable future? (choose one)

___ **1.** Very stabilizing

___ **2.** Somewhat stabilizing

___ **3.** Not stabilizing at all

Comment: ______________________________

____

ISSUE E. Should the U.S. and Russia jointly guarantee the stability of a post-Taliban Afghanistan? (choose one)

___ **1.** Yes

___ **2.** No

Comment: ______________________________

____

ISSUE C. How important is the role of the Russian state for Russia's economic development? (choose one)

___ **1.** Very important

___ **2.** Somewhat important

___ **3.** Not important

Comment: ______________________________

____

ISSUE D. How much of a stabilizing force is Russia going to be in world politics in the foreseeable future? (choose one)

___ **1.** Very stabilizing

___ **2.** Somewhat stabilizing

___ **3.** Not stabilizing at all

Comment: ______________________________

____

ISSUE E. Should the U.S. and Russia jointly guarantee the stability of a post-Taliban Afghanistan? (choose one)

___ **1.** Yes

___ **2.** No

Comment: ______________________________

____

ISSUE C. In order for the U.S. to reduce emissions, it is better to (choose one):

___ **1.** Curtail energy use

___ **2.** Promote more efficient use of existing resources

___ **3.** Develop new technologies

Comment: ______________________________

____

____

____

____

____

ISSUE D. How important is it for the U.S. to reduce its dependence on oil imports? (choose one)

___ **1.** Very important

___ **2.** Somewhat important

___ **3.** Not very important

Comment: ______________________________

____

____

____

____

____

____

ISSUE C. In order for the U.S. to reduce emissions, it is better to (choose one):

___ **1.** Curtail energy use

___ **2.** Promote more efficient use of existing resources

___ **3.** Develop new technologies

Comment: ______________________________

____

____

____

____

____

ISSUE D. How important is it for the U.S. to reduce its dependence on oil imports? (choose one)

___ **1.** Very important

___ **2.** Somewhat important

___ **3.** Not very important

Comment: ______________________________

____

____

____

____

____

____

Energy and the environment

The current energy crisis consists of two essentially separate problems: a deterioration of critical infrastructure in the U.S. electricity sector and a global squeeze on oil supplies.

by William Sweet

APWIDE WORLD PHOTOS

IN SAN GABRIEL, CALIFORNIA, *electric power transmission lines are seen at sundown spanning the horizon. In January 2001, California regulators ordered rotating blackouts throughout the state in an effort to cut back consumption of electricity.*

At the beginning of 2001, as President George W. Bush's new Administration took office, debates over U.S. energy policy seemed destined to evolve along predictable partisan lines, with the overall balance of power between Republicans and Democrats remaining closely divided, so that any changes in policy almost certainly would amount to mere changes of emphasis.

Admittedly, several factors were conspiring to create a sense of energy crisis: soaring electricity prices in California, which began in the summer of 2000, came on the heels of scattered but very widespread energy outages in the summer of 1999, raising questions both about the overall reliability of the nation's grid systems and about measures being taken to deregulate and restructure utilities; at the same time, sharp increases in oil and natural gas prices during the second half of 2000 were translating into much higher gasoline prices as well as higher home heating costs.

Recognizing that predecessors had allowed energy policy to slip, the new Administration clearly hoped to exploit the public's heightened concern to get some business done. Sharing a philosophical preference for production-oriented strategies, Bush and his rather conservative inner circle immediately began formulating a long-term strategy aiming to increase domestic production of fossil fuels, better secure foreign supplies, clear away bottlenecks in the electrical transmission systems and promote construction of new generating facilities, including nuclear power plants.

The Administration's plan assumed a steady and inexorable increase in U.S. energy consumption in the decades to come—a point sharply disputed, and not just by Democrats—and it advocated at least one hugely controversial measure, namely, opening the

WILLIAM SWEET, *an occasional contributor to* Great Decisions, *is senior news editor of IEEE* Spectrum *magazine, a monthly publication of the Institute for Electrical and Electronics Engineers, based in New York City. He covers energy and the environment for* Spectrum, *and has often written about other global issues, including resources, population, international finance and nuclear arms control.*

Arctic National Wildlife Refuge (ANWR) to oil exploration and ultimately drilling.

Thus, when Vice President Richard Cheney's energy task force issued its national energy report on May 17, 2001, the document met with an immediate hailstorm of criticism from conservationists and environmentalists, who complained that it undervalued the potential for improving energy efficiency and economizing on energy use, and overstated the need for finding new fuels and beefing up energy infrastructure. Yet even amid that storm, the dispassionate observer could not be but struck at how much the Cheney report had in common with ancestor studies prepared under the aegis of political leaders with ostensibly different agendas.

Just like an influential report prepared by President Bill Clinton's President's Committee of Advisers on Science and Technology (Pcast) in November 1997, the Cheney report squarely recognized the enormous gains in energy efficiency achieved by the U.S. in the 1980s and 1990s. True, the Pcast report made continued improvement of end-use efficiency its highest priority, while the Cheney team put increased production of fuels number one. But both reports advocated a robust R&D program to develop both renewable energy resources (such as wind, solar, biomass) and fuel systems based on hydrogen, such as fuel cells. Both considered a renewed program of nuclear construction highly desirable. And both recommended continuing strong support of the nation's clean-coal program, which the Department of Energy (DOE) had been managing for many years, and which seemed more important all the time in light of the country's greater-than-ever reliance on coal and the importance of cleaner coal in the context of national and global efforts to reduce both air pollutants and "greenhouse gases" thought to be warming the earth's atmosphere. Such gases, mainly carbon dioxide and methane originating from energy use, industrial processes and agriculture, trap the sun's radiation much as a greenhouse allows it in but not back out.

Impact of 9/11

As the U.S. Congress was reconvening at the beginning of the fall, the outlook was that some kind of comprehensive energy legislation incorporating elements of both the Cheney and Pcast reports would be enacted and signed into law. The Republican-controlled House had passed a bill during the summer based on the vice president's national energy plan, which included a clause opening the Alaskan refuge to drilling, despite complaints that even the most aggressive development program in ANWR would make little dent in the country's dependence on oil imports. Senate Democrats led by New Mexico's Jeff Bingaman were writing a competing bill, based on Pcast—and doing so four years after the report's release, basically because they too saw in the nation's new sense of energy crisis an opportunity to get overdue business done. (At the end of the year, Senate Majority Leader Tom Daschle had taken matters into his own hands and was trying to fashion a compromise.)

Yet, at the end of last summer, there also was some question as to whether the sense of crisis would persist long enough to motivate legislators and the White House to agree on a long-term strategic plan. The California electricity crisis seemed to be ending, and while Democrats and Republicans still bickered about who should foot the bill for bailing out the state's utilities and protecting consumers, nobody seemed inclined to rethink the question of whether electricity deregulation had been a good idea in the first place. Oil and gas prices were trending downward, defusing the potentially explosive question of whether the country should make some kind of crash effort either at conservation or production.

While the Bush Administration had renounced the Kyoto Protocol, which requires participating industrial countries to reduce their emissions of greenhouse gases by an average of 5.2% from 1990 levels between 2008 and 2012, and while the U.S. now found itself isolated in follow-on climate talks in Bonn, Germany, in July 2001, the Senate had passed a resolution calling on the government to remain a constructive participant in efforts to mitigate the dangers of climate change. Here, as in energy generally, signs pointed to some kind of closely negotiated bipartisan compromise.

Thus, at the beginning of September 2001, it seemed almost a foregone conclusion that the country would end up settling on some kind of watered-down strategic energy plan, incorporating elements of conservation, production and creative oil diplomacy. All that changed abruptly, however, on September 11, with the terrorist attacks on New York City and Washington.

If one asks what led to the suicide attacks, observed James R. Schlesinger, in a keynote address

AP/WIDE WORLD PHOTOS

KUWAITI OIL FIELD WORKER *kneels for midday prayer near an oil fire burning out of control near Kuwait City. The fires were probably set by retreating Iraqi soldiers during Persian Gulf war, March 1991.*

delivered to the National Academy of Engineering on October 9, it can be summarized in one word: oil. Schlesinger, who served as energy secretary (1977–79) to President Jimmy Carter and as defense secretary and Central Intelligence Agency (CIA) director before that, meant that U.S. troubles with Osama bin Laden began with the Persian Gulf war of 1990–91. Iraq's invasion and annexation of Kuwait would have doubled its petroleum production and export capacity, and so the U.S. and allies intervened—on the principle, to be sure, that wanton aggression had to be countered—to prevent Iraq from displacing U.S. ally Saudi Arabia as the arbiter of world oil prices. That in turn led to the decision to assemble allied forces for an invasion of Iraq in Saudi Arabia and, after the success of the Desert Storm operation, the still more consequential decision to leave them in Saudi Arabia on a semipermanent basis. The presence of those forces became bin Laden's number-one grievance, and a rallying cry for Islamic extremists throughout the Middle East, who considered the proximity of Western military bases to the holy sites of Mecca and Medina an absolutely unacceptable sacrilege.

Making the situation still more dangerous now, the U.S. and its allies find themselves at the dawn of the new millennium more crucially dependent than ever on Middle Eastern supplies. As noted in a report prepared at Rice University's James A. Baker III Institute for Public Policy at the end of 2000 (and well-timed to coincide with the transition to the new presidency):

- In 1985, when world oil prices collapsed after a long run following the second "petroleum shock" of 1979–80, the Organization of Petroleum Exporting Countries (OPEC, created in 1960), were thought to have spare capacity of about 15 million barrels per day (bpd)
- By 1990, when Iraq invaded Kuwait, global spare capacity was still about 5 to 5.5 million bpd, about 20% of OPEC's production capacity at the time and 8% of global demand
- But by the winter of 2000–2001, spare capacity was a negligible 2% of global demand.

"The surge in energy demand worldwide that combined with underinvestment to create these shortfalls has been stunning," the James Baker III panel concluded.

AN ESKIMO OIL WORKER *leans against a pipe at the KIC-1 well, the only one ever drilled into the rock beneath the Arctic National Wildlife Refuge.*

How policy issues look now

President Bush's energy team, much criticized at the time the Cheney report was released because of its closeness to the oil industry, can now be said, precisely because of that closeness, to be well acquainted with the key underlying factors that make bin Laden's attacks such a supremely dangerous threat. Not for nothing was the final chapter of the Cheney report devoted to oil diplomacy. The chapter's subtext could reasonably be read as, "You can count on us. We've all been in the petroleum business and know it through and through. We know what's required to get the oil."

In one respect, the September 11 attacks made things easier for the Administration. By inducing a sharp drop in airline travel and aggravating the onset of what may well be a stubborn global recession, they helped drive oil consumption down, taking the pressure off prices. But in the longer run, as the effects of the attacks themselves and of the U.S. military counterattack on global terrorism work their way through the volatile oil-producing states of the Middle East, Bush and his advisers will have their work cut out for them. Above all in Saudi Arabia itself, where the regime's promotion of Islamic fundamentalism at home is in glaring contradiction to its globally oriented oil diplomacy and its professed friendship with the U.S., Washington's diplomats must walk a swaying tightrope.

What then should be the fundamental approach of the U.S. in the coming years? Is an ever-greater military presence in the Middle East inevitable, as the campaign against terrorism progresses and Israel's situation continues to deteriorate, or can the U.S. somehow disengage to an extent, withdrawing from the bases that are fueling bin Laden's movement? Would that be a cowardly retreat, or would it be wisdom playing the better part of policy?

How much scope is there for reducing dependence on Middle Eastern oil by diversifying supply sources, for example by courting political elites in the Central Asian former Soviet republics, and in Russia itself? What are the pitfalls of cozying up to such rulers?

In light of the limits and risks of supply diversification, should the U.S. relaunch a renewed energy independence strategy, emphasizing conservation, new technology and domestic production, of the kind initiated under President Richard M. Nixon (1969–74) and pressed with determination by President Carter?

Before addressing these great decisions directly, it bears looking back to see how they have been handled in the past and how the U.S. got where it is today. It also will be necessary to take a sideward look at the question of global warming, which remains, even in the current critical situation, the great loom-

--- from Herblock: A Cartoonist's Life (Times Books, 1998)

ing global issue of the new century.

Energy independence and dependencies

Schlesinger, Carter's energy czar and as such the man responsible for devising and implementing the country's energy-independence drive in the late 1970s, made a startling admission at the end of his talk to assembled engineering fellows on October 9: even if the U.S. had succeeded in achieving independence from foreign suppliers, which was not in fact possible, he said, this still would not have saved the nation from dangerous foreign entanglements because, after all, the country's closest allies in Europe and Asia would remain critically dependent on Middle Eastern supplies, and those supplies would still have to be protected in a pinch. That is because—he really did not need to spell it out—any long interruption of oil supplies to Western Europe and Japan would cut their economic jugular, with near-fatal consequences for the U.S., too.

A certain absence of true conviction on the part of Carter's energy leader in that President's preferred energy strategy may partly account for why it went over so poorly with the public, and why the Administration's message seemed so fuzzy. Carter's speech to the people complaining of a national malaise was widely derided, and his policies were habitually ridiculed as "Chicken Little, the Sky is Falling." Yet in hindsight, despite some failure and misplaced effort, much of what that Administration accomplished now seems farsighted and consequential.

Almost all of what is being done to promote development of renewable-energy technology was first begun in a concerted way during the Carter years (1977–81), much of it under the aegis of the Solar Energy Research Institute (now the National Renewable Energy Laboratory) in Golden, Colo. In no small part as a result of such efforts, electricity generated by wind has been the fastest-growing share of the electricity supply in recent years—and in some countries like Germany, Sweden and India has become a truly significant share of the energy mix. Photovoltaics—solar cells made of light-sensitive materials that generate electricity from sunlight—are running a close second and seem sure to take first place soon (if they have not already).

Nuclear energy got a huge setback with the accident at Three Mile Island in 1979, but Carter—trained in reactor technology and nuclear physics—responded with a program of all-out regulatory reform which, though very costly in the short run, in the longer term has begun to pay dividends in the form of somewhat greater public confidence and much greater operating reliability. Reactors are now running a higher proportion of the time than ever before and many are being recommissioned to operate many more years than originally anticipated, making their economics more attractive.

Synthetic fuels or "synfuels," the Administration's effort to obtain liquid fuels for transportation from coal by building on technology devised primarily in Germany between the world wars, turned out to be by and large an expensive and embarrassing failure. Yet the program is taking on something of a second life now, in the form of integrated coal gasification technology, where the goal is to gasify and burn coal directly at the point of electricity generation, perhaps even capturing and "sequestering" carbon-dioxide emissions to prevent any climate impact.

More broadly, the synfuels effort was a constituent element in the nation's clean-coal program, one of its more important R&D efforts, not only in U.S. terms, but also for adaptation by coal-dependent countries like India and China.

Last, and by no means least, the Public Utility Regulatory Policies Act (Purpa) of 1978 made provision for industrial producers of electricity to "cogenerate," feeding extra power back into the grid. That provision helped stimulate development of new generating technology outside the traditional utility sector, known for its conservatism and unimaginativeness. Over the next decades, cogenerated electricity made a growing contribution to the electricity supply, making unnecessary the construction of many new central generating plants.

Increasingly troubled electricity sector

Efforts at formulating and implementing a comprehensive national energy program pretty much ended with Carter's defeat in 1980, when the public rejected his self-restraining style and instead embraced the optimism and confidence of Ronald Reagan, who, in his acceptance speech at the 1980 Republican convention, boldly repudiated those who said America had had its day in the sun. Yet even as the economy boomed under his leadership, and the country reasserted its dominant position in the world, policies adopted during the "environmental decade" of the 1970s continued to do their work. Demand for electricity grew just 25% from

1978 to 1988, as utilities adopted programs to discourage consumption. Deployment of new generating capacity roughly kept pace, with cogeneration accounting for a substantial share.

Construction of new generating plants was kept to the bare minimum required to meet demand in the Reagan years and beyond. With environmentalists and citizens' advocacy groups keeping very close tabs on utility plans, no new orders for nuclear plants were placed. New coal plants had to meet the stringent requirements of the 1970 Clean Air Act and subsequent amendments (though loopholes having to do with upgrading of old plants continue to be a big point of controversy).

The plot thickened in 1992, with enactment of the Energy Policy Act, requiring utilities to introduce competition in the wholesale purchase and sale of electricity, on the model of competitiveness in the long-distance telephone system. The idea, which found expression in the Federal Energy Regulatory Commission's Order No. 888, issued in 1996, was that independent power producers not only would have the right to sell into the market, but would have open and equal access to the transmission grid. The expectation, widely shared across the political spectrum, was that this would improve efficiency and bring down costs. Ultimately, it was assumed, most or all states would adopt rules introducing competition at the retail level as well, so that all consumers—residential as well as commercial—would be allowed to choose their electricity generator. By the end of the 1990s, indeed, half the states in the country had plans to deregulate and restructure their electricity systems along competitive lines.

But at this point, chickens came home to roost, and some of them were not little by any means. Utilities, required in many places to "unbundle" their generating assets—that is, separate the production of electricity from its distribution—found themselves in doubt as to what kinds of new investment would pay. Independent power producers initially bought existing assets rather than deploying new plants. Nobody had any idea who would end up owning the country's transmission lines, and how use of them would be billed. And meanwhile, as public utility commissions loosened their grip, as utilities were privatized and subjected to the "discipline of the market," demand-side management tools they had widely adopted in the 1970s and 1980s to encourage conservation began to atrophy.

The net result, as the economy underwent a second boom during the Clinton years, with a big boost from the Internet revolution in his second term, was that electricity demand started to grow at a brisker pace, without deployment of new generating and transmission assets keeping pace. Transmission capacity barely increased at all in the late 1990s, but there was an enormous increase in the scale and complexity of wholesale transactions carried by transmission lines—already an important factor in two massive outages experienced in the whole Western grid system in August 1996. Meanwhile, utilities sought to bolster their position with investors by trimming personnel and other expenses, even as the Internet itself and everything associated with networked computing began to make noticeable electricity demands.

By the summer of 1999, when significant outages occurred in Massachusetts, New York, the Middle West, and the Southwest, the signs of trouble were literally all around. When the energy department convened a panel to systematically review the situation that winter, the assembled experts found pretty much the same picture all over the country: whether it was a question of generation or transmission capacity, distribution lines or control equipment, service personnel or simulation engineers, everywhere there were too few resources to easily satisfy demands made on systems designed for radically different purposes.

The situation burst into the nation's consciousness as a full-blown crisis in the summer of 2000 in California, one

APWIDE WORLD PHOTOS

GERMANY IS A LEADER *in the use of renewable energy to provide electricity. This wind-power farm 80 miles south of Berlin, which opened in June 2000, is said to be Europe's biggest and provides electricity for 30,000 households.*

AP/WIDE WORLD PHOTOS

ENVIRONMENTALISTS DEMONSTRATE *in front of a 20-foot-high inflatable SUV at the state capitol, Tallahassee, Florida, May 2001. The women were lobbying for a proposal to increase fuel-efficiency requirements.*

of the first states to introduce a thoroughgoing electricity restructuring plan. Contrary to expectations held by pretty much everybody involved, an eccentric combination of factors conspired to drive wholesale prices much higher, rather than lower. Since legislators had placed caps on consumer prices and barred the state's three utilities from entering into long-term energy contracts (basically, to prevent "self-dealing" with the independent power producers they were required to sell their generating assets to), the power suppliers found themselves unable to pass along sky-rocketing wholesale costs of electricity to consumers. In short order, while the newly established Independent System Operator struggled valiantly to keep the system up and running—accomplishing this by declaring frequent emergencies and imposing intermittent rolling brownouts—the three utilities found themselves bankrupt or on the verge.

Liquid fuels a big problem, too

The California electricity crisis constitutes one half of Clinton's legacy of leadership failure on the nation's energy policy and it would be the incoming Bush Administration's first order of business to rectify the situation. The other half had to do with soaring prices in the fall and winter of 2000–2001 of gasoline, home heating oil and natural gas.

Here the essential story is so thoroughly familiar, a barebones treatment will surely suffice. Corporate fuel-efficiency standards (the so-called CAFE standards) first adopted during the years 1973–75 led to dramatic improvements in automobile gas mileage during the 1980s and into the 1990s. Between 1975 and 1985 the average fuel efficiency of the American car doubled, from 13.4 miles per gallon to 27.5 mpg. Had that trend continued, Vaclav Smil, the University of Manitoba's distinguished scientist has observed, the average rate would be well above 40 mpg today—considering that some existing cars do as well as 60 or 70 mpg.

But a loophole in the CAFE standards allowing sports-utility vehicles (SUVs) to be classified as light trucks soon led, when SUVs swept the country in a wholly unexpected fad, to stagnation of overall fleet efficiencies. Not only conservationists and environmentalists, but the Cheney group itself, acknowledged and highlighted the problem. As a result, total gas consumption began to rise sharply again.

With gasoline making more demands on refining capacity, prices for home heating oil also rose, as reserve inventories dropped. Prices for natural gas, also used prevalently in home heating, naturally followed suit. An aggravating factor here—and one that overlaps the California electricity crisis—was that during the previous decade, utilities in the U.S. and abroad as well had invested almost exclusively in new generating facilities powered by natural gas. (Among the states, California is one of the most dependent on natural gas for electricity production.)

From the American consumer's point of view, this aspect of the energy crisis naturally consisted of a perception that prices were much too high. Yet a case could be made that if all the costs and risks of relying heavily on fossil fuels for transportation and home heating were taken into account, prices were much too low to begin with, and arguably still too low even when they were two-to-four times higher than they had been before. After all, even at $2 a gallon, gasoline in the U.S. was still considerably cheaper than French bottled water—or even Poland Spring. In most European countries, even more dependent on oil, important tax policy sees to it that prices are closer to $4 a gallon.

Thus, in a report prepared during the Clinton years by several national laboratories to assess prospects for reducing greenhouse-gas emissions associated with energy use, it was concluded that fuel prices ought to better take into account their net social costs. Those costs, called "externalities" by economists because they are not internal to market prices, include "greenhouse gases,... air, water, and land pollution,... and economic impacts associated with the uneven geographic distribution of oil resources ... [including] military expenditures associated with [the] Persian Gulf," the report Scenarios for a Clean Energy Future noted.

That kind of consideration was emphatically not the kind of thing that the production-oriented Cheney team was inclined to dwell on when it began its work early in 2001. Its attitude, it seems not unfair to assume, was that members of the current Bush Administration knew how to get the country more oil, and they would just get the job done. But today, with the launch of a war against international terrorism, the task of securing added international oil supplies is no minor matter, and the question of whether that task should be somewhat lessened by forcing oil conservation by means of higher prices is back on the political agenda. ■

Global warming

WHAT THE CRISIS in the electricity sector and the global squeeze on petroleum supplies have in common is this: both production of electricity and use of oil-based fuels for transportation and heating represent threats to the global environment, inasmuch as any combustion of fossil fuels results in greenhouse gases that trap heat in the atmosphere and make the earth warmer. Therefore, any policies affecting the use and production of fossil fuels must be considered in terms of their impact on global warming, as well as in terms of securing supplies at acceptable prices.

The Cheney energy task force anticipated in its May 2001 report that U.S. energy consumption will increase by about 25% from 2000 to 2010, from about 100 quadrillion to roughly 125 quadrillion BTUs. With domestic production of fuels staying flat in the same period, the gap between U.S. energy needs and the country's ability to meet them from domestic sources would roughly double in that scenario, greatly increasing U.S. dependence on foreign supplies. At the same time, use of coal, which already accounts for more than half of the nation's electricity, having increased its share significantly in the last two decades despite the addition of costly emission-control technology, would increase still more. Reliance on natural gas, the fuel of choice for new generation, would triple.

That view of the future has not gone unchallenged. A report issued the previous year by several national laboratories (Scenarios for a Clean Energy Future) found that if all sensible efforts at energy conservation were made, but without heroic measures such as draconian taxes on energy use, energy consumption could be held flat or could even be made to decrease slightly over the next 20 years. Reliance on coal, of all fuels by far the greatest emitter per unit used of carbon dioxide, the most important greenhouse gas, could actually be made to decrease by as much as a third. In the labs' advanced conservation scenario, use of natural gas—in comparison to coal, not nearly as damaging to the global atmosphere, but still a significant source of greenhouse gases—could be kept close to current levels.

The labs' projections were carefully developed over a period of years on the assumption that the U.S. will need and want to make a concerted effort to limit its emissions of greenhouse gases. But how serious a problem is global warming? How much of a sacrifice is the country willing to make to limit its greenhouse-gas emissions, and what kinds of sacrifices might be necessary? Is the approach laid out in the Kyoto Protocol of 1997, which requires the advanced industrial countries to reduce their emissions at the end of this decade to levels below 1990, the right one?

The science of warming

When the Kyoto Protocol was formulated, the science underlying predictions that the earth was warming alarmingly was still immensely controversial. For every person who believed the ominous predictions issuing from the international community of atmospheric scientists assembled under the aegis of the Intergovernmental Panel on Climate Change (IPCC) to periodically assess the status of knowledge, there was someone else who dismissed them. To be sure, nobody disputed that the earth's atmosphere traps the sun's heat—without that greenhouse effect, the world would be uninhabitable. But there was serious question as to whether warming going beyond normal variations had been detected, and whether human activity was playing any role.

That situation has changed quite markedly in the last few years. Partly because of mutually consistent and confirming research done by many groups around the globe into the world's climate history (based on studies of gases in ice-core samples, ocean-floor borings, tree rings, the fossil record, and so on), and partly on elaborate computerized climate models constructed and refined at a handful of centers in Europe, the U.S. and Japan, earth and atmospheric scientists have come to have much greater confidence that the earth is indeed warming, is warming alarmingly, and that human activity is certainly a factor. Most disturbing of all is the real possibility that effects could ultimately be catastrophic on a global scale, going beyond just the serious inconvenience of regional climates becoming a few degrees warmer or cooler here or there (no small matter in itself). Since the earth's climate is a hugely

AP/WIDE WORLD PHOTOS

MENDENHALL GLACIER, *as seen from Skater's Cabin in Juneau, Alaska, March 2001: Visitors to the cabin can compare the extent of the glacier today with historical photographs showing it extending hundreds of yards farther into the lake it feeds.*

complex system of interacting variables in which combined effects are "nonlinear"—that is, out of proportion to individual causes—the prospect of a comprehensive climate catastrophe cannot be excluded.

Of course it is still possible that the science of global warming is somehow systematically flawed, and that in the fullness of time it will be radically revised or thrown out entirely. But this is equally true of Einsteinian relativity theory, quantum mechanics and the periodic table, genetics and evolution. They too may eventually turn out to be radically flawed—indeed, if the past is any guide, they probably will in fact turn out to be inadequate—but right now, they are the only physics, chemistry and biology extant. The science of global warming, likewise, is the only science known right now—that is, it is the consensus science developed and believed by those certified and qualified to have an opinion about it.

The most important and perplexing findings of atmospheric science, enshrined in a number of recent reports from the IPCC and the U.S. National Academy of Sciences, are roughly the following:

- The last decade of the 20th century was the warmest in the earth's recorded history, with almost every year warmer than the preceding one.
- The warming trend of the 20th century runs counter to a cooling trend registered during the previous 900 years in ice cores, tree rings, etc., and the earth is now warmer than it has been any time in the last millennium.
- At the scale of geologic time—hundreds of thousands of years—sharp changes in temperature, on the order of 7°–8°C, have occurred very abruptly, in a matter of decades.
- Actual measured concentrations of the two main greenhouse gases in the atmosphere—carbon dioxide and methane—are very much higher than they have been any time in the last 420,000 years, including the periods between and during the ice ages.

Since concentrations of carbon dioxide in the atmosphere have correlated very closely with the earth's climate over the last 420 millennia—albeit with some puzzling leads and lags—the fact that levels are higher than at any previous time in that period is frightening indeed.

The effects are to be seen all around, as noted in a recent survey of the subject by Donald Kennedy, former president of Stanford University and editor in chief of the American Association for the Advancement of Science's *Science* magazine. "Flowering seasons come weeks earlier for British plants than they did in the 19th century when parson-naturalists began recording the dates on which their favorite species first bloomed. Mountain glaciers all over the world are retreating, and sea levels have risen. Birds familiar to American birders have spread their ranges northward: cardinals now winter in New Hampshire, a state they never reached in summer when I was a boy. In the intertidal zones of Monterey the transects … are now occupied by species that had more southern distributions in the heyday of Cannery Row. And on the other coast bluefish and striped bass, unknown north of Cape Cod when I spent my first summer in Woods Hole, now delight anglers in the Gulf of Maine."

Not for nothing did Kennedy remind his audience of what the U.S. looked like the last time factors conspired nonlinearly to suddenly produce a drastic change in climate: "Present Chicago was covered [with ice] to a depth of three kilometers, and the edge of the ice went as far south as the Middle Atlantic states. …So much of the earth's water was tied up in ice that nearly all the continental shelves were exposed; you could walk from London to Paris. The mountain of ice changed weather circulation patterns, splitting the jet stream in North America into two limbs, the southernmost of which brought Oregon rain to Arizona and made it a verdant country, dotted with lakes."

Fast-changing politics

The developments in climate science are sufficiently dramatic to have begun to capture the attention of very smart people with leadership qualities all across the political spectrum, often confounding ideological expectations and rapidly transforming the landscape of interest groups influencing political processes in the U.S. and globally.

One of the first to part ways with usual allies was Britain's former prime minister Margaret Thatcher, an Oxford-educated chemist, who caught on to how climate science was evolving during her final years in office and so initiated the establishment of the Hadley Centre for Climate Prediction and Research. The idea was to colocate the center with England's Meteorological Office, near Reading, which is considered the world's premier weather-forecasting organization, and to make the center have similar prestige in climate forecasting. That project has been a success.

A second and even more important defection occurred a decade later, when John Browne, chairman of British Petroleum (BP), parted ways with most of

the oil industry—though Royal Dutch Shell had already paved the way—and announced BP would implement on its own initiative an emissions-reduction strategy roughly in keeping with Kyoto targets. BP, now flaunting the slogan "beyond petroleum," began to bill itself as the world's leading solar company, and—working with specialists at expert-driven environmental organizations like the Natural Resources Defense Council and Environmental Defense—prepared to reduce emissions from its own extraction and refining operations.

Cynics might complain that BP was only the world's largest solar company because it had acquired a U.S. manufacturer of photovoltaic cells when it merged with Amoco, and that the photovoltaic cells company (Solarex) represented a minuscule fraction of combined operations. They might object, still more pointedly, that BP is very heavily invested in Alaskan oil reserves and has good reason to curry favor with environmentalists.

Just the same, the impact of BP's bold moves has been enormous in the oil industry, and has left it split down the middle, between a faction led by BP arguing that global warming is a serious threat that must be urgently addressed, and a faction led by Exxon Mobil, arguing the science is still unproved. Scrutinized closely between the lines, Exxon Mobil can be heard saying: "We have not become the world's largest and most successful oil company by following the dictates of pseudoscience."

While "Exxon Mobil's environmental policy is marked by defiance," commented a reporter for *The Wall Sreet Journal*, the praise Shell and BP have got from environmentalists "points up the advantages of being marginally greener than the next guy."

It's a message that has been spreading. In May 2001, the Ford Motor Company issued a report saying that it considered the battle against global warming its highest corporate challenge. This was on the eve of a climate conference held in Bonn, Germany, to renegotiate implementation of the Kyoto Protocol, and shortly after President Bush had announced that the U.S. would not be bound by the Kyoto Protocol. The company's chairman William Clay Ford Jr., who took full operational control of the company in October 2001 as CEO, is a lifelong environmentalist who has made "green politics" a priority. He has said that global warming "stands out from other environmental issues because of its potentially serious consequences and its direct relationship to our industry."

That is a message, let it be said, that environmentalists need to heed themselves. The only two sources of large-scale power generation that are for all practical purposes free of greenhouse-gas emissions are nuclear energy and hydroelectricity. But nuclear power plants and large dams have ranked at the top of most environmentalists' most-hated lists. If the leading environmental organizations come to agree with Ford that global warming is the world's standout environmental issue, they will have to take a second look at nuclear energy and hydroelectricity.

One thing that has aroused particular disdain from Bush and his energy advisers has been the stubborn refusal of the Europeans, in the context of Kyoto talks, to provide any credits for those deploying new nuclear generating plants. From the U.S. perspective, the Europeans self-righteously criticize others for not doing more to prevent global warming, yet discourage one of the most effective means of addressing the problem.

The politics of Kyoto

Yet it is ironic that the U.S. President renounced the Kyoto process at just the point when so many major players in the oil and transportation industries were coming around to the view that global warming is indeed a serious problem—implicitly putting pressure on the environmental community, as noted, to reconsider some cherished positions.

Particularly disconcerting was Bush's stated reason for ditching Kyoto, which, if generalized, seemed to imply that nobody should have to go to any inconvenience to address a major problem, even if it represented a dire threat to the future of humanity. "The President has been unequivocal," explained spokesman Ari Fleischer. "He does not support the Kyoto treaty. It is not in the U.S.'s best economic interest." That would seem to imply that nobody need do anything about global warming, if it actually costs money.

Still, it bears noting that leading presidential advisers such as Condoleezza Rice have stated that the U.S. was repudiating the Kyoto Protocol not because the issue of global warming was unimportant as such, but rather because the Kyoto approach was deemed "ineffective." That position seemed to echo opinion widely held in Congress, by Senator Pete V. Domenici (R) of New Mexico, for example, a leader on energy and environmental issues who takes global warming very seriously but considers the Kyoto treaty hopelessly misguided.

Why is Kyoto so widely considered fatally flawed in the U.S., across the political and ideological spectrum, and among people of varied backgrounds and education? Two points figure prominently in all critiques. One is that developing nations are not required to meet mandated 1990 targets, but only to begin a process of national accounting and prepare, perhaps, to take advantage of specific Kyoto mechanisms designed to make it worth their while to reduce emissions. The Clean Development Mechanism, for example, is to provide credits for development of more-efficient energy technologies; another mechanism is the emissions-trading system being developed on models used very successfully in America to reduce pollutants, which would enable relatively poor countries to sell the right to emit on favorable terms to rich countries like the U.S.

The second major complaint is that in selecting 1990 as the base year for reduction targets, the Kyoto agreement essentially rigged the process in favor of the Europeans, Russia and the former Soviet republics. This is because, first, countries like Britain and Germany already were phasing out reliance on coal, mainly because of dwindling reserves, and therefore will much more easily meet targets because coal is such an important source of greenhouse gases. And second, because the former Soviet republics, deep in depression, have seen their energy use plummet with respect to 1990 levels, and therefore need do little to meet 1990 targets and in fact can reap a bonanza by selling emission rights to the advanced industrial countries.

Accordingly, when the Kyoto signatories met in Bonn last July and adopted a plan for detailed implementation of the Kyoto Protocol, leaving the U.S. isolated on the sidelines, what members of the U.S. delegation were saying to the press was roughly this: Kyoto is not an environmental treaty at all, it really is a trade treaty—because its provisions will have such a discriminatory adverse affect on the U.S., it is a weapon to bring the U.S. down a notch or two. In other words, in the Administration's view, the whole process is cooked up to subject the U.S. to what amounts to a tax, which will seriously disadvantage the country's producers in competition with the world's other manufacturers.

Rarely has an issue looked so radically different, like day or night, depending on what time zone one is in. What stands out in the minds of Europeans, Asians, and those in the fast-growing developing countries, is that the U.S. per capita energy consumption is much higher than anybody else's. To quote Professor Smil once again, "North America's energy consumption mean is now about 8 TOE [tons of oil equivalent] per capita, and the European average is approximately 4 TOE—but China's mean is 0.6, India's less than 0.3, and Bangladesh's not even 0.1 TOE."

From that point of view, it is only fair that the U.S. should be required to take disproportionately inconvenient measures to match the level of energy efficiency already achieved in Western Europe or Japan. And, given that developing countries will necessarily begin using more energy per person as their economies grow, it is only fair that they should play by quite different rules.

"The fact of the matter is," observed Norbert Walter, chief economist of the Deutsche Bank Group, in a *New York Times* column last June, "that if, from an energy policy perspective, the U.S. economy operated as efficiently as those of Europe and Japan, American energy consumption would fall by about 30%....If America had achieved European levels of efficiency in the 1990s, it would by now already exceed its Kyoto target for 2012, which was to be 7% below its 1990 carbon-dioxide emissions." What is more, if the U.S. continues to consume oil so gluttonously, it will no longer be able to make up its shortfall from abroad so very easily. "International supplies of energy will be increasingly scarce as China and India, the two most populous nations, are likely to continue growing at rates of 5% to 10% a year, with energy consumption expected to increase at substantial rates," said Walter. ■

U.S. policy options

❑ **1. The U.S should continue to seek some alternative approach to curbing global warming, or insist on renegotiation of the Kyoto Protocol, rather than rejoin the current Kyoto consensus.**

Pro: Several alternative strategies have been proposed. One possibility would be to demand, as a condition of U.S. ratification of the Kyoto Protocol, that developing countries pledge to meet specific emissions targets, or that the targets be reformulated so that countries are not able to get credit for measures they already are taking or trends already well established before Kyoto was negotiated in the first place.

Some eminent critics of the Kyoto agreement have proposed dropping the emphasis on targets (and, by implication, self-restraint), altogether. For example, Harvard economist Richard N. Cooper has suggested imposition of a global carbon tax that would affect all equally, regardless of how much energy they use per capita or what their relative economic status is. Rockefeller University's Jesse Ausubel has suggested that the world should determine what concentration of greenhouse gases in the atmosphere is safe, then figure out how to keep concentrations below that level by means of new technology and energy conservation.

Con: Any effort to renegotiate the Kyoto treaty runs the risk of sacrificing the doable for the unrealizable ideal. Developing countries will never agree to limit their emissions as long as their per-capita energy use is drastically lower than in the industrial countries. Nor will the Europeans and Asians ditch the Kyoto framework as long as U.S. energy use is seen as singularly profligate.

Already, any country is at liberty within the Kyoto framework to adopt a carbon tax, if the country sees that approach as the best way of attaining Kyoto targets. As for the idea of determining what levels of greenhouse gases are safe, that approach already is under discussion among climate negotiators and may well be incorporated into the Kyoto process as the next step.

❑ **2. The U.S. should drop the whole idea of curtailing energy use so as to reduce emissions, and instead concentrate on development of technologies to capture or "seques-**

ter" carbon dioxide and methane.
Pro: It already is known how to extract and capture carbon dioxide from power plant and industrial emissions, and there are a number of facilities in the world where this is done in order to produce carbon dioxide for specialized applications. Methane, four times as potent a greenhouse gas as carbon dioxide, is contained in excrement from farm animals and is a significant factor in overall greenhouse-gas emissions in places where commercial livestock farming is widespread. Yet it can be captured and used as fuel. The same kind of double economy can be achieved, and has likewise been demonstrated, by injecting carbon dioxide into deep coal beds to enhance extraction of methane for use as fuel.
Con: Extraction of carbon dioxide from plant emissions, though feasible, would double the generating cost of electricity at current prices; if imposed as a general policy, its adverse effects would be far more onerous than a general carbon or energy tax. The national laboratories' Scenarios for a Clean Energy Future report concludes that this kind of carbon sequestration cannot be a significant factor in greenhouse strategy during the next 15–20 years. As for technologies for enhanced recovery and exploitation of methane, while they are very promising in many specific situations—where there are a lot of pig farms, for example, or a lot of depleted coal mines—such situations are too limited for this strategy to be a panacea.

❑ **3. However the problem of global warming is addressed in the long run, the much more urgent problem for the U.S. is to diversify its foreign supplies of petroleum, so that consumers can be guaranteed adequate gasoline and home heating oil in the years immediately to come.**
Pro: All reputable sources agree that the U.S. once again has become dangerously dependent on OPEC oil supplies—the cartel's share of crude oil production dropped from 56% in 1973 to 29% in 1985 but now is back over 40%, and could climb above 50% by 2010, according to Smil. With major oil-producing countries like Saudi Arabia and the United Arab Emirates destabilized by the ongoing war between the U.S. and Islamic terrorism, it is essential to cut dependence on those states by reaching out to new suppliers. Russia and Uzbekistan have large reserves that should be developed and exploited as fast as possible, and many other countries around the world are in a position to contribute significantly more to world production than they do at present. The emphasis of U.S. policy should be to provide the major petroleum companies all the diplomatic and financial help possible to further new production.
Con: That strategy is doomed to failure, if only because total reserves are reaching their limits and total world demand is bound to increase markedly as huge developing countries like India and China import more petroleum. Senator Richard G. Lugar (R-Ind.) and former CIA director R. James Woolsey have predicted that total world production will peak by the end of this decade. Besides, making all policy subordinate to furthering oil production necessarily will require the U.S. to make unseemly deals with many unsavory regimes, often endangering long-term interests. It would be better to shore up relations with current U.S. suppliers in the short run, minimizing the military operations and presence that are destabilizing Islamic regimes, while in the long run doing everything possible to reduce consumption of gasoline.

SIZABLE INVESTMENT *in both pipeline and explorations, such as the Astra platform in the Caspian Sea, has promoted much greater oil production. Russia is the third country to tap the fields beneath the Caspian.*

❑ **4. The best overall energy strategy for the U.S. would be a concerted effort to reduce both dependence on imported oil and combustion of fossil fuels that warm the atmosphere.**
Pro: This means robustly developing more energy-efficient technologies, encouraging their adoption by means of taxes on energy use or carbon emissions, promoting early deployment of automotive vehicles that rely on natural gas or hydrogen fuel rather than gasoline, and switching to carbon-free modes of central (large-scale) electricity generation, including nuclear energy and hydroelectricity.
Con: There are plenty of good reasons to develop more energy-efficient technologies and alternatives to fossil fuels without throwing government money at these challenges. Photovoltaics, hydrogen-fed fuel cells, wind turbines, hybrid-electric cars powered by batteries or fuel cells in combination with gasoline—all will mature in their own good time. In the meantime, it would be foolish to sacrifice other critical environmental interests—natural habitats destroyed by gargantuan dams, unborn generations threatened by ill-secured nuclear wastes—in the name of minimizing risks that have yet to materialize. ■

OPINION BALLOTS are on pages 91–92

DISCUSSION QUESTIONS

1. Is there truly an energy crisis in the U.S., and if so, what are its most important ingredients?

2. How did electricity deregulation originate, and is it a good idea? Can electricity still be reregulated?

3. Should tax policy or revised CAFE standards strongly discourage continued purchase of SUVs?

4. Which U.S. President did most to encourage development of a comprehensive energy policy, and which one did least?

5. How is knowledge about the earth's climate history acquired, and how are the consequences of emitting greenhouse gases calculated?

6. What are the main findings of climate science that have convinced experts that the danger of global warming is real?

7. Why has the Kyoto Protocol encountered such sharp resistance in the U.S., and why is America's attitude regarded with such impatience in the rest of the world?

8. How far should the U.S. go to ingratiate itself with OPEC oil suppliers or with alternative suppliers, say among the former Soviet republics?

9. How has the conflict between Israel and the Palestinians affected the U.S. energy situation? Should energy policy include a plan to further settlement of that conflict?

10. Can relations with the Islamic world be stabilized and "returned to normalcy," or should energy policy assume an enduring "clash of civilizations"?

READINGS AND RESOURCES

Cheney, Dick, and Lundquist, Andrew D., **National Energy Policy: Report of the National Energy Policy Development Group,** May 2001. Available at **www.whitehouse.gov/energy**

Cohn, Laura, Crock, Stan, et al., "What To Do About Oil." **Business Week,** October 29, 2001, pp. 30–33.

Cooper, Richard N., "Toward a Real Global Warming Treaty." **Foreign Affairs,** March/April 1998, pp. 66–79.

Holdren, John P., **Report to the President on Federal Energy Research and Development for the Challenges of the Twenty-First Century.** President's Committee of Advisors on Science and Technology (Pcast), Panel on Energy Research and Development, November 1997. Available at **www.ostp.gov/energy**

Jacoby, Henry D., Prinn, Ronald G., and Schmalensee, Richard, "Kyoto's Unfinished Business." **Foreign Affairs,** July/August 1998, pp. 54–66.

Kennedy, Donald, **Climate and Civilization: The Scientific Evidence for Climate Change, and How Our Response to It May Influence National Policy.** A lecture on the science of climate warming delivered at the State University of New York College at Oneonta, October 4, 2000. Available at **www.oneonta.edu/faculty/allenth/climate_and_civilization**

Lugar, Richard G., and Woolsey, R. James, "The New Petroleum." **Foreign Affairs,** Jan./Feb. 1999, pp. 88–102. This article makes a pitch for greater reliance on ethanol from crops.

Morse, Edward L., and Jaffe, Amy Myers, **Strategic Energy Policy: Challenges for the 21st Century.** Report of an independent task force cosponsored by the James A. Baker III Institute for Public Policy of Rice University and the Council on Foreign Relations. Washington D.C., Brookings Institution, 2001. 45 pp. $10.00.

Nordhaus, William D., and Boyer, Joseph, **Warming the World: Economic Models of Global Warming.** Cambridge, Mass., MIT Press, 2000. 246 pp. $35.00.

Smil, Vaclav, "The Energy Question, Again." **Current History,** December 2000, pp. 408–12. An analysis of fuel-efficiency standards, part of a general account of today's energy picture.

Sweet, William, "Restructuring the Thin-Stretched Grid." **IEEE Spectrum** magazine, June 2000, pp. 43–49. Background information on the electricity crisis.

Victor, David G., **The Collapse of the Kyoto Protocol and the Struggle to Slow Global Warming.** New York, Council on Foreign Relations, 2001. 178 pp. $19.95.

ENVIRONMENTAL PROTECTION AGENCY, Ariel Rios Building, 1200 Pennsylvania Ave., NW, Washington, DC 20460; (202) 260-2090. **www.epa.gov** ■ This governmental agency is responsible for clean air and water and deals with international environmental standards.

INTERNATIONAL ATOMIC ENERGY AGENCY, P.O. Box 100, Wagramer Strasse 5, A-1400 Vienna, Austria; (431) 2600-0; Fax (431) 2600-7. **www.iaea.org** ■ As an intergovernmental organization under the UN's umbrella, the IAEA deals with nuclear energy.

U.S. DEPARTMENT OF ENERGY, 1000 Independence Ave., SW, Washington, DC 20585; (800) 342-5363; Fax (202) 586-4403. **www.energy.gov** ■ This agency is responsible for a secure and reliable energy system that is both environmentally and economically sound. The agency oversees nuclear energy and the development of science and technology.

INDEX TO GREAT DECISIONS TOPICS (1991–2001)

AFRICA

'01—Conflict Resolution in Africa: Can It Succeed?
'00—Africa: Prospects for the Future
'98—Africa Today: Worst of Times, Best of Times
'96—Africa: Should the U.S. Care?
'94—South Africa: Forging a Democratic Union
'94—Islam and Politics: Egypt, Algeria and Tunisia
'92—Africa South of the Sahara: Fresh Winds of Democracy?

ASIA

'01—China and Taiwan: What Role for the U.S.?
'00—Indonesia in Aftershock: Prospects for Recovery
'99—The Asian Financial Crisis: The IMF and Its Critics
'99—Japan: The Shadow of the Miracle
'98—China and the U.S.: What Priorities in a Changing Relationship?
'98—Turkey: Emerging Regional Power or State in Crisis?
'97—Northeast Asia: Strategic Crossroads
'96—Economic Cooperation in the Asia-Pacific: Openings for the U.S.?
'95—China, Taiwan, Hong Kong: U.S. Challenges
'93—China: New Reforms, Old Politics?
'93—India & Pakistan: Collision or Compromise?
'91—Japanese-U.S. Trade: Harmony or Discord?

LATIN AMERICA

'01—Prospects for Mexico: New Path in the 21st Century?
'99—Latin America: A Broad Overview
'98—Cuba: Time to Rethink U.S. Strategy?
'96—Mexico: Embattled Neighbor
'94—Argentina, Brazil, Chile: Democracy & Market Economics
'92—Latin America's New Course: Bridge to Closer U.S. Ties?
'91—Cuba: What Future for Castro and Communism?

MIDDLE EAST

'01—Dealing with Iraq: Which Way Forward?
'00—The Middle East at the Millennium
'99—Iran and the Caspian Basin: Tradition and Transformation
'97—Middle East: Peace and the Changing Order
'95—Middle East: Lasting Steps to Peace?
'92—Middle East After Desert Storm: As the Dust Settles
'91—The Middle East: New Frictions, New Alignments

RUSSIA, FORMER U.S.S.R. AND EASTERN EUROPE

'00—Russia: Report Card on Survival
'97—Russia and the U.S.: Growing Cooperation?
'95—Russia and Its Neighbors: U.S. Policy Choices
'94—Conflict in Former Yugoslavia: Quest for Solutions
'93—Russia & the Central Asian Republics: After Independence, New Directions?
'92—Breakup of the Soviet Union: U.S. Dilemmas
'91—Nationalism's Revival: Soviet Republics & Eastern Europe

WESTERN EUROPE

'01—European Integration: Past, Present and Future
'00—The Euro's Challenge to the Dollar
'99—Implementing NATO Enlargement: Difficult Choices Ahead
'98—Turkey: Emerging Regional Power or State in Crisis?
'97—European Integration: What Future for Europe and the U.S.?
'93—Germany's Role: In Europe? in the Atlantic Alliance?
'91—The New Europe: What Role for the U.S.?

DEFENSE AND SECURITY

'01—Missile Defense: A Cold-War Debate Continues
'00—The Military: What Role in U.S. Foreign Policy?
'99—Implementing NATO Enlargement: Difficult Choices Ahead
'99—Weapons of Mass Destruction: Reemerging Threat?
'96—What Future Role for NATO?
'96—Failing Nations: What U.S. Response?
'96—The Intelligence Community: Time for Reform?
'95—Nuclear Proliferation: Can It Be Capped?
'94—Defense: Redefining U.S. Needs and Priorities

ECONOMIC ISSUES

'01—U.S. Trade Policy: Coping with Globalization
'00—The Euro's Challenge to the Dollar
'99—The Asian Financial Crisis: The IMF and Its Critics
'98—Financing Development: Time for a New Look?
'97—Globalization: Workplace Winners and Losers
'95—Global Finance: America's Role and Stakes
'94—Trade with the Pacific Rim: Pressure or Cooperation?
'93—Trade & the Global Economy: Projecting U.S. Interests

ENVIRONMENT

'97—Environmental Threats to Stability: The Role of Population Growth
'96—Water: A Dangerous Endangered Resource?
'94—Environmental Crisis in Former Soviet Bloc: Whose Problem? Who Pays?
'92—Planet Earth: Dying Species, Disappearing Habitats
'91—Women, Population & the Environment

U.S. FOREIGN POLICY

'00—U.S. Role in the World: What Are the Choices?
'00—The Military: What Role in U.S. Foreign Policy?
'99—The Information Age: New Dimensions for U.S. Foreign Policy
'98—Special Interests: Is U.S. Foreign Policy for Sale?
'98—Human Rights: What Role in U.S. Policy?
'96—Foreign Policy and the U.S. Political System
'95—Promoting Democracy: America's Mission?
'94—New World Disorder? U.S. in Search of a Role
'93—U.S. in a New World: What Goals? What Priorities?
'92—U.S. Agenda for the '90s: Domestic Needs, Global Priorities
'91—Rethinking Foreign Aid: What Kind? How Much?

OTHER CRITICAL ISSUES

'01—The Global Disease Crisis: What Is America's Role?
'00—Humanitarianism: Facing New Challenges
'99—U.S. Role in the UN: A Changing Dynamic?
'98—Religion's Role in World Affairs: Challenges for the U.S.
'97—Today's Media: What Voice in Foreign Policy?
'97—Terrorism and Crime: A More Dangerous World
'95—United Nations at Fifty: Reaching Out or Overreaching?
'95—Immigration: An End to Open Doors?
'93—UN: What Role in the New World?
'93—Children at Risk: Abroad and at Home
'92—The Refugee Crisis: How Should the U.S. Respond?
'92—The AIDS Pandemic: Global Scourge, U.S. Challenge
'91—Media's Role in Shaping Foreign Policy

OPINION BALLOT 2001 HIGHLIGHTS

TOPIC 1: U.S. TRADE POLICY

ISSUE A. Is the increasing globalization of the U.S. economy making life better in your community, or is it making life worse?

Making life better	75%
Making life worse	10%

ISSUE B. In response to the globalization of trade and the economy, the U.S. should:

	AGREE	DISAGREE
Continue efforts to expand U.S. exports.	93%	3%
Curb imports by raising tariffs and quotas.	13%	79%
Encourage the growth of multilateral trade through the WTO.	84%	9%
Encourage foreign investment in the U.S.	69%	22%
Reduce regulations in the U.S. to facilitate the exchange of goods and services.	51%	40%

ISSUE C. What is your opinion of antiglobalization protesters such as those who took to the streets in Seattle:

Very favorable	6%
Somewhat favorable	22%
Somewhat unfavorable	30%
Very unfavorable	31%

ISSUE D. As globalization increases, how much attention should the U.S. pay to such conditions in the developing countries as:

	MORE	LESS	JUST ENOUGH
Human rights	54%	7%	29%
The rights of workers	55%	7%	27%
Child labor	66%	5%	18%
Environmental standards	69%	4%	16%

TOPIC 2: CHINA AND TAIWAN

ISSUE A. Which of the following is better for the U.S. national interest: defending Taiwan, or letting China proceed with reunification efforts?

Defending Taiwan	31%
Letting China proceed with reunification	43%

ISSUE B. Do you agree or disagree with the following statements?

	AGREE	DISAGREE
The U.S. should make an explicit pledge to defend Taiwan against an invasion from the mainland.	23%	70%
The U.S. should offer to mediate the dispute between China and Taiwan.	50%	44%
Now that Taiwan is a democracy, the U.S. should encourage its quest for independence.	39%	52%
The U.S. should urge Taiwan to enter into reunification talks with China.	38%	52%
China and Taiwan should reach an interim agreement preserving the status quo.	75%	16%
The U.S. should link trade with China to that country's human-rights record.	35%	57%

Results of 30,472 ballots received as of June 30, 2001, and tabulated by Calculogic Corporation of Englewood, New Jersey.

TOPIC 3: MISSILE DEFENSE

ISSUE A. Given the many demands on U.S. defense spending during the coming decade, which of the following items are most important, just important, or not important at all?

	MOST IMPORTANT	JUST IMPORTANT	NOT IMPORTANT
Purchasing the next generation of fighter aircraft and other tactical weaponry.	18%	56%	21%
Sufficient funding for overseas operations.	18%	66%	11%
Boosting military pay to spur recruitment and retention of personnel.	56%	36%	5%
Fielding defenses against possible attacks by states of concern.	24%	46%	24%

ISSUE B. Considering the 1972 ABM Treaty, do you think:

The treaty has outlived its purpose.	27%
The treaty is still useful as a means of limiting the arms race.	64%

ISSUE C. Regarding the issue of a missile-defense system, which of the following options should the U.S. government adopt?

No national missile defense at all.	34%
The 100-interceptor NMD system now being planned.	21%
A forward-based boost-phase antimissile system.	29%

ISSUE D. Considering the estimate of $60 billion being spent on national missile defense and early-warning upgrades over the next decade and a half, do you think that:

More should be spent.	9%
Less should be spent.	49%
That is about the right amount.	28%

TOPIC 4: DEALING WITH IRAQ

ISSUE A. What circumstances would justify a U.S. military strike on Iraq?

	AGREE	DISAGREE
An Iraqi invasion of Kuwait.	73%	21%
An Iraqi reoccupation of the northern Kurdish zone.	38%	52%
An Iraqi refusal to readmit UN weapons inspectors.	19%	72%
Evidence that Iraq is reviving its WMD programs.	57%	33%
A joint effort with the Iraqi opposition to unseat the regime.	25%	66%

ISSUE B. In its policy toward Iraq, the U.S. should:

	AGREE	DISAGREE
Maintain sanctions until Iraq complies fully with UN resolutions.	32%	54%
Relax sanctions to permit humanitarian relief.	71%	18%
Support a military overthrow of Saddam Hussein's government.	36%	50%

ISSUE C. In dealing with Iraq, should the U.S. take the following steps under the conditions indicated?

	YES	NO
Maintain the no-fly zones even in light of opposition from allies.	49%	39%
Accept the opinion of the UN Security Council on Iraq, even if it goes against U.S. policy.	62%	26%
Continue to fund the Iraqi opposition, even if its chances of overthrowing the regime appear small.	41%	46%

TOPIC 5: GLOBAL DISEASE CRISIS

ISSUE A. Do you agree or disagree with the following statements?

	AGREE	DISAGREE
The U.S. has an obligation to help countries in Africa and elsewhere afflicted by epidemics.	82%	14%
It is in America's own self-interest to contain epidemic diseases in Africa and elsewhere.	93%	4%
The global AIDS epidemic is a security threat to the U.S.	70%	24%

ISSUE B. Concerning the availability of drugs against lethal diseases overseas, the U.S. should:

Defend the property rights of U.S. drug companies	16%
Make exceptions for countries unable to afford brand-name drugs	72%

ISSUE C. Which of the following measures should the U.S. adopt to protect itself from infectious diseases overseas?

	YES	NO
Tighter immigration controls	68%	19%
Physical examination of travelers	46%	36%
More immunizations for Americans	76%	11%
Deportation of infected immigrants	39%	41%

ISSUE D. Should the U.S. along with other wealthy countries launch an aid program of Marshall Plan proportions to help African countries stricken by epidemics?

Yes	72%
No	17%

TOPIC 6: PROSPECTS FOR MEXICO

ISSUE A. In its relations with Mexico, the most important issue for the U.S. is:

Illegal immigraton	20%
Drug trafficking	25%
Trade	24%
Political reform in Mexico	25%

ISSUE B. In dealing with Mexico, the U.S. should:

	AGREE	DISAGREE
Emulate the European Union and create a common currency and lower its border.	10%	79%
Impose sanctions on Mexico to force it to curb the drug trade.	21%	68%
Relax limits on immigration by instituting a guest-worker program.	58%	33%

ISSUE C. How important are the following issues facing President Fox at home:

	MOST IMPORTANT	IMPORTANT	NOT IMPORTANT
Bringing peace to Chiapas.	22%	66%	3%
Attracting private capital to state-owned industries.	36%	50%	6%
Ending political and administrative centralism.	35%	51%	5%
Increasing social spending in such areas as education and health care.	66%	27%	1%

**Note: These percentages and others reported may not add up to 100 because some repondents did not mark particular ballots or volunteered other information.*

TOPIC 7: EUROPEAN INTEGRATION

ISSUE A. Should the European Union admit the countries of Eastern Europe before they meet all the economic and political requirements?

Yes, admit	25%
No, don't admit	69%

ISSUE B. Should the U.S. support or oppose the European Union's attempt to create its own military task force (CESDP)?

Support	82%
Oppose	12%

ISSUE C. In the foreseeable future, is integration in the European Union more likely to flourish, or to stagnate?

Flourish	70%
Stagnate	21%

ISSUE D. As regards the euro, should the U.S. intervene to prop up the euro, or should the U.S. see to it that the dollar remains strong?

Prop up euro	23%
Keep dollar strong	59%

ISSUE E. Is the European Union going to become a new superpower, or is that not going to happen in the foreseeable future?

Yes, the European Union will become a superpower	45%
No, not likely	45%

TOPIC 8: CONFLICT RESOLUTION IN AFRICA

ISSUE A. Given the newness of most African states, conflicts in that continent are no worse than they were in other nations at comparable stages of their political development.

Yes	50%
No	42%

ISSUE B. Regional organizations in Africa such as OAU or SADC are ineffective at settling disputes.

Yes	52%
No	35%

ISSUE C. Do you agree or disagree with the following statements?

	AGREE	DISAGREE
The U.S. has no vital security interest in Africa.	36%	56%
The U.S. should support African leaders who achieve political stability and economic reform even if they do not promote democracy.	74%	18%
The U.S. should intervene militarily in African countries engaged in genocide.	32%	57%

ISSUE D. As for dealing with African conflicts, which of the following tools are appropriate for U.S. foreign policy and which ones are not?

	APPROPRIATE	NOT APPROPRIATE
Noninvolvement	26%	61%
Diplomacy	92%	1%
Economic aid	85%	7%
Military aid	22%	65%
Covert intervention	19%	69%
Direct military intervention	12%	75%

TEACHER'S GUIDE Prepared by Marcel Lewinski, master teacher and curriculum developer, this valuable resource contains glossaries for each article, teaching strategies and activities, and reproducible handouts. $25.00 (including shipping and handling). Product Order No. 31512.

TELEVISION SERIES The longest-running television program devoted solely to international affairs, the **Great Decisions Television Series** is a valuable and instructive tool for the classroom and in discussion groups. The series features the expert, informed opinions of policymakers, scholars and journalists. Past guests include:

- Ambassador Charlene Barshefsky, *Senior International Partner,* Wilmer, Cutles & Pickering
- Lee H. Hamilton, *Director,* the Woodrow Wilson Center
- Ambassador Robert E. Hunter, *Senior Adviser,* RAND Corp.
- Charles A. Kupchan, *Associate Professor,* Georgetown University
- Marina S. Ottaway, *Senior Associate/Co-director,* Democracy and Rule of Law Project, CEIP
- Daniel Yergin, *President,* Cambridge Energy Research Associates

The 2002 Series (13 half-hour programs) will begin airing on PBS affiliates across the country in late winter. A two-tape VHS video set containing the eight **Great Decisions 2002** topics is also available. $35.00 (plus $5.00 shipping and handling). Product order No. 31515.

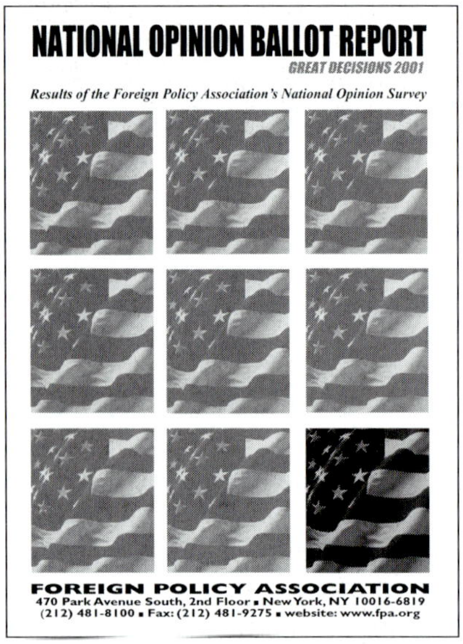

OPINION BALLOTS Vote for the foreign policy option of your choice! You can make your opinions count by filling in a ballot after you read and discuss each topic. If you prefer to wait until you have finished discussing all eight topics, you can use the ballot envelope that is bound into this book to mail your ballots to the Foreign Policy Association. Either way, please send your ballots no later than the June 30th cutoff date in order to have your opinions included in the final *National Opinion Ballot Report.* The *Ballot Report* will be prepared by the FPA, with the advice of a public opinion analyst, and will be presented to the White House, the Departments of State and Defense, and members of Congress, as well as the nation's media.

UPDATES Concise, informative supplements to the briefing book topics on developments since the book went to press. They are available free in February and August.

PROGRAM MATERIALS **Great Decisions Program Handbook** and **Tips for Discussion Group Leaders.** Upon request, FPA will provide this material, free of charge, to help you create a better program.

---

visit FPA online, you can:

FPA.org

- Take part in a discussion on foreign policy with other FPA members
- Get the latest updates to the **Great Decisions** articles
- Download the **Tips for Discussion Group Leaders** booklet
- Read the results of our latest *National Opinion Ballot Report*
- Get the latest information on FPA events and speakers.

To order FPA materials or to request a free catalog, contact:

Foreign Policy Association • 470 Park Ave. So. • New York, NY 10016-6819 • (800) 477 5836 • Fax (212) 481 9275

★ ★ ★ ★ JUST PUBLISHED HEADLINE SERIES

MEXICO: CHANGING OF THE GUARD

by George W. Grayson

George W. Grayson teaches government at the College of William & Mary and has written 15 books and monographs on Mexico, including *A Guide to the 2000 Mexican Presidential Election,* published by the Center for Strategic & International Studies (CSIS), where he is an adjunct fellow.

Vicente Fox Quesada of the center-right National Action party (PAN) became president of Mexico on December 1, 2000, with ambitious goals for domestic and foreign policy. Yet the populist leader, formerly a business executive at Coca-Cola, faces opposition both within his party and from outside, with an array of potent foes trying to stymie his plans. This Headline Series looks at the initiatives Fox has tackled so far, including defusing the Chiapas conflict, economic reform and relations with the United States, European countries and other nations in the Western Hemisphere. Evaluating the successes and failures of his first year in office, Grayson provides an analysis and forecast of Fox's ability to transform Mexico into a truly modern, democratic, humanitarian country.

HS 323 ▪ $5.95, 80 pages, Fall 2001. ISBN: 0-87124-199-4.

★ ★ ★ ★ ★ SOUTH ASIA SPECIAL OFFER

PAKISTAN: FLAWED NOT FAILED STATE

by Dennis Kux

Dennis Kux, retired State Department South Asia specialist and author of *The United States and Pakistan, 1947–2000: Disenchanted Allies,* has just returned from India and Pakistan. He is currently a Senior Scholar at the Woodrow Wilson Center in Washington, D.C.

HS 322 ▪ 88 pages, Summer 2001. ISBN: 0-87124-198-6.

INDIA: OLD CIVILIZATION IN A NEW WORLD

by Barbara Crossette

Barbara Crossette, a journalist at *The New York Times* since 1973, is now chief of that paper's UN bureau. Previously a correspondent in Southeast Asia and in South Asia, Ms. Crossette won the George Polk Award for foreign reporting for her coverage of the assassination of Indian Prime Minister Rajiv Gandhi.

HS 320 ▪ 88 pages, Spring 2000. ISBN: 0-87124-193-5.

special price for these two: $10.00 (incl. S&H)—a saving of $5.00

FPA Invites You to...

Become a National Associate.

Your participation as a National Associate will enable FPA, an independent, nonpartisan educational organization, to carry out its mission to develop awareness and understanding of global issues and informed opinion on U.S. foreign policy. To become a National Associate, or to make a tax-deductible contribution, please use the envelope bound into this book.

Become an FPA Civic Volunteer.

Lead your community in a dialogue on "great decisons" that affect our daily lives. FPA's volunteer corps of civic leaders organizes and leads Great Decisions discussion groups supplemented by lecture series, town meetings, media programs and other forums that encourage thoughtful deliberation and civic action.

Through their efforts, citizens across the country join together to share viewpoints and strengthen the democratic process.

Participate in the Foreign Policy Process.

- Join a Great Decisions foreign policy discussion group in your community.
- Participate in the opinion ballot process (ballots are bound into this book).
- Lead a new Great Decisions group in your area.
- Coordinate several groups by becoming a Great Decisions Regional Organizer, acting as the liaison between the Foreign Policy Association and Great Decisions groups in your area, as well as introducing the program to new audiences.

FPA wishes to thank the following Great Decisions participants who generously supported the program.

National Associates

Albert Adams
Benjamin F. Adams
William L. Bell
William J. Bond
Ann S. Bowen
Jeffrey M. Busch
Karen Campbell
Mark Diestler
Robert M. du Roy
R. Glenn Elliott
Charles J. Fitzgerald
Alison M. Harwood
Charles M. Holmes
Thomas A. Hood
Jerome Horowitz
Susanne W. Howe
Monica Hunt
Albert H. Huntington
Legean Hyppolite
Walter O. Isaac
Jed P. Kaplan
Edib Kirdar
Donald P. Knode
Spiridon Koulouris
John H. Lawson
Laura Lester
Erma A. Mair
Gerald Meloy
Frank P. Morello
Robert D. Nagel
Ralph H. Nestmann
Noel Neushehir
Joseph P. Nguyen
Lindsey H. Parham
John S. Reinhardt
Ronald K. Ritter
Emmeline Rocha-Sinha
Jeanne-Marie Silk
James H. Stanford
Alan Sullivan
Allan W. Sydney
Richard J. Vogel
Johnathan M. Walker
Timothy N. Wineland
Stephen G. Yeonas
Robert W. Zimmerman

Student Members *

Andrew H. Bauer
David Borchard
Michael A. Hennig
Marcus C. Holmes
Lonnie Lucien
Laura D. Milazzo
Jennifer Nemcovic
Gary E. Oldenburger
Colette M. Pollitt
Debra L. Rivera
Jamie J. Sanchez
Hannie M. Santana
Cristina Stephens
Roy Zhou

* *New membership category.*

With Bristol-Myers Squibb research, a tiny pair of chromosomes could make a huge difference to this pair of Armstrongs.

Three-time Tour de France winner
Lance Armstrong, with his son Luke.

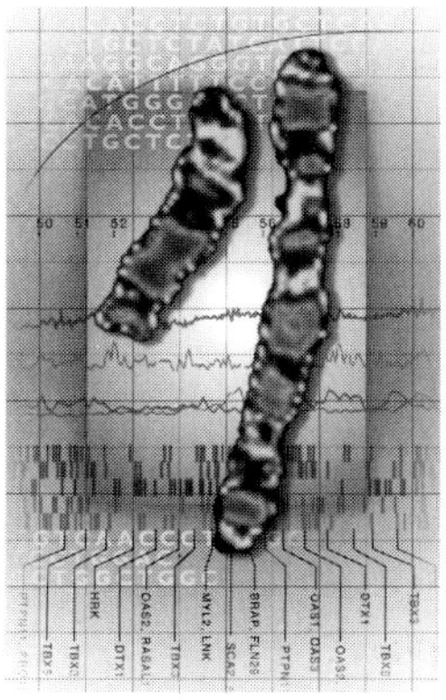

Five years ago, cyclist Lance Armstrong was diagnosed with testicular cancer. It had already spread to his abdomen, lungs and brain. But with aggressive treatments, including three Bristol-Myers Squibb medicines, Lance conquered his cancer. He went on to win the Tour de France three times, and even to have a wonderful son—Luke.

Today, there are more miracles in store for little Luke and his generation. At the Bristol-Myers Squibb Center for Applied Genomics, researchers strive to unlock the genetic secrets of breast and colon cancer, Alzheimer's, and diabetes. Someday—perhaps someday soon—mutant cancer genes will be identified, repaired, even "switched off." Imagine the hope this brings to a cancer survivor raising his young son.

At Bristol-Myers Squibb, we're leading the way in new frontiers against disease. And little Luke—and all of us—could ultimately benefit.

Bristol-Myers Squibb Company *Hope, Triumph, and the Miracle of Medicine*